T0127921

Get the eBook FREE!

(PDF, ePub, Kindle, and liveBook all included)

We believe that once you buy a book from us, you should be able to read it in any format we have available. To get electronic versions of this book at no additional cost to you, purchase and then register this book at the Manning website.

Go to https://www.manning.com/freebook and follow the instructions to complete your pBook registration.

That's it!
Thanks from Manning!

AI as a Service

Serverless machine learning with AWS

AI as a Service

SERVERLESS MACHINE LEARNING WITH AWS

PETER ELGER
EÓIN SHANAGHY

MANNING
SHELTER ISLAND

For online information and ordering of this and other Manning books, please visit
www.manning.com. The publisher offers discounts on this book when ordered in quantity.
For more information, please contact

Special Sales Department
Manning Publications Co.
20 Baldwin Road
PO Box 761
Shelter Island, NY 11964
Email: orders@manning.com

Manning Publications Co.   Development editor: Lesley Trites
20 Baldwin Road   Technical development editor: Al Krinker
PO Box 761   Review editor: Ivan Martinović
Shelter Island, NY 11964   Production editor: Deirdre S. Hiam
                                          Copy editor: Ben Berg
                                          Proofreader: Melody Dolab
                              Technical proofreader: Guillaume Alleon
                         Typesetter and cover designer: Marija Tudor

ISBN 9781617296154
Printed in the United States of America

For my parents, Noel and Kay—Eóin
For my daughters Isobel and Katie, my parents Jacky and Julian,
and my brother Jonathon—Peter

contents

foreword

For the past two decades, AI has played an increasingly significant role in our lives. It has done so quietly behind the scenes, as AI technologies have been employed by companies around the world to improve search results, product recommendations, and advertising, and even to assist healthcare workers to provide a better diagnosis. AI technologies are all around us, and soon, we'll all travel in cars that drive themselves!

With this rise in prominence came a rise in demand for relevant skills. Engineers with expertise in machine learning or deep learning are often hoovered up by the big tech companies at huge salaries. Meanwhile, every application on the surface of the earth wants to use AI to improve its user experience. But the ability to hire the relevant skillsets and acquire the necessary volume of data to train these AI models remains a significant barrier to entry.

Fortunately, cloud providers are offering more and more AI services that remove the need for you to steep yourself in the art of collecting and cleaning up data and training AI models. AWS, for instance, lets you use the same technologies that power product recommendations for Amazon.com through Amazon Personalize, or the speech recognition technology that powers Alexa with Amazon Transcribe. Other cloud providers (GCP, Azure, IBM, and so on) also offer similar services, and it will be through these services that we will see AI-powered features in everyday applications. And as these services become better and more accessible, there will be less need for people to train their own AI models, except for more specialised workloads.

It's great to finally see a book that focuses on leveraging these AI services rather than the nitty-gritty details of training AI models. This book explains the important concepts in AI and machine learning in layman's terms, and describes them for exactly what they are, without all the hype and hyperbole that often accompany AI-related conversations. And the beauty of this book is that it is way more than "how to use these AI services from AWS," but also how to build applications the serverless way. It covers everything from project organization, to continuous deployment, all the way to effective logging strategies and how to monitor your application using both service and application metrics. The later chapters of the book are also a treasure trove of integration patterns and real-world examples of how to sprinkle some AI magic into an existing application.

Serverless is a state of mind, a way of thinking about software development that puts the needs of the business and its customers at the forefront, and aims to create maximum business value with minimum effort by leveraging as many managed services as possible. This way of thinking leads to increased developer productivity and feature velocity, and often results in more scalable, resilient, and secure applications by building on the shoulders of giants such as AWS.

Serverless is not the future of how we build businesses around software; it's the present and now, and it's here to stay. This book will help you get started with Serverless development and show you how to integrate AI services into a Serverless application to enhance its user experience. Talk about hitting two birds with one stone!

YAN CUI
AWS SERVERLESS HERO
INDEPENDENT CONSULTANT

preface

The fourth industrial revolution is upon us! The coming decade will likely see huge advances in areas such as gene editing, quantum computing, and, of course, artificial intelligence (AI). Most of us already interact with AI technology on a daily basis. This doesn't just mean self-driving cars or automated lawn mowers. AI is far more pervasive than these obvious examples. Consider the product recommendation that Amazon just made when you visited their site, the online chat conversation you just had with your airline to re-book a flight, or the text that your bank just sent you warning of a possibly fraudulent transaction on your account. All of these examples are driven by AI and machine learning technology.

Increasingly, developers will be required to add "smart" AI-enabled features and interfaces to the products and platforms that they build. Early adopters of AI and machine learning have been doing this for some time, of course; however, this required a large investment in research and development, typically requiring a team of data scientists to train, test, deploy, and operate custom AI models. This picture is changing rapidly due to the powerful force of commoditization.

In his 2010 bestselling book, *The Big Switch*, Nicholas Carr compared cloud computing to electricity, predicting that eventually we would consume computing resources as a utility. Though we are not quite at the point of true utility computing, it is becoming clearer that this consumption model is fast becoming a reality.

You can see this in the explosive growth in the range and capability of cloud-native services. Commoditization of the cloud stack has given rise to the serverless computing paradigm. It is our belief that serverless computing will become the de facto standard architecture for building software platforms and products in the future.

In conjunction with the commoditization of the wider application stack, AI is also rapidly becoming a commodity. Witness the number of AI services that are available from the major cloud providers in areas such as image recognition, natural language processing, and chatbot interfaces. These AI services grow in number and capability month by month.

At our company, fourTheorem, we use these technologies on a daily basis to help our clients extend and improve their existing systems through the application of AI services. We help our clients to adopt serverless architectures and tools to accelerate their platform development efforts, and we use our experience to help restructure legacy systems so that they can run more efficiently on cloud.

It is the rapid growth and commoditization of these two technologies, Serverless and AI services, along with our experience of applying them to real-world projects, that led us to write this book. We wanted to provide an engineer's guide to help you succeed with AI as a Service, and we wish you luck as you begin to master this brave new world of software development!

acknowledgments

Ask any technical book author ,and they will tell you that completing a book takes a lot of time and effort. It also requires the fantastic support of others. We are incredibly grateful for the many people who made completing this book possible.

First we would like to thank our families for their support, understanding, and patience while we worked to complete the book. Eóin would like to thank his amazing wife, Keelin, for her unending patience, moral support, and indispensable technical reviews. He would also like to thank Aoife and Cormac for being the best children in the world. Peter would like to thank his daughters, Isobel and Katie, just for being awesome.

Eóin and Peter would like to thank fourTheorem co-founder Fiona McKenna for her belief in this book, and her constant support and expertise in so many areas. We could not have done it without you.

Starting a project like this is the hardest part, and we are grateful for the people who helped in the beginning. Johannes Ahlmann contributed ideas, writing, and discussion that helped to shape what this book became. James Dadd and Robert Paulus provided invaluable support and feedback.

We would also like to thank the awesome team at Manning for making this book possible. In particular, we want to thank Lesley Trites, our development editor, for her patience and support. We would also like to thank Palak Mathur and Al Krinker, our technical development editors, for their review and feedback. Thank you to our project editor, Deirdre Hiam; Ben Berg, our copyeditor; Melody Dolab, our proofreader, and Ivan Martinović, our reviewing editor.

We would like to thank Yan Cui for writing the foreword to this book. Yan is an outstanding architect and champion of all things serverless, and we are grateful for his endorsement.

A big thanks to all of the reviewers for their feedback and suggestions for improvement to the text and examples: Alain Couniot, Alex Gascon, Andrew Hamor, Dwight Barry, Earl B. Bingham, Eros Pedrini, Greg Andress, Guillaume Alleon, Leemay Nassery, Manu Sareena, Maria Gemini, Matt Welke, Michael Jensen, Mykhaylo Rubezhanskyy, Nirupam Sharma, Philippe Vialatte, Polina Keselman, Rob Pacheco, Roger M. Meli, Sowmya Vajjala, Yvon Vieville,

A special thanks to Guillaume Alleon, technical proofreader, for his careful review and testing of the code examples.

Finally we wish to acknowledge the broader open source community, of which we are proud to participate in. We truly do stand on the shoulders of giants!

about this book

AI as a Service was written as an engineer's guide to building AI-enabled platforms and services. The aim of the book is to get you up and running, and able to produce results quickly, without getting stuck in the weeds. AI and machine learning are big topics, and there is an awful lot to learn if you wish to master these disciplines. It is not our intent to discourage anyone from doing this, however if you need to get results quickly, this book will help you get up to speed.

The book examines two growing and increasingly important technologies: serverless computing and artificial intelligence. We examine these from a developer's perspective to provide a practical, hands-on guide.

All of the major cloud vendors are engaged in a race to provide relevant AI services, such as

- Image recognition
- Speech-to-text, text-to-speech
- Chatbots
- Language translation
- Natural language processing
- Recommendations

This list will only expand over time!

The good news is that you do not need to be an AI or machine learning expert to use these offerings. This book will guide you in applying these services in your day-to-day work as a developer.

In tandem with the grown of AI services, it is now possible to build and deploy applications with a minimum of operational overhead using the serverless approach. Our belief is that within the next few years, the tools, techniques, and architectures described in this book will become part of the standard toolkit for enterprise platform development. This book will bring you up to speed quickly, and help you build new systems using serverless architectures and to apply AI services to your existing platforms.

Who should read this book

AI as a Service was written for full stack and back-end developers who are tasked with implementing AI-enhanced platforms and services. The book will also be of value to solution architects and product owners looking to understand how their systems can be augmented and improved with AI. DevOps professionals will gain valuable insights into the "serverless way" of building and deploying systems.

How this book is organized: a roadmap

This book is broken down into three sections covering nine chapters.

Part 1 provides some background and examines a simple serverless AI system:

- Chapter 1 discusses the rise of serverless computing over the last few years, explaining why Serverless represents true utility cloud computing. Following this, it provides a brief overview of AI in order to bring readers with no experience with the topic up to speed.
- Chapters 2 and 3 rapidly construct a serverless AI system that uses off-the-shelf image recognition technology. Readers can deploy and experiment with this system to explore how image recognition can be used.

Part 2 goes much deeper into the individual tools and techniques that developers need to know to become effective with serverless and off-the-shelf AI:

- Chapter 4 examines how to build and deploy a simple serverless web application and then, perhaps more importantly, how to secure the application the serverless way.
- Chapter 5 explores how we can add AI-driven interfaces to a serverless web application, including speech-to-text, text-to-speech, and a conversational chatbot interface.
- Chapter 6 provides some specific advice on how to be an effective developer with this new technology set, including project structure, CI/CD, and observability—things that most developers getting to grips with this technology will need in their tool chest.
- Chapter 7 looks in detail at how serverless AI can be applied to existing or legacy platforms. Here we provide advice on the generic patterns that can be applied, and also look at some point solutions to illustrate application of these patterns.

Part 3 looks at how we can bring together what you've learned from the first two parts in the context of a full-scale AI-driven system:

- Chapter 8 examines gathering data at scale, using the example of a serverless web crawler.

- Chapter 9 looks at how we can extract value from large data sets using AI as a Service, using the data collected from the serverless web crawler.

Readers should review the material in chapter 1 to get a basic grounding of the subject matter, and pay close attention to the content in chapter 2, where we describe how to set up a development environment. The book is best read in order, as each chapter builds on the examples and learning from the previous one.

About the code

This book contains many examples of source code, both in numbered listings and inline with normal text. In both cases, source code is formatted in a `fixed-width font like this` to separate it from ordinary text. Sometimes code is also in bold to highlight code that has changed from previous steps in the chapter, such as when a new feature adds to an existing line of code.

In many cases, the original source code has been reformatted; we've added line breaks and reworked indentation to accommodate the available page space in the book. In rare cases, even this was not enough, and listings include line-continuation markers (➥). Additionally, comments in the source code have often been removed from the listings when the code is described in the text. Code annotations accompany many of the listings, highlighting important concepts. Source code for the examples in this book is available for download from the publisher's website.

All of the source code for this book is available at this repository: https://github.com/fourTheorem/ai-as-a-service.

liveBook discussion forum

Purchase of AI as a Service includes free access to a private web forum run by Manning Publications where you can make comments about the book, ask technical questions, and receive help from the author and from other users. To access the forum, go to https://livebook.manning.com/#!/book/ai-as-a-service/discussion. You can also learn more about Manning's forums and the rules of conduct at https://livebook.manning.com/#!/discussion.

Manning's commitment to our readers is to provide a venue where a meaningful dialogue between individual readers and between readers and the author can take place. It is not a commitment to any specific amount of participation on the part of the author, whose contribution to the forum remains voluntary (and unpaid). We suggest you try asking the author some challenging questions lest his interest stray! The forum and the archives of previous discussions will be accessible from the publisher's website as long as the book is in print.

about the authors

PETER ELGER is a co-founder and CEO of fourTheorem. Peter started his career at the JET Joint Undertaking in the UK, where he spent seven years building acquisition, control, and data analytics systems for nuclear fusion research. He has held technical leadership roles across a broad base of the software industry in both the research and commercial sectors, including software disaster recovery, telecommunications, and social media. Prior to founding fourTheorem, Peter was co-founder and CTO of two companies: Stitcher Ads, a social advertising platform; and nearForm, a Node.js consultancy. Peter's current focus is on delivering business value to his clients through the application of cutting edge serverless technology, cloud architectures, and machine learning. His experience covers everything from architecting large-scale distributed software systems to leading the international teams that implement them. Peter holds degrees in physics and computer science.

EÓIN SHANAGHY was fortunate enough to have been able to start programming on a Sinclair ZX Spectrum in the mid-1980s. It was the first piece of electronics he didn't try to disassemble. These days, he tries to take software systems apart instead. Eóin is the CTO and co-founder of fourTheorem, a technology consulting firm and AWS Partner. He is an architect and developer with experience in building and scaling systems for both startups and large enterprises. Eóin has worked in many different technology eras, from Java-based distributed systems back in 2000 to full-stack polyglot container and serverless applications in recent years. Eóin holds a B.A. in computer science from Trinity College, Dublin.

about the cover illustration

The figure on the cover of *AI as a Service* is captioned "Homme de la Forêt Noire," or "The man from the Black Forest." The illustration is taken from a collection of dress costumes from various countries by Jacques Grasset de Saint-Sauveur (1757-1810), titled *Costumes civils actuels de tous les peuples connus*, published in France in 1788. Each illustration is finely drawn and colored by hand. The rich variety of Grasset de Saint-Sauveur's collection reminds us vividly of how culturally apart the world's towns and regions were just 200 years ago. Isolated from each other, people spoke different dialects and languages. In the streets or in the countryside, it was easy to identify where they lived and what their trade or station in life was just by their dress.

The way we dress has changed since then and the diversity by region, so rich at the time, has faded away. It is now hard to tell apart the inhabitants of different continents, let alone different towns, regions, or countries. Perhaps we have traded cultural diversity for a more varied personal life—certainly for a more varied and fast-paced technological life.

At a time when it is hard to tell one computer book from another, Manning celebrates the inventiveness and initiative of the computer business with book covers based on the rich diversity of regional life of two centuries ago, brought back to life by Grasset de Saint-Sauveur's pictures.

Part 1

First steps

In part I we provide the ground work to get you up to speed on AI as a Service. In chapter 1 we look at the development and history of artificial intelligence and serverless computing. We review the current state of the art, and we categorize the available services on AWS into a standard architectural structure. In chapters 2 and 3 we dive right in and build a serverless image recognition system as our first AI as a Service platform.

A tale of two technologies

1

Welcome to our book! In these pages we are going to explore two exploding technologies: *serverless computing* and *artificial intelligence*. We will do this from an engineering perspective. When we say an engineering perspective, we mean that this book will provide you with a practical hands-on guide to get you up and running with AI as a Service, without getting bogged down in a lot of theory.

We imagine that like most people, you have heard of these topics and will be wondering why we've combined both of these seemingly disparate subjects into a single book. As we will see throughout the following chapters, the combination of these technologies has the potential to become the de facto standard for enterprise and business-to-consumer platform development. It is a combination that will provide software developers—and by implication the businesses they work for—with enormous power to augment and improve existing systems and to rapidly develop and deploy new AI-enabled platforms.

The world is becoming increasingly digital—you may have heard of the phrase "digital transformation." This generally refers to the process of transforming existing manual business processes that are currently run using spreadsheets, local databases, or even no software at all into platforms running on the cloud. Serverless provides us with a tool chain to accelerate digital transformation, and increasingly AI forms a core part of these transformations, replacing all or part of these human-driven business processes with computers.

Software developers will increasingly be required to implement these platforms; most of us who are involved in the software industry will need to become skilled at designing, developing, and maintaining these types of systems if we aren't already.

Are you currently thinking, "I don't know anything about AI! Do I need to become an AI expert, because that sounds really difficult?" Don't panic! You don't need to become a data scientist or a machine learning expert in order to build serverless AI systems. As we will see throughout this book, most of the hard work has already been done for you in the form of "off-the-shelf" cloud AI services. Our job as software professionals is to engineer solutions using these components.

Let's consider a simple example to illustrate the concept. Imagine a chain of hotels. There are a lot of processes that must occur in order for the company running the hotels to be successful and operate at a profit. Take, for example, the problem of deciding what the room rate should be on a certain day. If this is priced too high, no one will book, and if it is priced too low, the company will lose out on revenue. Humans operating this process rely on their experience to set the room rates, and will take into account factors such as the local competition, time of year, the expected weather, and any events of interest that may be occurring in the locality. Once decided upon, these rates will be advertised but will constantly change as the local conditions change and rooms are booked up.

This process is a great fit for an AI as a Service platform, as it is a problem in optimization. Using cloud-native services, we can imagine rapidly developing services to ingest and store the appropriate data, either through API access or scraping web sites with information on local events. We can use off-the-shelf AI models to interpret the scraped data, and we could cross-train an existing neural network to compute the optimal room rate for us. Rates could be automatically published through another service. This could be achieved today with a very limited knowledge of AI, purely through connecting cloud-native AI and data services.

If your primary interest is developing simple web sites, or low-level communication protocols, AI as a Service is not going to be of interest. However, for the vast majority of software professionals, AI as a Service will be something that will have a major impact on your professional life, and soon!

1.1 Cloud landscape

Anyone involved in the software industry will have at least a basic understanding of *cloud computing*. Cloud computing began as a mechanism to run virtual servers on someone else's hardware—what is commonly know as *Infrastructure as a Service (IaaS)*. It has since evolved into a much richer suite of on-demand services that can cater to a wide variety of compute loads. There are three major players at present: Amazon, Google, and Microsoft. Amazon Web Services (AWS) has been and continues to be the dominant provider of cloud infrastructure, delivering a bewildering array of offerings.

As of March 2020, the three major platforms provide a very similar range of services. Table 1.1 lists the number of available services from Amazon, Google, and Microsoft under a set of common categories as listed on their product pages.[1]

Table 1.1 Cloud service counts, March 2020

Service type	AWS	Google	Azure
AI and Machine Learning	24	20	42
Compute	10	7	20
Containers	4	8	10
Developer	12	16	11
Database	12	6	12
Storage	10	6	17
IoT	12	2	22
Network	11	11	20
Security	18	28	10
Other	85	119	115
Total	198	223	279

That's a lot of services to try to understand, each of which comes with its own specific API. How can we best make sense of all of this and be effective engineers, given that we can never understand the entire landscape in detail? This landscape is also in a constant state of flux as new services are added and updated.

Our goal should be to understand the architectural principles and how we can compose systems from these services to achieve a specific business goal. We should aim to keep a mental inventory of the types of services that are available and to deep dive on a subset so that we can quickly assimilate and utilize a new service as needed, depending on the result that we want to achieve.

---

[1] Sources: https://aws.amazon.com/products/, https://cloud.google.com/products/, and https://azure .microsoft.com/en-us/services/.

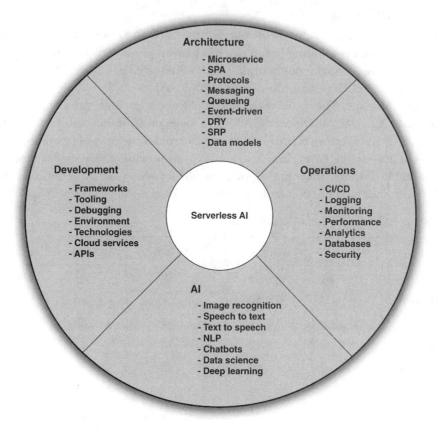

Figure 1.1   Effective AI as a Service engineering

Figure 1.1 outlines a mental frame of reference for thinking about AI as a Service platforms.

The model is built on understanding four pillars:

- *Architecture*—What are the effective architectural patterns for adopting serverless computing?
- *Development*—What are the best development tools, frameworks, and techniques?
- *AI*—What are the available machine learning and data processing services, and how can they best be applied to solve business problems?
- *Operations*—How do we effectively put these services into production and manage their operation?

In this book, we will explore the application of each of the AI subtopics through building an example software system that incorporates machine learning services such as chatbots and speech-to-text. We will explore frameworks and tools for effective serverless development, and provide help and advice on how to effectively debug in the serverless environment. Later in the book, we will discover how to apply AI tools and techniques to platform operations and how to secure a serverless platform.

We will also see how our existing experience of software architecture transfers to the serverless domain, and develop a canonical architecture for AI as a Service platforms that will help us to place each of the available cloud services into context. We will use this architecture throughout the book a reference model for the example systems that we will develop.

For the rest of this chapter, we will explore the development of Serverless and AI and provide an abridged history of each topic. This important background context will help us understand how we arrived where we are today as an industry and how the seemingly complex fields of AI and cloud computing evolved. Most of the theory is in this chapter; from chapter 2 onward we will get right into the code!

1.2 What is Serverless?

Given that there is no official definition of the term *Serverless*, we offer the following as a working solution.

Serverless computing is a form of cloud utility computing where the cloud provider dynamically manages the underlying resources for the user of the service. It provides a level of abstraction over the underlying infrastructure, removing the burden of management from the end user.

Serverless software is a form of cloud software which avoids the explicit creation and management of infrastructure; for example, servers or containers. These traditional computing resources are replaced by functions managed and run by the cloud provider. This is known as *Functions-as-a-Service (FaaS)*. Serverless applications also avoid creating heavy, dedicated resources such as databases, file storage, or message queues. Instead, they rely on managed services offered by cloud providers which scale automatically to handle vast workloads. The pricing model for serverless applications is also significant. Instead of paying for resources regardless of whether they are in use or idle, the cloud provider typically charges when functions are called and managed services are consumed. This can enable large cost savings and ensure that infrastructure costs grow in line with use.

The principles of serverless computing can be summarized as follows:

- Servers and containers are replaced by cloud functions, executed on demand.
- Managed services and third-party APIs are preferred over custom-built resources.
- Architectures are primarily event-driven and distributed.
- Developers focus on building the core product, not low-level infrastructure.

The term *Serverless* is a bit of a misnomer, because, of course, there is always a server involved somewhere in the chain! The point is that with Serverless we, as users of the technology, no longer have to care about the underlying infrastructure. The cloud vendor, through FaaS and other managed services, provides a level of abstraction over the underlying infrastructure.

The history of computing has in one sense been all about creating levels of abstraction. Early users had to be concerned with physical disk sectors and registers until the abstraction of the operating system was created. Languages have evolved from a low level such as assembly language, to dynamic modern dialects such as Python, through the creation of a series of increasingly sophisticated abstractions. So it is with Serverless.

Anyone engaged in the craft of software development, be it as a developer, DevOps specialist, manager, or senior technologist, understands that the rate of change in our industry is unlike any other. Imagine for a moment, if you will, other professions, such as doctors, dentists, lawyers, or civil engineers, having to update their knowledge base at the frenetic rate that the software industry does. If you're finding it difficult to imagine, we agree with you!

This both a boon and a curse. Many of us enjoy working with the latest and greatest technology stacks, yet we often suffer from a paradox of choice in that there are perhaps too many languages, platforms, and technologies to choose from.

> **The paradox of choice**
> *The Paradox of Choice: Why More is Less* is a book by psychologist Barry Schwartz, in which he develops the thesis that more choice in fact leads to consumer anxiety. He argues that a successful product should limit the amount of choice into a few distinct categories. It is a similar situation with programming languages, frameworks, and platforms, in that we literally have too many options to choose from!

Many who have been in the industry for a while become justifiably skeptical of the latest technology trend or framework. However, it is our belief that Serverless and the current wave of AI represent a true paradigm shift, and not just a short-term trend.

To understand what Serverless really means, we first need to understand how the industry got to where it is today, and to do that, we need to explore the key driver behind the industry: speed!

1.3   *The need for speed*

The history and development of the computer industry is a fascinating topic, and many worthy books have been written on the subject. While we could not do the topic full justice here, it is important to understand some key historical trends and the forces behind them. This will help us to see that Serverless is, in fact, the next logical step in this history.

1.3.1   *The early days*

The history of computing can be traced back to ancient times, with devices such as the abacus. Historians identify the first known computer algorithm as that implemented by Ada Lovelace in the 19th century for Charles Babbage. The early development of computing was concerned with single-purpose, unwieldy systems, designed to accomplish a single goal. The modern software era only really started with the development of the first multitasking operating system, MULTICS, in 1964, followed thereafter by the development of the Unix operating system.

1.3.2 The Unix philosophy

The Unix operating system was created at Bell Labs in the 1970s by Ken Thompson and Dennis Ritchie. The original AT&T version spawned many derivative works; the most famous, perhaps, is the Linux kernel and associated distributions. For those of you with an interest in the history of computing, figure 1.2 depicts the main branches of the Unix family tree. As you can see, the original system spawned many successful derivatives, including Linux, Mac OS X, and the BSD family of operating systems.

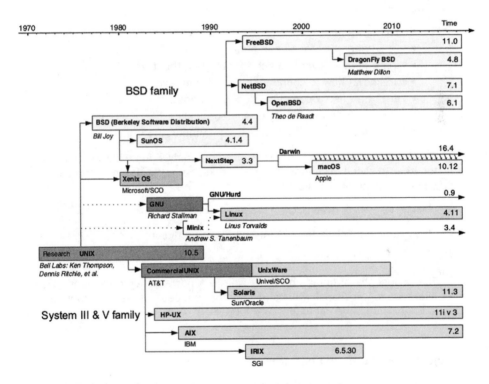

Figure 1.2   Unix family tree. Source: http://mng.bz/6AGR.

Perhaps of greater importance than the operating system is the philosophy that developed around the original Unix culture, which can be summarized as

- Write programs that do one thing and do it well.
- Write programs to work together.
- Write programs to handle text streams, because that is a universal interface.

TIP   For a full explanation of this topic, see *The Unix Programming Environment* by Brian Kernigan and Rob Pike (Prentice-Hall, 1983).

This approach to system design first introduced the concept of modularity to software development. We should note at this point that these principles may be applied irrespective of the underlying operating system or language. It is perfectly valid to apply the Unix philosophy in a Windows programming environment using C#, for instance.

The key point to understand here is that of the Single Responsibility Principle—write programs or modules with a single focus.

Single focus

To illustrate the concept of a single focus for a program, consider the following Unix command-line tools:

- `ls` knows how to list files in a directory.
- `find` searches for files in a directory tree.
- `grep` knows how to search for strings within text.
- `wc` knows how to count lines or words in text.
- `netstat` lists open network connections.
- `sort>` sorts numerically or alphabetically.
- `head` returns the top *n* lines from its input.

Each of these tools in and of themselves are fairly simple, but we can combine them together to accomplish more complex tasks. For example, the following code gives a count of the number of listening TCP sockets on a system:

```
$ netstat -an | grep -i listen | grep -i tcp | wc -1
```

This example displays the five largest files in a directory tree:

```
find . -type f -exec ls -s {} \; | sort -n -r | head -5
```

The philosophy of doing one thing well is a powerful force for good in software. It allows us to write smaller units of code that are easier to reason about and easier to get right than large interconnected monoliths.

1.3.3   *Object orientation and patterns*

This original clean and modular approach was in large part forgotten by the industry in favor of the object-oriented paradigm. During the late 1980s and early 1990s, languages such as C++ gained increasing popularity. Driven by the software pattern movement, the promise of object orientation was that code could be reused at the object level through mechanisms such as inheritance and polymorphism. It turned out that this vision was never realized, as ironically stated in the famous Banana, Monkey, Jungle problem.

Banana, Monkey, Jungle

The Banana, Monkey, Jungle problem refers to the problem of reuse in real-world object-oriented code bases. It can be stated as "I wanted a banana, but when I reached for it, I got a monkey as well holding onto the banana. Not only that, but the monkey was holding onto a tree so I got the whole jungle as well."

The following snippet illustrates the problem:

```
public class Banana {
    public Monkey Owner {get;}
}

public class Monkey {
    public Jungle Habitat {get;}
}

public class Jungle {
}
```

In order to use the Banana class, I first need to provide a Monkey instance to it. In order to use the Monkey class, I need to provide it with an instance of Jungle, and so on. This coupling is a real problem in most object-oriented code bases that the authors have come across.

During this period, before the web, systems tended to be developed and built as monoliths, and it was not atypical for large systems to have over a million lines of code comprising a single executable.

1.3.4 Java, J2EE, .NET,

The trend of object orientation continued through the 1990s into the 2000s, with languages like Java and C# gaining prominence. However, the nature of these systems started to shift away from desktop delivery to more-distributed, network-aware applications. This period saw the rise of the application server model, and was characterized by large monolithic code bases, massive relational databases with plenty of stored procedures, and CORBA/COM for distributed communication and interoperability. Deployment was typically every three to six months, and required weeks of planning and an outage period.

CORBA and COM

The *Common Object Request Broker Architecture* is a legacy binary communication protocol that was very much in vogue in the early 2000s. The *Common Object Model (COM)* was a Microsoft-specific alternative to CORBA. Both technologies are now thankfully mostly replaced with RESTful APIs.

Figure 1.3   Enterprise software development circa 2000 (or *Ploughing with Oxen*, George H. Harvey, 1881). Source: http://mng.bz/oRVD.

On reflection, early 21st century development could be compared to the early days of agriculture. Of its time, it was revolutionary. By comparison to what came later, it was slow, unwieldy, inflexible, and labor-intensive.

1.3.5   *XML and SOAXML (Extensible Markup Language) SOA (service-oriented architecture)*

From here, the industry moved to adopt *XML (Extensible Markup Language)* as a means to configure and communicate everything, peaking with the emergence of SOAP and a drive toward the so-called *service-oriented architecture (SOA)*. This was driven by an appetite for decoupling and interoperability, and underpinned by a dawning understanding of the benefits of open standards.

> **SOAP**
>
> The *Simple Object Access Protocol* is an XML-based text protocol touted as a superior alternative to CORBA and COM. Due to its text-based nature, SOAP had better cross-platform interoperability characteristics than CORBA or COM; however, it was still heavyweight and cumbersome to use compared with modern JSON-based RESTful APIs.

1.3.6   *Web speed*

In parallel with the changes in enterprise software development, fueled by the dot-com boom (and subsequent crash), the *Software as a Service (SaaS)* model began to gain traction. The industry was shifting toward the web as the primary application delivery mechanism, initially for external customer-facing use, but increasingly for internal enterprise delivery. This period saw an increasing need for rapid delivery of software, including initial deployments as well as feature additions which could now be deployed onto a server with instant effect. At this time, the predominant SaaS hosting model was to deploy to on-premise servers or machines co-located in a data center.

Thus the industry had two major problems. First, there was the need to predict ahead of time the required capacity so that enough capital expenditure could be allocated to purchase the required hardware to deal with the expected load. Secondly, large, monolithic, object-oriented code bases did not really lend themselves to the web-speed development model.

It was clear that the heavyweight, closed enterprise model was not a good fit for web-speed delivery. This led to an increasing adoption of open standards-based approaches, and to the increased use of open source technologies. This movement was led by organizations such as FSF (Free Software Foundation), Apache, and GNU/Linux.

The shift toward open source caused a crucial, irreversible change in the way enterprise software architectures were defined. Best practices, standards, and tools were once dictated by the interests of enterprise leaders like Sun Microsystems, Oracle, and Microsoft. Open source empowered hobbyists, startups, and academics to innovate quickly, and to share and iterate with unprecedented frequency. Where the industry once waited for the big players to agree on complex standards documentation, the model shifted to utilize the combined power and agility of the community to demonstrate working, pragmatic solutions that not only worked right away, but continuously improved at a blistering pace.

1.3.7 *Cloud computing*

Cloud computing first came to prominence in 2006 when Amazon launched their Elastic Compute Cloud product, now known as Amazon EC2. This was followed in 2008 by Google's App Engine, and in 2010 by Microsoft Azure. To say that cloud computing has fundamentally changed the software industry would be an understatement. In 2017, Amazon Web Services (AWS) reported revenues of 17.46 billion USD.

The availability of on-demand compute power made it affordable and fast for individuals and cash-strapped startups to build truly innovative projects and have a disproportionate impact on the industry. Critically, the industry started looking to the most innovative end users of software tooling for leadership, not the enterprise software vendors. For the enterprise, the rise of cloud computing caused several seismic shifts. Key among these were

- Shift of cost models from large up-front capital expenditure to lower ongoing operational expenditure.
- Elastic scaling—Resources could now be used and paid for on demand.
- DevOps and infrastructure as code—As cloud APIs matured, tooling was developed to capture the entire deployment stack as code.

1.3.8 *Microservices (rediscovery)*

The widespread adoption of open source combined with the shift to operational expenditure and elastic scaling led to a rediscovery of the Unix philosophy when it came to enterprise platform development, and helped to drive the adoption of the so-called microservice architecture. While there is no agreed-upon formal definition for a microservice, most practitioners in the industry would agree with the following characterization:

- Microservices are small, fine-grained, and perform a single function.
- The organization culture must embrace automation of testing and deployment. This eases the burden on management and operations, and allows for different development teams to work on independently deployable units of code.
- The culture and design principles must embrace failure and faults, similar to anti-fragile systems.
- Each service is elastic, resilient, composable, minimal, and complete.
- The services can be individually and horizontally scaled.

The ideas behind microservices are nothing new. Distributed systems have existed since the 1970s. Erlang was doing microservices in the 1980s, and everything since, from CORBA to SOA, tried to achieve the goal of distributed, networked components. The enablers for the mass adoption of microservices were cloud, containers, and community:

- Cloud infrastructure like AWS gave us the ability to quickly and cheaply deploy and destroy secure clusters of machines with high availability.
- Containers (Docker) gave us the ability to build, package, and deploy immutable units containing software at a microservice unit of scale. Previously, it wasn't feasible or comprehensible to deploy a few hundred lines of code as a single unit!
- Community offerings gave us the tooling to manage the new form of complexity that emerges when you start dealing with numerous, small units of deployment. This includes orchestration in the form of Kubernetes, monitoring in the form of *ELK (Elasticsearch, Logstash, and Kibana)* or Zipkin, as well as the massive range of tooling, such as the work open sourced by the Netflix engineering team.

The microservice model is a great fit for modern cloud infrastructures because each component can be scaled individually. Moreover, each component can also be deployed individually. This enables much more rapid development cycles and, indeed, led to the development of what has since been termed *continuous deployment,* where code committed by a developer moves immediately to production with no human intervention, provided, of course, that it passes a series of stringent automated tests.

For a full treatment of microservices, we can recommend *The Tao of Microservices* by Richard Rodger, also published by Manning.

1.3.9   *Cloud native services*

Services such as Amazon's EC2 are typically referred to as *Infrastructure as a Service* or *IaaS.* While this is a powerful concept, it still places the burden of operations and management on the end user of the service. Most systems will require some form of database and other pieces of infrastructure to operate. If we build a system on top of IaaS, then we would need to install and maintain a cluster of database servers and deal with issues like backup, geographical redundancy, and scaling the cluster to handle the requisite load. We can avoid all of this overhead by instead using cloud native services. Under this model, the cloud provider handles the management and operation of our database for us; we simply tell the system what to do through configuration or the use of an API.

To provide a more concrete example, let's look at Amazon's DynamoDB service. This is a fully managed high-scale key value store. To use DynamoDB, we need only go to the DynamoDB setup page on the AWS console, enter a few pieces of configuration information, and we have a table ready to read and write to in less than 60 seconds. Contrast this with the setup that would be required to install our own key value store on EC2 instances, which would require hours of setup and continued maintenance.

One of the most exciting developments in cloud services is the ability to run managed code units on the cloud without caring about the underlying server. This is usually referred to as *Function as a Service* or *FaaS*. On AWS, FaaS is implemented using the *Lambda* service, whereas Google's offering is called *Cloud Functions*.

1.3.10 *The trend: speed*

If we pull on all of these threads, it becomes apparent that with a few missteps, the main driving force is the need for speed. After all, time is money! By this, we mean that there is an increasing need to get code into production as quickly as possible, and to be able to manage and scale it quickly. This has driven the adoption of microservices and cloud native services, because these technologies provide a path to rapid development and deployment of functionality.

In tandem with the changing technology landscape, there has been an evolution in the methodologies that the industry has applied to the development of software. These trends are summarised in figure 1.4.

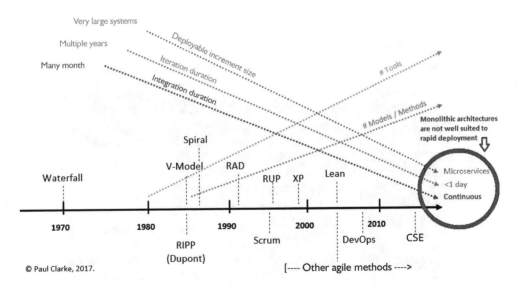

Figure 1.4   Changes in iteration times and code volumes. Courtesy of Clarke, Paul. 2017. Computer science lecture notes. Dublin City University and Lero, the Irish Software Research Center.

As illustrated, iteration times have been rapidly decreasing. In the 1980s and early 1990s, using waterfall-based methodologies, what could be called an iteration would be the length of the entire project—perhaps a year or more for most projects. As we moved into the mid 1990s, iteration times dropped with the adoption of early agile-like approaches such as the Rational Unified Process (RUP). With the advent of agile methodologies like Extreme Programming (XP) around the 2000s, iteration times dropped to two to three weeks in duration, and now some more-hyper agile practices use iteration times of around a week.

Software concomitant release cycles—the time between releases of production—have been decreasing, from more than a year in the 1980s and 1990s to today's far more rapid release schedules. Indeed, the highest performing organizations using continuous deployment techniques can release software to production many times a day.

The ability to release at this frenetic pace has been enabled by another trend: namely, the decreasing unit of scale. The volume of code per deployment unit has been decreasing. In the 1980s and 1990s, large, monolithic code bases were the order of the day. Due to the coupled nature of these code bases, testing and deployment was a difficult and time-consuming process. With the advent of service-oriented architecture in the late 1990s and early 2000s, the deployment unit decreased in size. This was followed by a much more significant drop as microservices were adopted.

Figure 1.5 illustrates how the decreasing unit of scale and accelerated deployment cycles have been accompanied by increasing levels of abstraction away from the underlying hardware.

The industry has in large part moved away from installing and running physical hardware, through virtual servers to container-based deployment. The current state of the art is typically to deploy small services built as containers to some kind of

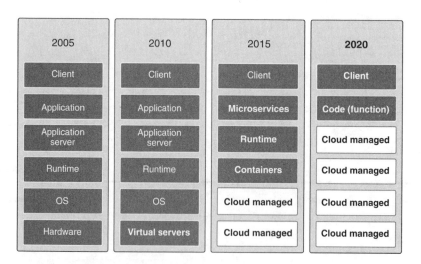

Figure 1.5   Unit of scale change

orchestration platform such as Kubernetes. Services will typically then consume either IaaS-configured databases or cloud-native data services. However, it seems clear that if the trend of increased deployment speed and reduced unit of scale is to continue—and the economic incentive would indicate that this is a desirable goal—then the next logical step in this progression is to move to fully serverless systems.

Figure 1.6 illustrates the path and technology milestones that have led the industry to the development of Serverless.

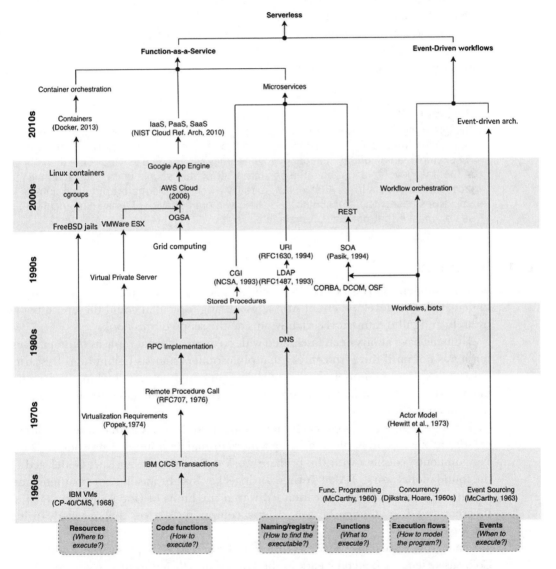

Figure 1.6 A history of computing concepts leading to serverless computing. E. van Eyk et al, "Serverless is More: From PaaS to Present Cloud Computing." *IEEE Internet Computing* 22, no. 5 (Sept/Oct. 2018): 8-17, doi: 10.1109/ MIC.2018.053681358.

In summary, the need for rapid development and deployment of software has led to a decreasing unit of scale. The next logical step in this progression is the adoption of fully serverless architectures.

1.4   What is AI?

Artificial intelligence (AI) is a term that has grown to encompass a range of techniques and algorithmic approaches in computer science. To many people, it can often conjure up images of out-of-control killer robots, mainly due to the dystopian futures portrayed in the Matrix and Terminator movies!

A more sober and sensible definition of the term might be this:

Artificial Intelligence refers to the capacity of a computer to exhibit learning and decision making capabilities, as seen in humans and other animal species.

> ### It's just code
> Though some of the capabilities exhibited by modern AI systems can often appear miraculous, we should always bear in mind that at the end of the day it's just code. For example, an algorithm that can recognize images may be a very powerful tool, but at the base level it is just an interconnected set of very simple units. The "learning" process that occurs in an AI algorithm is really a very simple matter of tuning numerical values based on training data. It is the emergent behavior of these numerical values en masse that produces remarkable results.

1.4.1   History of AI

Why the sudden interest in AI? How come AI and machine learning are increasingly in demand? The development of AI is a fascinating topic that could fill several books by itself, and full treatment is certainly outside the scope of this book.

Humans have always been fascinated with creating artificial replicas of themselves, but it was not until the 17th century that philosophers such as Leibniz and Descartes began to explore the notion that human thought could be described in a systematic, mathematical manner, and therefore could perhaps be amenable to replication by nonhuman machines.

From these first philosophical forays, it took until the early 20th century for thinkers such as Russel and Boole to develop a more formal definition of these ideas. These developments, coupled with the brilliant work of mathematician Kurt Godel, led to the foundational work of Alan Turing. Turing's key insight was that any mathematical problem that could be formally defined within the limits of Godel's incompleteness theorem could, in theory, be solved by a computing device, the so-called Turing Machine.

The groundbreaking work of Turing and Flowers, developing the Bombe and Colossus systems at Bletchley Park in the UK, eventually led to the now famous Dartmouth Collage conference in the summer of 1956, which is generally recognized as the formal founding of the discipline of AI.

There was much early optimism, leading to some wildly optimistic predictions such as

- H.A. Simon and A. Newell, 1958: "Within ten years, a digital computer will be the world's chess champion."
- H.A. Simon, 1965: "Machines will be capable, within twenty years, of doing any work a man can do."
- M. Minsky, 1967: "Within a generation … the problem of creating artificial intelligence will substantially be solved."

Progress in the field through the early years of the 1970s did not match these expectations. As time passed with no substantial progress, funding sources dried up and research in the field slowed. This period is known as the *first AI winter*.

The 1980s witnessed the rise of *expert systems*: rule-based problem-solving languages like Prolog gained traction and much interest from the business community. History repeated itself, and toward the end of the 1980s it became clear that the early promise of expert systems was not going to be realized. This fact, coupled with the rise of commodity PC hardware, meant that companies would no longer invest in the expensive custom hardware required for these systems, and the second AI winter began.

In the background, researchers had made strides in advancing the field of neural network development, both in network architecture and improved training algorithms such as back propagation. The field was lacking one key ingredient: computational power.

Throughout the 1990s and early 2000s, Moore's law (the exponential growth in compute power) continued apace. This growth in power allowed researchers to build increasingly more complex neural networks and to shorten the training cycles, providing a boost to the field and the ability to innovate at a much more rapid pace. Beginning with IMB's Deep Blue beating Gary Kasparov in 1997, AI has been expanding into many areas and has been rapidly commoditizing, meaning that the technology is now available for use in many business contexts at low cost, without requiring a team of expert researchers.

1.4.2 *Real world AI*

Since the 1950s, efforts have been made to create machines that can exhibit the capabilities of humans, that can take an objective and figure out a way to fulfil it. The last few years have seen the emergence of real-world AI solutions that are being used every day. Whether you are watching the latest TV drama, listening to music, shopping online, or getting the latest news updates, there's a high probability that you are using technology that is driven by the latest advances in AI. Let's take a look at some of the areas where artificial intelligence technology has had a major impact.

RETAIL AND E-COMMERCE

In online retail and physical retail stores, AI is applied in recommending products that shoppers are most likely to buy. In the early days of e-commerce, we saw simple examples of recommenders ("People who bought this also bought…."). These days, many retailers are monitoring user browsing behavior in great detail, and using this data with real-time AI algorithms to prominently place products that are more likely to be bought.

ENTERTAINMENT

The significant rise of online movies, TV, and music consumption has given providers a huge volume of consumption data. This data is being used by all the major providers to drive consumption further. Netflix has stated that 80% of subscriber choices come from the platform's recommendation algorithm. Spotify is another example of a streaming platform that learns from user behavior and suggests further music recommendations.[2]

NEWS AND MEDIA

The use of AI in social media and online news has been much publicised. Facebook and Twitter both use AI extensively to select posts to appear in users' timelines. About two-thirds of U.S. adults get news from social media sites, so AI is having a significant impact on the news we see (source: http://www.journalism.org/2018/09/10/news-use-across-social-media-platforms-2018/).

ADVERTISING

Advertising is an area that has been massively impacted by AI. AI is used for matching ads to users based on online behaviour and preferences. The process of advertisers bidding for consumer attention across mobile and web is real-time and automated by AI. Google and Facebook, both with large AI research divisions, use AI extensively in this process. In 2017, Facebook and Google accounted for 90% of new advertising business (source: https://www.marketingaiinstitute.com/blog/ai-in-advertising-what-you-need-to-know).

CUSTOMER CONTACT

The ways in which consumers interact with businesses are changing as the online world evolves. Many people are used to automated telephone answering systems that guide us through options by selecting numbers on a keypad, or using voice recognition of questionable accuracy. Customer support operations are now using a variety of advances to reduce costs and improve customer experience. One example is to use sentiment analysis to detect tone and prioritise the importance of some interactions. Another example is the use of chatbots to answer common queries without any staff being required.

Voice recognition and voice synthesis are also extremely useful in these scenarios as the capability of those systems improves. The 2018 Google Duplex demo was a fantastic example of how good these capabilities have become (http://mng.bz/v9Oa). Every day more people are using Alexa, Siri, or Google Assistant as an interface to the online world, getting information, organising their lives, and making purchases.

---

[2] Sources: http://mng.bz/4BvQ and http://mng.bz/Qxg4.

DATA AND SECURITY

Businesses, consumers, and regulators are becoming increasingly aware of the importance of data privacy and security. This is seen in the regulations forming around how data is stored, retained, and processed. Additionally, security breaches are an increasing cause for concern. AI has a role to play in addressing both sides. Document processing, classification, and identification of personal data is already possible and implemented in services such as Amazon Macie. In the area of threat and breach detection, AI is being used to both prevent and alert. Amazon GuardDuty is a good example of this.

Apart from information security, AI is finding many real-world applications in the field of physical security. The recent major improvements in image processing and facial recognition are being applied for urban, building, and airport security. AI can also be applied effectively for the detection of physical threats from objects such as explosives, firearms, and other weapons.

FINANCE

Often, data in financial applications is time-series data. Think of a data set containing the number of sales of a product per day in a given year. Time-series data of this nature is amenable to predictive AI models. These models can be used for forecasting and resource planning.

HEALTH CARE

Development of AI in health care has largely been concerned with diagnostic tools, and particularly image interpretation in the fields of radiology and microbiology. A recent survey of deep learning research in this field demonstrates the explosion of interest in the area and dramatic improvements in performance in recent years. While some works already claim to outperform medical experts, AI is more typically expected to be used as an assistant in detection and measurement of subtle abnormalities.[3]

In many parts of the developing world, there is a shortage of medical expertise, which makes the application of AI even more valuable. For example, detection of tuberculosis is being carried out by automated interpretation of chest x-ray images using AI.

Figure 1.7   AI assists in the diagnosis of tuberculosis using mobile x-ray units in the developing world. (Reproduced with permission courtesy of Delft Imaging Systems.)

---

[3] Sources: (1) Geert Litjens, Thijs Kooi, Babak Ehteshami Bejnordi, Arnaud Arindra Adiyoso Setio, Francesco Ciompi, Mohsen Ghafoorian, Jeroen A.W.M. van der Laak, Bram van Ginneken, Clara I. Sánchez. "A survey on deep learning in medical image analysis." *Medical Image Analysis*, Volume 42, 2017, Pages 60-88. (2) and (3) work by Esteva et al. (2017) and Gulshan et al. (2016) in the fields of dermatology and ophthalmology.

1.4.3   *AI services*

Table 1.3 shows some common applications of artificial intelligence, and AWS (and other cloud providers) offer services built on pre-trained models for many of these use cases.

Table 1.2   AI applications and services

Application	Use	Service
Natural language processing	Machine translation	AWS Translate
Document analysis	AWS Textract	
Key phrases	AWS Comprehend	
Sentiment analysis		
Topic modelling		
Document classification		
Entity extraction		
Conversational interfaces	Chatbots	AWS Lex
Speech	Speech-to-text	AWS Transcribe
Text-to-speech	AWS Polly	
Machine vision	Object, scene, and activity detection	AWS Rekognition
Facial recognition		
Facial analysis		
Text in images		
Others	Time series forecasting	AWS Forecast
Real-time personalization and recommendation	AWS Personalize	

We will use most of these services in later chapters, so they will become very familiar to you, but we'll summarize each service here for reference:

- *AWS Translate* is a neural machine translation service. This means that it uses deep learning models to deliver more accurate and more natural-sounding translation than traditional statistical and rule-based translation algorithms.
- *AWS Textract* automatically extracts text and data from scanned documents using a combination of optical character recognition (OCR) and text classification models.
- *AWS Comprehend* is a natural language processing (NLP) service that uses machine learning to find insights and relationships in text.

- *AWS Lex* is a service for building conversational interfaces voice and text, also known as *chatbots*. It accomplishes this by using deep learning models for natural language understanding (NLU) and automatic speech recognition (ASR).
- *AWS Transcribe* uses deep learning models to convert speech to text from audio files.
- *AWS Polly* turns text into lifelike speech using advanced deep learning models.
- *AWS Rekognition* is an image recognition services that uses deep learning models to identify objects, people, text, scenes, and activities in images and videos, as well as detect any inappropriate content.
- *AWS Forecast* is based on the same technology used at Amazon.com. It uses machine learning to combine time series data with additional variables to build forecasts.
- *AWS Personalize* provides personalized product and content recommendations. It's based on the recommendation technology used on Amazon.com.

1.4.4 AI and machine learning

Much of the focus and progress in AI in the past 10 years has been made in the area of machine learning, which is the *"study of computer algorithms that improve automatically through experience"* (Tom Mitchell, *Machine Learning*, McGraw Hill, 1991). There is some debate as to the specific meanings of AI and machine learning, and their subtle difference. In this book, when we talk about AI applications in software systems, we are talking about machine learning.

The practice of machine learning typically involves a training phase, followed by a test phase. Regardless of the algorithm, the machine learning algorithm is trained on a set of data. This could be a set of images in the case of an image recognition algorithm, or a set of structured records in the case of a financial prediction model. The algorithm's purpose is to make judgments about the test data based on features it has "learned" from the training data.

Machine learning can be divided into these categories, as illustrated in figure 1.8.

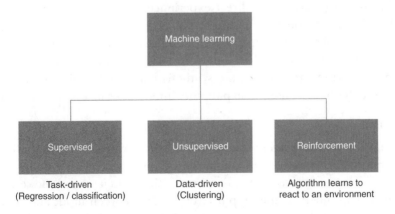

Figure 1.8 Types of machine learning (Source: Analytics Vidhya)

NOTE   *Features* are an important concept in machine learning. In order to recognize a cat in an image, you might look for features such as triangular ears, whiskers, and a tail. Selecting the right set of features is critical to effective performance of the algorithm.

In traditional machine learning algorithms, features are created by hand. In neural networks, features are selected automatically by the network.

Machine learning can be divided into these categories:

- Supervised learning
- Unsupervised learning
- Reinforcement learning

SUPERVISED LEARNING

Supervised learning is when the algorithm is provided with a set of labeled training data. Take, for example, a set of documents labelled with their classification. These labels might represent the topic of each document. By training a given algorithm with this data set, you would expect the algorithm to predict the topic of unlabeled test documents. This can be very effective with sufficient, well-labeled training data. The drawback, of course, is that it can be difficult to find or create such labelled training data in sufficient volume.

UNSUPERVISED LEARNING

Unsupervised machine learning tries to extract relevant patterns in data without access to any annotated training data (labels). Examples of unsupervised algorithms would be clustering, dimensionality reduction, and anomaly detection. We can use unsupervised learning when we want to extract patterns from a data set without specific expectations as to the outcome. The unsupervised approach has a clear advantage, as it doesn't require labelled data. On the other hand, the results can be difficult for humans to interpret, and the learned patterns may be different from what is desired.

REINFORCEMENT LEARNING

Reinforcement learning learns from direct experience. It is provided with an environment and a reward function, and aims to maximize its reward. We allow the algorithm to take actions and observe the outcomes from those actions. Then we try to calculate a reward function of how desirable the outcome was. The most likely applications for reinforcement learning at this time are synthetic computer-simulated environments that allow for millions or billions of exploratory interactions in a short period of time.

1.4.5   *Deep learning*

Deep learning is based on *artificial neural networks (ANNs)*, which were first studied in the 1950s. Artificial neural networks are organized as connected layers of nodes, or *perceptrons*. The input is provided as a set of numbers in the input layer, and the result is usually provided as numbers in the output layer. Layers between input and output are called "hidden" layers. The objective of ANNs is to iteratively learn weights for each perceptron so as to produce an approximation of the desired result in the output layer. The word "deep" refers to the fact that there are many layers in the network (at least 7-8 but probably hundreds). A deep learning network is illustrated in figure 1.9.

The concept of modelling the human brain with neural networks has been around since the dawn of AI research. However, the raw compute power was just not available for these approaches to realise their potential. As more powerful processing became available during the late 2000s and early 2010s, neural networks and deep learning began to become the predominant approach to AI. Progress in deep learning was further aided by advances in the algorithms as well as the availability of large volumes of training data coming from the internet. The task of labelling training data is often solved by crowdsourcing (e.g. Amazon Mechanical Turk).

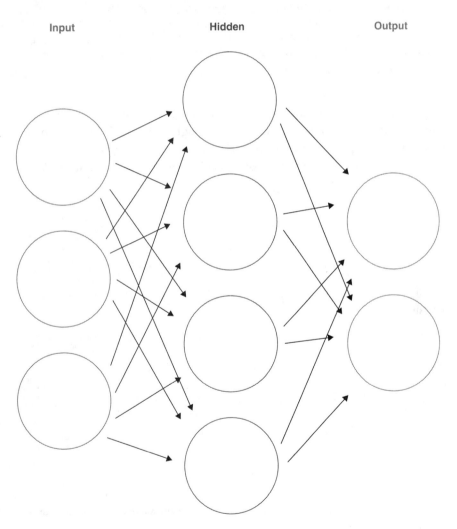

Figure 1.9   Deep neural network layers

Alpha Go

One key event that demonstrated the massive progress in deep learning was the triumph of Alpha Go over the best human Go masters. Alpha Go was initially developed by UK-based company DeepMind Technologies. The company was acquired by Google in 2014.

The key thing to understand about this is that the network had to "learn" Go. This is significantly different from the approach that Deep Blue was able to take in beating Gary Kasparov. This is due to the number of possible game states. In Chess, there are approximately 10^{45} game states, whereas in Go there are approximately 10^{170}. Because of this, it is possible to use a combination of game knowledge and algorithmic ML techniques to essentially program Deep Blue to be expert at Chess. However, when we consider that the number of atoms in the observable universe is estimated to be 10^{80}, we get an understanding of the complexity of the game of Go and the impossibility of attempting to use an expert systems-like approach. Instead, Alpha Go used a deep neural network that was trained in the game of Go by observing millions of games.

Figure 1.10 attempts to categorize the preceding summary of machine learning tools and techniques into a single diagram. Though a detailed description of all of the nuances in this space is beyond the scope of this chapter, figure 1.10 should provide a basic reference frame when discussing machine learning at a high level.

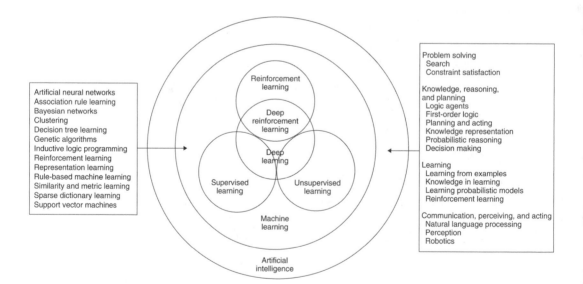

Figure 1.10   AI and machine learning algorithms and applications. Deep reinforcement learning: an overview. Yuxi Li. https://arxiv.org/abs/1701.07274.

1.4.6   AI challenges

At present, AI is dominated by supervised learning, which requires data for training. One of the challenges is having labeled data representing all scenarios to be learned by the network. Development of unsupervised models is a hot topic of research for this reason. For many users who wish to leverage AI, it is often impossible to obtain sufficient data. Training with a limited data set often leaves algorithms with biases, leading to incorrect judgments on data which is not similar to the training set.

There are also challenges in the area of law and ethics when AI is employed. If a machine learning algorithm makes an undesirable judgment, it is difficult to know what party is liable. If a bank makes a decision that an individual is not entitled to a mortgage, it might be unclear why that decision has been made and who can be held accountable.

1.5   The democratization of compute power and artificial intelligence

It is interesting to observe the democratizing power that Moore's Law has had over the decades. Consider that there are still programmers working today who remember submitting programs for execution on punch cards! During the era of the mainframe and minicomputer, access to computer time was a scare resource granted to only the privileged few. Now, of course, most of us carry more compute power in our pockets in the form of a smartphone than those early systems had.

Cloud computing has had a similar effect. Back in the dot-com era, specialist hardware engineers were required to construct racks of servers in co-located facilities. Today we can script up the equivalent of an entire data center and tear it down just as easily—if we have sufficient funds available, that is!

So it is with AI. Previously, in order to build a system with say, speech recognition, we would need to use highly specialist bespoke hardware and software, or even perform research into the topic ourselves. Today we need only plug into one of the cloud native speech recognition services and we can add a speech interface to our platform.

1.6   Canonical AI as a Service architecture

When approaching any new topic as broad as AI as a Service, it is important to build a picture of how the pieces fit together. Figure 1.11 is a high-level view of the typical structure of a serverless AI platform: an architectural frame of reference. We will refer back to this canonical architecture throughout the book as a common reference mental model.

The key points to realize about this architecture are

- It can be implemented entirely with cloud native services—no physical or virtual machines are required, and no containers.
- It can be realized on multiple cloud platforms provided by the major vendors.

Let's review each of the elements of this architecture in turn.

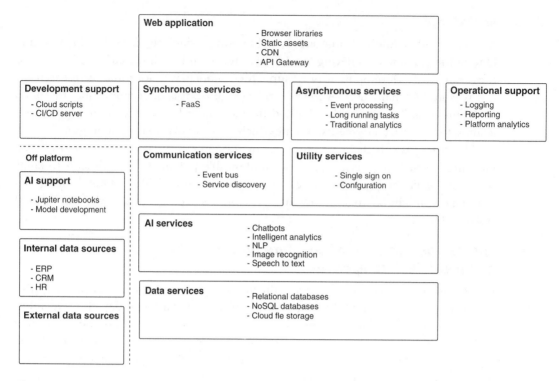

Figure 1.11   Canonical AI as a Service platform architecture

1.6.1   *Web application*

A typical platform will deliver functionality through a web application layer, that is to say using the HTTP(S) protocol. This layer is usually comprised of a number of elements, including

- Static assets such as images, style sheets, and client-side JavaScript
- Some form of content-delivery network or page cache
- RESTful API
- GraphQL interface
- User registration login/logout
- Mobile API
- Application firewall

This layer acts as a gateway to the main platform for client requests.

1.6.2   *Realtime services*

These services are typically consumed by the Web Application layer in order to return an immediate response to a client request. These services represent a common glue layer between all parts of the platform. For example, one service may be responsible for fetching an image and passing it to an AI service for analysis, and then returning the results to the client.

1.6.3   *Batch services*

Typically these services are for longer-running, asynchronous tasks and will include things like *ETL (Extract Transform Load)* processes, long-running data loads, and traditional analytics. The batch services will typically use well-known analytical engines such as Hadoop or Spark, consumed as cloud native services rather than self-managed.

1.6.4   *Communication services*

Most platforms will require some form of asynchronous communication, typically implemented on top of some form of message-passing infrastructure or event bus. Within this communication fabric, we also expect to find things like service registration and discovery.

1.6.5   *Utility services*

Utility services include security services such as single sign-on and federated identities, and also network and configuration management services such as *VPC (Virtual Private Cloud)* and certificate handling.

1.6.6   *AI services*

This forms the intelligent core of the serverless AI platform, and can comprise a range of AI services depending on the focus of the platform. For example, here you may find chatbot implementations, natural language processing, or image recognition models and services. In many cases these services are wired into the platform using pre-canned off-the-shelf cloud-native AI services; in other cases, some cross-training of models may be required before deployment into the platform.

1.6.7   *Data services*

Underpinning our serverless AI stack are the data services. These will typically use a mixture of relational databases, NoSQL databases, cloud file storage, and anything in between. As with the other areas of the system, the data tier is implemented through consumption of cloud-native data services rather than self-installed and managed instances.

1.6.8   *Operational support*

This grouping holds the management tools required for successful operation of the platform such as logging, log analysis, message tracing alerting, and so on. As with the other parts of the system, the operational support services may be implemented without the need to install and manage infrastructure. It is interesting to note that these operational support services may themselves use AI services in order to help with alerting and anomaly detection. We cover this in more detail in later chapters.

1.6.9   *Development support*

This grouping is concerned with the deployment of the platform, and will hold the scripts needed to create the cloud fabric for the other service groupings. It will also provide support for continuous integration/continuous delivery pipelines for each of the other service groups, and for end-to-end testing of the platform.

1.6.10   *Off-platform*

We have included an off-platform grouping of elements. These may or may not be present, depending on the platform operational model.

AI SUPPORT

This includes data-science-type investigations, bespoke model training, and investigation. We will see later that the process of training a machine learning system is very different from that of using it operationally. For many use cases, training is not required.

INTERNAL DATA SOURCES

Enterprise platforms will typically have touch points to internal or legacy systems. This could include CRM (customer relationship management) and ERP (enterprise resource planning) type systems or connections to legacy internal APIs.

EXTERNAL DATA SOURCES

Most platforms do not live in isolation and may consume data and services from third-party APIs; these act as external data sources to our serverless AI platform.

1.7   *Realization on Amazon Web Services*

In order to make this more concrete, figure 1.12 depicts how the canonical architecture might map onto Amazon Web Services.

This is, of course, not an exhaustive list of all of the available cloud native services on the AWS platform; however, it does illustrate how these services may be grouped together into a coherent architectural structure.

Why AWS?

Throughout this book, we will be providing code and examples against the AWS platform. We have chosen to do this for two reasons:

- AWS is by far the market leader in the cloud computing space in terms of market penetration. At time of writing, AWS commands a 48% share. This means that the examples in the book will be familiar to a broader base of readers.
- AWS is the leader in terms of innovation. We recently compared the release dates of services across a number of categories, between AWS and other cloud providers. We found that on average AWS released services 2.5 years ahead of the competition. This also implies that the AWS service offerings are more mature and complete.

Additionally, of course, it would make for a lot of work to build the example systems on three difference clouds!

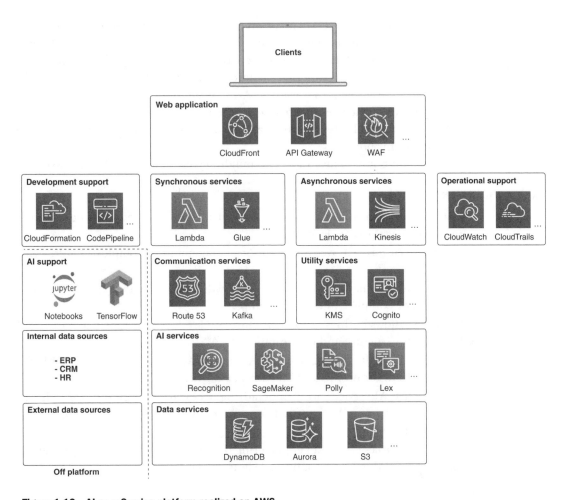

Figure 1.12   AI as a Service platform realized on AWS

The key points to take away from this mapping exercise are

- At no point in this system are we required to install and manage a server. This removes a large amount of operational overhead with regard to management, scaling, capacity planning, and so on.
- All of the creation and deployment of these services is controlled through a set of deployment scripts which can be version-controlled and managed as code assets.
- Our AI services can be consumed off the shelf; in other words, a machine learning expert is not required to construct the system.

We hope that this first chapter has provided you with enough background information on industry trends to convince you that AI as a Service and Serverless in general will become the de facto standard for platform development over the coming years.

For the rest of this book, we will focus on practical recipes and examples to enable you to move right to the cutting edge of serverless AI development. We will cover building a range of AI-enabled systems of increasing complexity, all the time referring back to our canonical architecture that we developed in this chapter.

We would stress that while we will use AWS throughout this book, the architectures, principles, and practices are readily transferable to other clouds. Both Azure and GCP provide parallel offerings that can be composed in a similar manner to the AWS examples in this book.

Next up, we are going to dive right into building your first AI as a Service system!

1.8   Summary

- The unit of scale has been reducing in size. The next logical progression is function-as-a-service or FaaS.
- Serverless largely removes the need for management of complex IT infrastructure.
- Service scaling is handled by the cloud provider, removing the need for capacity planning or complex auto-scaling setups.
- Serverless allows businesses to focus more on developing platform features, and less on infrastructure and operations.
- There will be an increasing need for AI services as data volumes and complexity increase, both for business and technical analytics.
- Cloud-native AI services are democratizing access to AI technology, which can now be used by non AI experts. The range of available offerings will only grow over the coming cycles.
- All of these forces enable an engineering-driven approach to building serverless platforms and the consumption of AI as a service.

Building a serverless image
recognition system, part 1

This chapter covers

- Building a simple AI as a Service system
- Setting up the cloud environment
- Setting up a local development environment
- Implementing a simple asynchronous service
- Deploying to the cloud

In this chapter and in chapter 3 we will focus on building our first AI-enabled serverless system. By the end, you will have configured and deployed to the cloud a small system that is capable of reading and recognizing images from a web page and displaying the results for review. This may sound like an awful lot of work for a single chapter and indeed, before the advent of Serverless and off-the-shelf AI, the progress that we will make in this chapter would have taken a small team of engineers many person-months to complete. As Isaac Newton stated, we stand on the shoulders of giants! In this chapter we will stand on the shoulders of countless software engineers and AI experts to rapidly assemble our "hello world" system.

If you are new to AWS and serverless technology, there is an awful lot to take in over the course of these two chapters. Our aim is go slowly and to provide a lot of detail in order to bring everyone up to speed. We will take a "paint by numbers" approach, so if you follow the code and deployment instructions carefully, you should be just fine.

As you progress through these pages, no doubt several questions will pop into your head, such as "How do I debug this?" or "How should I unit test this?" Rest assured that we will provide more detail in subsequent chapters; for now, grab some coffee and buckle up!

2.1   *Our first system*

Our first serverless AI system will use Amazon Rekognition to analyze the images on a web page. From an analysis of these images, the system will generate a word cloud and provide a list of tags for each image. We will develop the system as a number of discrete, decoupled services. A screenshot of the finished user interface is shown in figure 2.1.

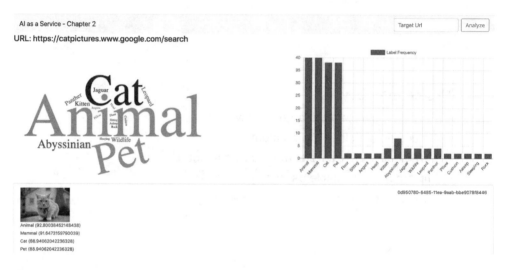

Figure 2.1   Finished UI

In this case, we pointed our system to a web page that contains images of cats. The image recognition AI has correctly identified the cats and allowed us to construct a word cloud and a histogram of the detected label frequency from this analysis. The system then shows us each image that was analyzed, along with the results of the analysis and a confidence level for each tag.

2.2   *Architecture*

Before we dive into implementation, let's take a look at the architecture for this simple system to see how it maps to the canonical architecture that we developed in chapter 1, and how the services collaborate to delver this functionality. Figure 2.2 depicts the overall structure of the system.

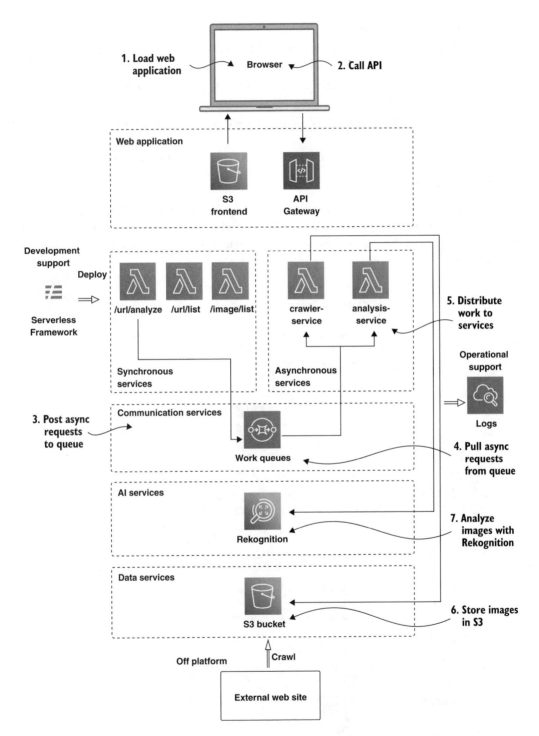

Figure 2.2 System architecture. The system is composed of custom services built using AWS Lambda and API Gateway. SQS is used for message communication. The managed services used here are S3 and Rekognition.

The system architecture shows the layers of the system:

- Starting with the front end, served from S3 (Simple Storage Service), APIs are invoked through the API Gateway.
- The asynchronous Lambda functions are triggered by SQS (Simple Queue Service) messages.
- The synchronous Lambda functions are triggered by events coming from the API Gateway.
- AWS Rekognition is a fully managed AI image analysis service.

2.2.1 Web application

The front end of the system is a single-page application comprising HTML, CSS, and some simple JavaScript to render the UI, as highlighted in figure 2.3. You will see this figure repeated throughout the chapter as we walk through the building blocks of our system.

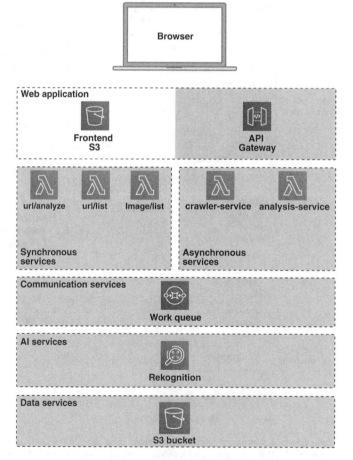

Figure 2.3   Web application

The front end is deployed into an S3 bucket. Also in this tier, we are using API Gateway to provide a route into the synchronous services that provide data for the front end to render.

2.2.2 Synchronous services

There are three synchronous services implemented as Lambda functions, as shown in figure 2.4.

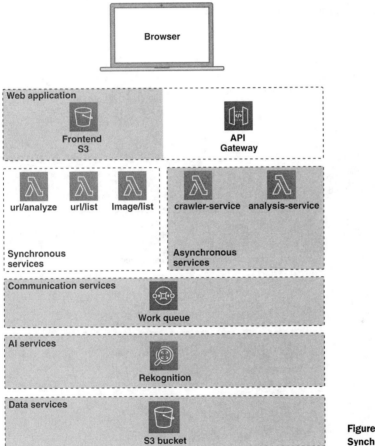

Figure 2.4
Synchronous services

These services are available as RESTful endpoints accessed through the API gateway:

- POST /url/analyze—This endpoint takes a URL in the body and submits it to an SQS queue for analysis.
- GET /url/list—Used by the front end to fetch the list of URLs that have been processed by the system.
- GET /image/list—Returns the set of images and analysis results that have been processed for a given URL.

To trigger the analysis, the user of our system inputs a URL into the input field at the top of the UI and clicks the Analysis button. This will make a POST request to /url/analyze, which will result in a JSON message post to an SQS queue of the form:

```
{body: {action: "download", msg: {url: "http://ai-as-a-service.s3-website-eu-
    west-1.amazonaws.com"}}}
```

2.2.3 Asynchronous services

The asynchronous services form the main processing engine of the system. There are two main services, highlighted in figure 2.5.

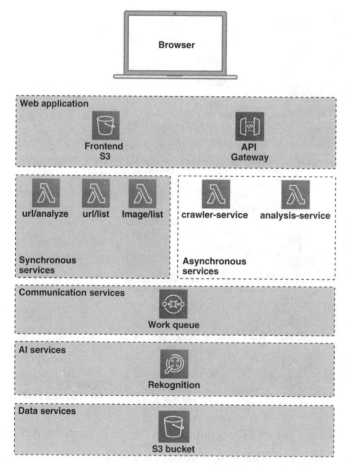

Figure 2.5
Asynchronous services

The crawler service extracts images from an HTML page. The analysis service provides an interface to AWS Rekognition, submitting images for analysis and collating the results.

On receipt of a "download" message, the crawler service will fetch the HTML from the provided URL. The crawler will then parse this HTML and extract the source attributes for each of the inline image tags in the page. The crawler will then download each image and store it in an S3 bucket. Once all of the images have been downloaded, the crawler will post an analyze message to the analysis SQS queue of the form:

```
{body: {action: "analyze", msg: {domain: "ai-as-a-service.s3-website-eu-west-
    1.amazonaws.com"}}}
```

This message will be picked up by the analysis service, which will call out to the image recognition AI for each downloaded image, collect the results, and write them into the bucket for later display by the front end.

2.2.4 Communication services

Internally, the system uses the Simple Queue Service (SQS) as a message pipeline, as shown in figure 2.6.

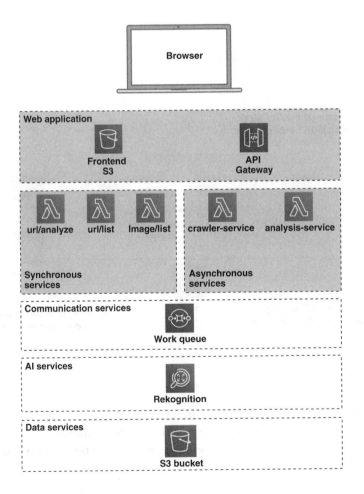

Figure 2.6 Communication and data services

As we will see throughout this book, this messaging approach is a powerful pattern that allows us to add services to and remove them from our system with little or no perturbation to the system as a whole. It also forces us to keep our services decoupled and provides a clean model to individually scale services.

For this system, we are using SQS as our primary communication mechanism, but we use the term *communication services* to encompass any infrastructural technology that can be used to facilitate communication between consumers and services. Typically this will require some form of service discovery and one or more communication protocols. Figure 2.7 depicts an isolated view of the communication services for our system.

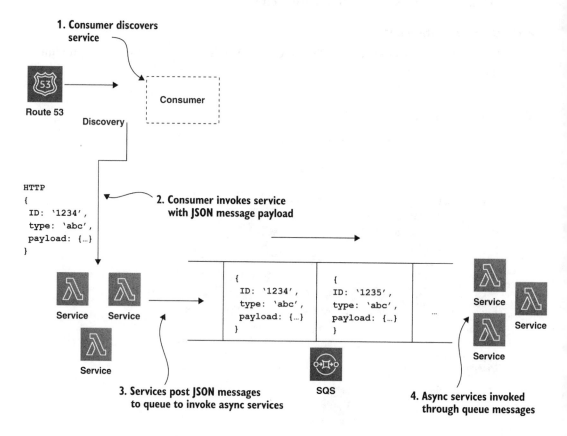

Figure 2.7   Communication services

The communication services shown are Route 53 DNS (Domain Name System) for service discovery and HTTP and SQS as the communication protocols. Typically we will use the JSON data format to encode messages between parties. This is independent of the underlying communication protocol.

> **Messaging technology**
>
> Messaging systems, queuing, and related technology are a large topic and we won't cover them in detail in this book. However you should be aware of the concepts if you aren't already. In brief, messaging systems typically support either of two models—point to point or publish/subscribe:
>
> - *Point to point*—Under this model, a message that is placed into a queue is delivered to one consumer and one consumer only.
> - *Publish/subscribe*—Under this model, all consumers that have registered an interest in a message type receive the message.
>
> Queue systems also differ in how consumers are informed of a new message. Broadly, this can happen in one of three ways:
>
> - *Push*—The queue system will push the message to the consumer(s).
> - *Poll*—The consumers will poll the queue for messages.
> - *Long poll*—the consumes will poll for an extended period of time.
>
> In this chapter, SQS will push messages to our consuming Lambda function.
>
> For a primer on this subject we recommend *Enterprise Integration Patterns* by Gregor Hohpe and Bobby Woolf (Addison-Wesley Professional, 2003).

2.2.5 *AI services*

This system uses only a single AI service, Amazon Rekognition. This AI service provides a number of different image recognition modes including object and scene detection, facial recognition, facial analysis, celebrity recognition, and text detection in images. For this first system, we are using the default object and scene detection API.

2.2.6 *Data services*

In the Data Services tier, we are using only the Simple Storage Service (S3). This is sufficient for our needs in this initial platform; we will explore other data services in subsequent chapters.

2.2.7 *Development support and operational support*

We are using the serverless framework as our main development-support system. All logging data is collected using CloudWatch. We will discuss each of these in more detail in the following sections.

2.3 *Getting ready*

Now that we have seen the end goal, let's dive in and put the system together. You will need an active AWS account. If you don't already have an AWS account, you will need to create one. If you are new to AWS, then please refer to appendix A, which has instructions to get you set up.

For those of you familiar with AWS, we suggest that you create a separate sub-account to keep the examples in this book clear of any other systems you may be running.

Appendix A also contains instructions for creating API keys and configuring command-line and API access, so we suggest that even experienced AWS developers review this material to ensure a correct development environment.

TIP All example code has been tested in the `eu-west-1` region; we suggest that you also use this region for deployment of code.

WARNING Using AWS costs money! Please ensure that any cloud infrastructure is destroyed once you are finished with it. We have provided scripts to help with resource removal at the end of each chapter.

2.3.1   *DNS domain and SSL/TLS certificate*

The example in this chapter and others throughout the book require that a DNS domain and associated certificate be in place. These can be set up easily on AWS, and full instructions on how to do this are provided in appendix D. Before attempting to run the examples, please ensure that you have set up your AWS environment as per the instructions provided in appendix D.

NODE.JS

We use Node.js as our main development platform in this book. If you haven't installed it already, you need to.

> **Why Node.js?**
>
> We selected Node.js as our development platform for this book because of the ubiquity of JavaScript, which is available in every major web browser as well as server-side with the Node.js platform. Additionally, JavaScript is available as an implementation language for all of the major FaaS offerings, all of which makes it the natural choice.
>
> Don't worry if you haven't used Node.js before. If you know even a small amount of JavaScript, you'll be just fine. We can highly recommend the tutorial series at Node School if you want to brush up on Node (and even JavaScript). Head over to https://nodeschool.io/ to get started.

At the time of writing, the current LTS (long term supported) versions of Node.js are 10.x and 12.x. Binary installers are available from https://nodejs.org/. Download and install the appropriate binary for your development machine.

NOTE The latest supported version of Node.js on AWS where we will be building this system is 12.x. For consistency, it's best to choose the latest 12.x LTS release in your local development environment.

Once the installer has run, check that all is well by opening a console window and checking the Node.js and NPM versions using these commands:

```
$ node -v
$ npm -v
```

NPM

NPM is the package management system for Node.js. For each of our example systems, we will use NPM to manage dependent software units called *node modules*. If you are unfamiliar with NPM, we can recommend the NPM tutorial at Node School: https://nodeschool.io/#workshopper-list.

THE SERVERLESS FRAMEWORK

Next, we will need to install the Serverless Framework. This provides a layer of abstraction and configuration above the base AWS API, and helps us to more easily create and consume cloud services. We will make extensive use of the Serverless Framework throughout this book, so it should become familiar. We install Serverless using NPM. Open a console window and run

```
$ npm install -g serverless
```

NPM global installs

Running `npm install` with the `-g` flag tells NPM to install a module globally. This makes the module available on the path so that it can be executed as a system command.

Check that Serverless installed successfully by running

```
$ serverless -v
```

The Serverless Framework

There are several frameworks available to help support serverless development. The leading framework at the time of writing is the Serverless Framework, which is implemented in Node.js. Under the hood, the framework uses the Node.js AWS API to accomplish its work, and for AWS it leans heavily on CloudFormation. In this chapter we will just use the framework without going into detail about how it works. For now the key point to understand is that the framework allows us to define infrastructure and Lambda functions as code, which means that we can manage our operational resources in a similar manner to how we manage the rest of the source code for our system.

NOTE If you're curious to know more about Serverless, we have provided an in-depth look at how the framework operates in appendix E.

TIP Chapter 6 covers some advanced serverless topics and provides a production grade template for your projects.

2.3.2   Setup checklist

Before we proceed with the code. Please review this checklist to ensure that everything is in place:

- Appendix A
  - AWS account created
  - AWS command line installed
  - AWS access keys created
  - Development shell configured with access keys and verified
- Appendix D
  - Route 53 domain registered
  - SSL/TLS Certificate created
- This chapter
  - Node.js installed
  - Serverless Framework installed

If all of the this is in place, we are good to go!

> **WARNING**   Please ensure that all of the items in this checklist are completed; otherwise you may encounter issues when trying to run the example code. In particular, please ensure that *both* the environment variables AWS_REGION and AWS_DEFAULT_REGION are set and point to the same AWS region, as described in appendix A.

2.3.3   Get the code

Now that we have a basic setup done, we can proceed to grab the code for the system. The source code for this chapter is available in this repository: https://github.com/fourTheorem/ai-as-a-service in the chapter2-3 subdirectory. To get started, go ahead and clone this repository:

```
$ git clone https://github.com/fourTheorem/ai-as-a-service.git
```

The code maps to the architecture as you might expect. There is a top-level directory for each defined service, as shown in the following listing.

Listing 2.1   Repository structure

```
├── analysis-service
├── crawler-service
├── frontend-service
├── resources
└── ui-service
```

2.3.4   Setting up cloud resources

In addition to our services folders, we also have a top-level directory called *resources*. Our system relies on a number of cloud resources, and before we can deploy any of the service elements, we need these resources to be in place. For the case of our simple system, we will need an SQS queue for asynchronous communication and an S3 bucket to hold downloaded images. We will deploy these using a dedicated Serverless Framework configuration file. Let's take a look at how this is done. `cd` into the `chapter2-3/resources` resources directory and take a look at the `server-less.yml` file, shown in the next listing.

Listing 2.2   Serverless configuration for resources

```
service: resources                                          ◁─┐ Service
 frameworkVersion: ">=1.30.0"                                  │ name
custom:                                          ◁─┐ Custom
   bucket: ${env:CHAPTER2_BUCKET}                   │ definitions
   crawlerqueue: Chap2CrawlerQueue
   analysisqueue: Chap2AnalysisQueue
   region: ${env:AWS_DEFAULT_REGION, 'eu-west-1'}
   accountid: ${env:AWS_ACCOUNT_ID}

provider:                          ◁─┐ Provider-
   name: aws                         │ specific
   runtime: nodejs12.x
   stage: dev
   region: ${env:AWS_DEFAULT_REGION, 'eu-west-1'}

resources:
   Resources:
     WebAppS3Bucket:                              ◁─┐ Bucket
       Type: AWS::S3::Bucket                         │ definition
       Properties:
         BucketName: ${self:custom.bucket}
         AccessControl: PublicRead
         WebsiteConfiguration:
           IndexDocument: index.html
           ErrorDocument: index.html
     WebAppS3BucketPolicy:                      ◁─┐ Bucket
       Type: AWS::S3::BucketPolicy                 │ policy
       Properties:
         Bucket:
           Ref: WebAppS3Bucket
         PolicyDocument:
           Statement:
             - Sid: PublicReadGetObject
               Effect: Allow
               Principal: "*"
               Action:
                 - s3:GetObject
               Resource: arn:aws:s3:::${self:custom.bucket}/*
     Chap2CrawlerQueue:                                    ◁─┐ Queue
       Type: "AWS::SQS::Queue"                                │ definitions
       Properties:
         QueueName: "${self:custom.crawlerqueue}"
     Chap2AnalysisQueue:
       Type: "AWS::SQS::Queue"
       Properties:
         QueueName: "${self:custom.analysisqueue}"
```

> **TIP**   Serverless uses the *YAML* file format for its configuration. YAML stands for *YAML Ain't Markup Language*; you can find more information on YAML at this site: http://yaml.org/.

Don't worry if this looks overwhelming at first. We will be using the Serverless Framework throughout this book, so these configuration files will become very familiar. Let's take a look at the overall structure of this file.

> **TIP**   Full documentation for the Serverless Framework and its configuration can be found at the project's main site: https://serverless.com/framework/docs/.

The Serverless configuration is broken down into several top-level sections. The key ones to understand are

- `custom`—Defines attributes to be used elsewhere in the configuration.
- `provider`—Defines provider-specific configuration to the framework. In this example we are using AWS as the provider; however, the framework supports multiple cloud platforms
- `functions`—Defines function endpoints that the service implements. In this example we don't have any functions to define, so this section is not present in this example.
- `resources`—Defines supporting resources on the cloud platform. In this example we are defining two SQS queues and an S3 bucket. When we deploy this configuration, the Serverless Framework will create the queues and bucket for us.

> **NOTE**   There are many other tools that can be used to deploy cloud resources, such as AWS CloudFormation or Hashicorp's Terraform, both of which are great tools for managing infrastructure as code. We would recommend investigating these if you have an infrastructure-intensive project. For this book we will be using the Serverless Framework almost exclusively. We also note that the Serverless Framework uses CloudFormation on AWS under the hood; we cover this in more detail in appendix E.

Before we can go ahead and deploy our resources, we need to decide on a bucket name. The AWS bucket name space is global, so you should pick a name that is available and add an additional environment variable, `CHAPTER2_BUCKET`, to your shell in the same way that we set up the AWS environment variables:

```
export CHAPTER2_BUCKET=<YOUR BUCKET NAME>
```

Replace `<YOUR BUCKET NAME>` with a unique name of your choosing. Now we are all set, so let's go ahead and deploy our resources. From a command shell in the `chapter2-3/resources` directory, run

```
$ serverless deploy
```

Serverless will go ahead and deploy our resources, and you should see output similar to the following listing.

Listing 2.3 Serverless deploy output

```
Serverless: Packaging service...
Serverless: Creating Stack...
Serverless: Checking Stack create progress...
.....
Serverless: Stack create finished...
Serverless: Uploading CloudFormation file to S3...
Serverless: Uploading artifacts...
Serverless: Validating template...
Serverless: Updating Stack...
Serverless: Checking Stack update progress...
.............
Serverless: Stack update finished...
Service Information
service: resources
stage: dev
region: eu-west-1
stack: resources-dev
api keys:
  None
endpoints:
  None
functions:
  None
```

Serverless has created an S3 bucket and an SQS queues for us. Now that we have our supporting infrastructure, we can move on to the actual implementation!

2.4   *Implementing the asynchronous services*

With our basic setup done, we can proceed to write our first services. In this section we will put together the crawler and analysis asynchronous services and test them in isolation.

2.4.1   *Crawler service*

First up, let's take a look at the `crawler-service` code. Figure 2.8 illustrates the process flow inside this service.

The `crawler-service` is invoked when a message is placed on the `crawler` queue. The message contains a target URL for the service to crawl. Once invoked, the crawler fetches the HTML page at the specified URL, and parses out the image tags. Then, for each image in turn, it downloads the image into an S3 folder. Finally, once all of the images have been downloaded, it posts an `analyze` message to the `analysis` queue, including the domain name of the analyzed URL for further processing.

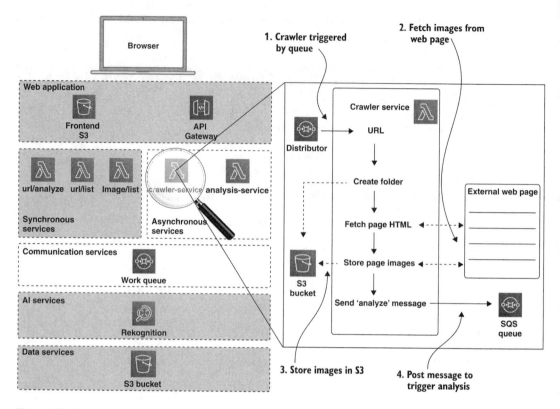

Figure 2.8   Crawler service

The code for the crawler service is located at `chapter2-3/crawler-service`. `cd` into this directory and you should see the files listed here:

```
handler.js
images.js
package.json
serverless.yml
```

To get an understanding of the resources used by this service and the overall structure, we should first look at the file `serverless.yml`, which contains the configuration shown in the next listing.

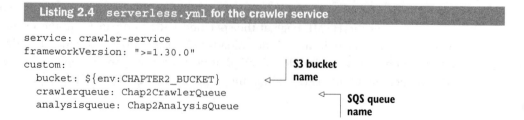

Listing 2.4   `serverless.yml` for the crawler service

```
service: crawler-service
frameworkVersion: ">=1.30.0"
custom:
  bucket: ${env:CHAPTER2_BUCKET}
  crawlerqueue: Chap2CrawlerQueue
  analysisqueue: Chap2AnalysisQueue
```

S3 bucket name

SQS queue name

```
    region: ${env:AWS_DEFAULT_REGION, 'eu-west-1'}
    accountid: ${env:AWS_ACCOUNT_ID}                    ⟵⎤ Account ID from
                                                          ⎦ local environment
provider:
  name: aws
  runtime: nodejs12.x
  stage: dev
  region: ${env:AWS_DEFAULT_REGION, 'eu-west-1'}
  iamRoleStatements:
    - Effect: Allow            ⟵── S3 permissions
      Action:
        - s3:PutObject
      Resource: "arn:aws:s3:::${self:custom.bucket}/*"
    - Effect: Allow
      Action:
        - sqs:ListQueues
      Resource: "arn:aws:sqs:${self:provider.region}:*:*"
    - Effect: Allow            ⟵⎤ Allow receipt from
      Action:                    ⎦ crawler queue
        - sqs:ReceiveMessage
        - sqs:DeleteMessage
        - sqs:GetQueueUrl
      Resource: "arn:aws:sqs:*:*:${self:custom.crawlerqueue}"
    - Effect: Allow            ⟵⎤ Allow posts to the
      Action:                    ⎦ analysis queue
        - sqs:SendMessage
        - sqs:DeleteMessage
        - sqs:GetQueueUrl
      Resource: "arn:aws:sqs:*:*:${self:custom.analysisqueue}"

functions:                   ⎤ Define the handler
  crawlImages:            ⟵  ⎦ function entry point
    handler: handler.crawlImages
    environment:
      BUCKET: ${self:custom.bucket}
      ANALYSIS_QUEUE: ${self:custom.analysisqueue}
      REGION: ${self:custom.region}
      ACCOUNTID: ${self:custom.accountid}
    events:                           ⎤ Function triggered
      - sqs:                      ⟵  ⎦ by crawler queue
          arn: "arn:aws:sqs:${self:provider.region}:${env:AWS_ACCOUNT_ID} \
            :${self:custom.crawlerqueue}"
```

The effect of this configuration is to define and deploy our crawler service function to
AWS, and allow it to be triggered by the crawler SQS queue that we deployed through
the resource's configuration. The key sections are

- custom—Define attributes to be used elsewhere in the configuration.
- provider—The provider section in this configuration sets up the AWS permissions to allow the service to access the SQS queues, and also to give it permission to write to our S3 bucket.
- functions—This section defines the service Lambda. The handler setting references the implementation, which we will look at shortly. The events entry

connects the function to our previously deployed SQS crawler queue. Finally, the environment block defines the environment variables that will be available to our function.

> **NOTE** The permissions defined in the `iamRoleStatements` block maps directly to the AWS Identity and Access Management (IAM) model. Full documentation on this can be found on AWS at https://aws.amazon.com/iam.

Unlike the previous `serverless.yml` file for our resources, this file does not define any resources. That is because we chose to define our resources outside of the scope of this service. In general, a good rule of thumb to adopt is that global or shared resources should be deployed in a common resource stack; resources that are used by a single service should be deployed with that specific service.

> **TIP** Resource sections in Serverless YAML files define resources that will be created on deployment. Other services depending on this resource must be deployed after the resource has been created. We find that it is best to put global resources in a separate configuration.

Let's now take a look at the main implementation file for the crawler, which is in `handler.js`. At the top of the file we include a number of modules, as shown in the following listing.

Listing 2.5 Crawler handler.js required modules

request is a node module that implements a fully featured HTTP client.

url is a core node module that understands how to parse URLs.

```
const request = require('request') 1((CO3-1))
const urlParser = require('url')
const AWS = require('aws-sdk')
const s3 = new AWS.S3()
const sqs = new AWS.SQS({region: process.env.REGION})
const images = require('./images')()
```

Include the AWS SDK node module. In this case, we instantiate an S3 and an SQS object in order to interface with our S3 bucket and queue respectively.

./images refers to our own module in the file images.js.

The main entry point to this service is `crawlImages`. This function takes three parameters: `event`, `context`, and `cb`. The code for this is shown next.

Listing 2.6 Crawler service entry point

```
module.exports.crawlImages = function (event, context, cb) {
  asnc.eachSeries(event.Records, (record, asnCb) => {
    let { body } = record

    try {
      body = JSON.parse(body)
```

Loop over messages

```
    } catch (exp) {
      return asnCb('message parse error: ' + record)
    }

    if (body.action === 'download' && body.msg && body.msg.url) {
      const udomain = createUniqueDomain(body.msg.url)
      crawl(udomain, body.msg.url, context).then(result => {
        queueAnalysis(udomain, body.msg.url, context).
          then(result => {
            asnCb(null, result)
          })
      })
    } else {
      asnCb('malformed message')
    }
  }, (err) => {
    if (err) { console.log(err) }
    cb()
  })
}
```

Crawl the URL
for images.

Send message to SQS
to trigger analysis

The function takes three parameters as follows:

1 event—Supplies information about the current event that is being processed. In this case, the event object holds an array of records taken from the SQS queue.

2 context—Used by AWS to supply contextual information for the call, such as the amount of available memory, execution time, and the client call context.

3 cb—Callback function. This should be called by the handler with a result once processing is complete.

Callbacks and asynchronous I/O

Callback functions are a staple of JavaScript, allowing code to execute asynchronously and return a result through execution of a passed-in callback parameter. Callbacks are a natural syntactic fit for asynchronous I/O (as opposed to synchronous I/O), which is one of the reasons for the success of the Node.js platform. If you need to brush up on JavaScript functions and callbacks, we can recommend the Node School "Javascripting" tutorial which can be found at https://nodeschool.io/.

Finally, for the crawler service, let's take a brief look at the file package.json shown in the next listing. This file provides a set of Node module dependencies.

Listing 2.7 Crawler service package.json

```
{
  "name": "crawler-service",
  "version": "1.0.0",
  "description": "",
  "main": "handler.js",
```

Sets the module
version number

```
"scripts": {
  "test": "echo \"Error: no test specified\" && exit 1"
},
"author": "",
"license": "ISC",
"dependencies": {
  "async": "^3.2.0",
  "aws-sdk": "^2.286.2",              ◁──┐ Sets the aws-sdk
  "htmlparser2": "^3.9.2",              │ module version
  "request": "^2.87.0",
  "shortid": "^2.2.15",
  "uuid": "^3.3.2"
}
}
```

package.json

Though the format of the `package.json` file is relatively straightforward, there are a few nuances, such as semantic version support and scripts. It would be beyond the scope of this book to describe the full details here. In-depth coverage of this topic is provided by NPM at https://docs.npmjs.com/files/package.json.

This entry point function is pretty simple. It just calls the `crawl` function to download images from the URL provided in the event object, and once the crawl is complete, it queues a message to SQS indicating that the downloaded images are ready for analysis.

The main `crawl` function is shown in the following listing.

Listing 2.8   `crawl` function

```
function crawl (url, context) {                          │ The domain part is extracted
  const domain = urlParser.parse(url).hostname   ◁──┘ from the requested URL.

  return new Promise(resolve => {                        │ The request module is used to
    request(url, (err, response, body) => {    ◁──┘ fetch the HTML for the given URL.
      if (err || response.statusCode !== 200) {
        return resolve({statusCode: 500, body: err})
      }
      images.parseImageUrls(body, url).then(urls => {              ◁──
        images.fetchImages(urls, domain).then(results =>      ◁──
          writeStatus(url, domain, results).then(result => {
            resolve({statusCode: 200, body: JSON.stringify(result)})
          })
        })
      })
    })
  })
}
```

The list of images is passed into the fetchImages function, which downloads each image to the nominated bucket.

The parsed HTML content is handed off to the parseImageUrls function, which returns a list of images for download.

Finally, the function writes a status file to the bucket for downstream services to consume before resolving the promise.

Promises and fat arrow

If you are a little out of practice with JavaScript, you might be wondering what the construct `.then(result => {...` means. The fat arrow operator is a replacement for the `function` keyword (with a slight twist). For pragmatic purposes you can think of the following as equivalent:

```
result => { console.log(result) }

function (result) { console.log(result) }
```

The `.then` construct defines a handler function to be called on resolution of a promise. Promises provide an alternative mechanism to callbacks for asynchronous I/O. Many folks prefer to use promises as opposed to callbacks, as it helps to keep code cleaner and avoid what is colloquially known as "Callback Hell." If you are unfamiliar with promises, full details can be found at https://www.promisejs.org/.

The `queueAnalysis` function, shown in the next listing, uses the AWS SQS interface to post a message to the analysis queue, which will later be picked up by the analysis service.

Listing 2.9 `queueAnalysis` function

```
function queueAnalysis (url, context) {
  let domain = urlParser.parse(url).hostname
  let accountId = process.env.ACCOUNTID
  if (!accountId) {
    accountId = context.invokedFunctionArn.split(':')[4]    Build the SQS
  }                                                          endpoint URL.
  let queueUrl = `https://sqs.${process.env.REGION}.amazonaws.com/
    ${accountId}/
    ${process.env.ANALYSIS_QUEUE}`
                                          Construct the
  let params = {                          message body.
    MessageBody: JSON.stringify({action: 'analyze', msg: {domain: domain}}),
    QueueUrl: queueUrl
  }

  return new Promise(resolve => {
    sqs.sendMessage(params, (err, data) => {      Post the
      ...                                         message to SQS.
    })
  })
}
```

Now that we understand the code for the crawler, let's deploy the service. First we will need to install the supporting node modules. To do this, `cd` into the `crawler-service` directory and run

```
$ npm install
```

We can now deploy our service by running the Serverless Framework's `deploy` command:

```
$ serverless deploy
```

Once this command has completed, we can check that all is well by inspecting the AWS Lambda console, which should look similar to figure 2.9.

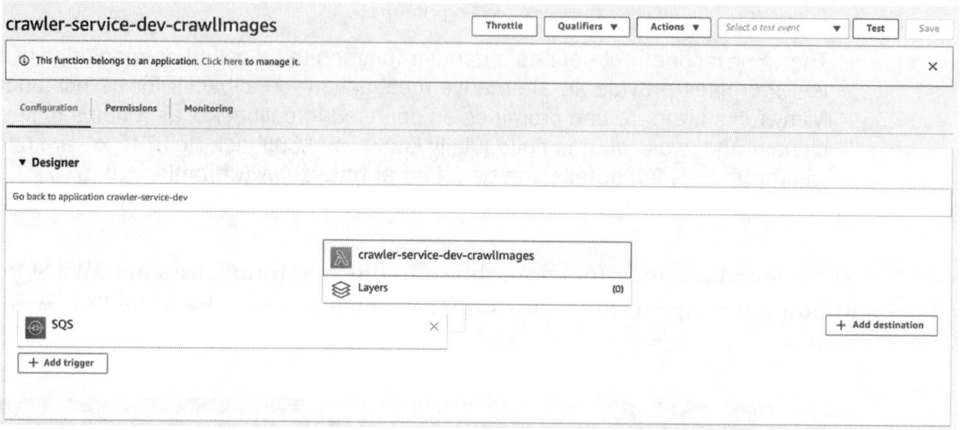

Figure 2.9   Crawler service Lambda

Before we move on to the analysis function, let's test out the crawler by sending a message to SQS. Open the AWS console, go to the SQS service page, and select the `Chap2CrawlerQueue` in the appropriate region. Then select Send Message from the Queue Action drop-down.

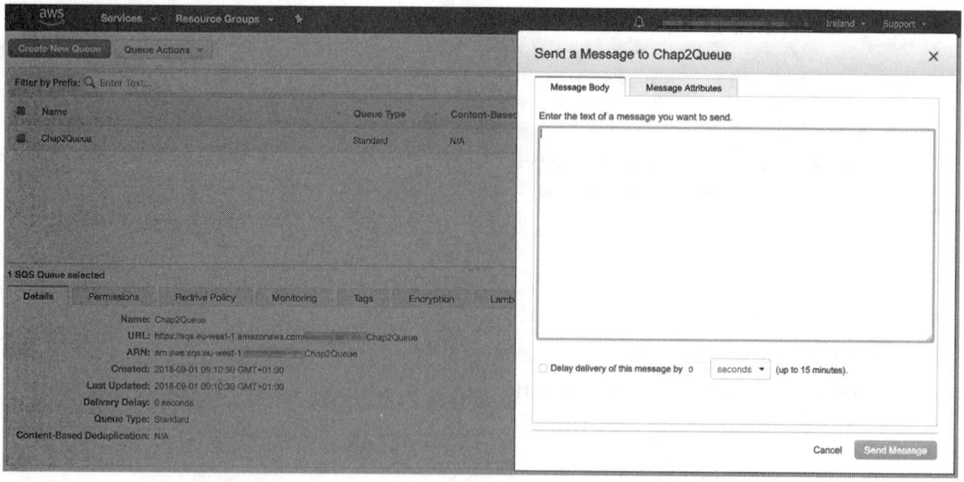

Figure 2.10   Send SQS message

Paste the JSON shown here into the message window and click Send Message:

```
{
  "action": "download",
  "msg": {
    "url": "http://ai-as-a-service.s3-website-eu-west-1.amazonaws.com"
  }
}
```

> **NOTE** We have created a simple static website using S3 for testing purposes
> that has some example images at the URL in the test message, but you can use
> a different URL if you prefer—for example, the results of a Google image
> search.

The message will be appended to the SQS queue and picked up by the crawler service.
We can take a look at the crawler logs to confirm that this indeed happened. Open
up the AWS console and then open up CloudWatch. Click on the Logs menu item
on the left side and then select the crawler service, listed as `crawler-service`
`-dev-crawlimages`, to inspect the logs. You should see output similar to that shown
in figure 2.11.

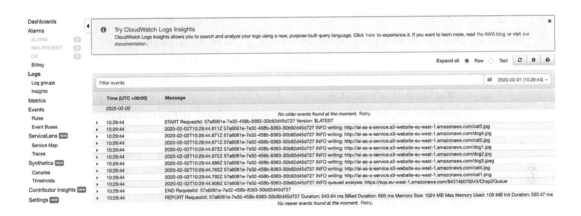

Figure 2.11 CloudWatch logs for crawler

Finally let's check that our images were downloaded correctly. Open up the AWS console and go to the S3 service. Select your bucket. You should see a folder named
`ai-as-a-service.s3-website-eu-west-1.amazonaws.com`. Click into this to
view the downloaded images, as shown in figure 2.12.

	Name ▾	Last modified ▾	Size ▾	Storage class ▾
☐ ▢	edccc890-45a6-11ea-b2e6-272c2d971cd2	Feb 2, 2020 10:29:45 AM GMT+0000	21.4 KB	Standard
☐ ▢	edd2e310-45a6-11ea-b2e6-272c2d971cd2	Feb 2, 2020 10:29:45 AM GMT+0000	83.5 KB	Standard
☐ ▢	edd35840-45a6-11ea-b2e6-272c2d971cd2	Feb 2, 2020 10:29:45 AM GMT+0000	125.7 KB	Standard
☐ ▢	edd505f0-45a6-11ea-b2e6-272c2d971cd2	Feb 2, 2020 10:29:45 AM GMT+0000	65.3 KB	Standard
☐ ▢	edd5a230-45a6-11ea-b2e6-272c2d971cd2	Feb 2, 2020 10:29:45 AM GMT+0000	297.2 KB	Standard
☐ ▢	eddc0ad0-45a6-11ea-b2e6-272c2d971cd2	Feb 2, 2020 10:29:45 AM GMT+0000	26.5 KB	Standard
☐ ▢	eddfb450-45a6-11ea-b2e6-272c2d971cd2	Feb 2, 2020 10:29:45 AM GMT+0000	561.2 KB	Standard
☐ ▢	ede27370-45a6-11ea-b2e6-272c2d971cd2	Feb 2, 2020 10:29:45 AM GMT+0000	1.2 MB	Standard
☐ ▢	status.json	Feb 2, 2020 10:29:47 AM GMT+0000	4.3 KB	Standard

Figure 2.12   Downloaded images

In the next chapter we will turn our attention to the analysis service and complete the deployment of the asynchronous services, before deploying the rest of the system. For now take a well-earned break and congratulate yourself on your hard work so far!

Summary

- AWS provides a growing range of cloud native services that we can leverage. In this chapter we used S3, Route53, Lambda, and SQS.
- AWS provides a web-based console that we can use to set up an account and configure API access keys
- The Serverless Framework is used to deploy cloud infrastructure, including an S3 bucket, SQS queue, and Route53 DNS records. A `serverless.yml` file allows us to define and deploy our infrastructure in a predictable and logical way.
- An SQS queue connects to a crawler Lambda function.
- The crawler service is a Lambda function that downloads images and places them in an S3 bucket.

WARNING Chapter 3 continues to build on this system, and we provide instructions on how to remove the deployed resources at the end of chapter 3. If you are not planning on working on chapter 3 for some time, please ensure that you fully remove all cloud resources deployed in this chapter in order to avoid additional charges!

Building a serverless image recognition system, part 2

This chapter covers

- Building a simple AI as a Service system
- Consuming an AI image recognition service
- Implementing synchronous and asynchronous services
- Deploying a UI
- Deploying to the cloud

In this chapter we will continue building our serverless image recognition system that we started in chapter 2. We will add our image recognition service that will call AWS Rekognition to do the hard work for us. Once this is done, we will build a simple front end for our system that will allow us to test our image recognition capabilities.

If you haven't worked through chapter 2, you should go back and do so now before proceeding with this chapter, as we will be building directly on top of the work that we started there. If you're good with the content from chapter 2, we can dive right in where we left off and deploy the analysis service.

3.1   Deploying the asynchronous services

In chapter 2 we set up our development environment and deployed the crawler service. In this chapter we will continue with the deployment of the rest of the system, starting with the analysis service.

3.1.1   Analysis service

Let's take a look at the `analysis-service`. In a similar manner to the `crawler-service`, this service is triggered by a message from the Analysis SQS queue once there are images available for analysis in our S3 bucket. An outline of the logic for this service is depicted in figure 3.1.

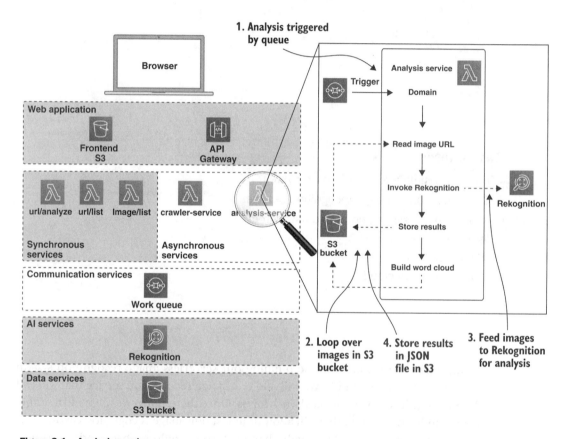

Figure 3.1   Analysis service

In essence the `analysis-service` forms a bridge between the downloaded images and the Amazon Rekognition service. Each image downloaded by the `crawler-service` is fed into Rekognition, and a set of labels is returned. Each label is a word describing the object recognized by the model in the image and a confidence level (a number between 0 and 100, where 100 is full confidence in the image label).

Following this analysis, the service processes the returned data to create a set of word counts that can be fed into a word cloud generator. The idea behind this is to try to visually determine a common thread between the images available at the given URL.

Let's take a look at the code in the `analysis-service`, starting with the `serverless.yml` configuration to see how this is achieved. This is shown in the next listing.

Listing 3.1   Analysis service `serverless.yml`

```yaml
service: analysis-service
custom:
  bucket: ${env:CHAPTER2_BUCKET}
  ...

provider:
  ...
  iamRoleStatements:
    - Effect: "Allow"          Allow access to the
      Action:                  Rekognition API.
        - "rekognition:*"
      Resource: "*"
  ...

functions:
  analyzeImages:
    handler: handler.analyzeImages    Define main
    ...                                entry point
```

We should note at this point that the `serverless.yml` configuration file for this service is very similar to the previous ones. The main difference is that it allows access from this Lambda function to the Rekognition API. Let's see how this interface works. The file `handler.js` in the `analysis-service` code implements this interface.

The following listing shows the `require` statements for the `analysis-service`.

Listing 3.2   Analysis service require

```javascript
                                   The AWS SDK module      The S3 interface is created
                                   is loaded.               for dealing with buckets
const AWS = require('aws-sdk')                              and their objects.
const s3 = new AWS.S3()
const rek = new AWS.Rekognition()    The Rekognition
                                     interface is created.
```

The next listing shows how the Rekognition object is used in the function `analyzeImageLabels`

Listing 3.3   Using the Rekognition API

```javascript
function analyzeImageLabels (imageBucketKey) {
  const params = {              The Rekognition call
    Image: {                    parameters are created.
      S3Object: {
        Bucket: process.env.BUCKET,
        Name: imageBucketKey
```

```
        }
      },
      MaxLabels: 10,
      MinConfidence: 80
    }
    return new Promise((resolve, reject) => {          Rekognition's detectLabel
      rek.detectLabels(params, (err, data) => {   ◁──┘ API is invoked.
        if (err) {
          return resolve({image: imageBucketKey, labels: [], err: err})
        }
        return resolve({image: imageBucketKey,
          labels: data.Labels})                  ◁──┐ The promise resolves
      })                                              │ with the results.
    })
}
```

This simple function achieves an awful lot! It triggers an image recognition AI service to run against an image file stored in an S3 bucket, and then returns a set of results for further processing. All of this in a rather small amount of code!

It should be noted that we can do a lot more with Rekognition; however, for the purposes of this code, we are just using the default settings. We will explore this in more detail in later chapters.

TIP Rekognition works on video as well as still images, and can be used to detect a range of features within images, such as smiling or frowning faces, text in images, and well-known people. Can you think of applications that would benefit your end users? For example, we have recently used it for address and zip code detection in images.

The final listing for the `analysis-service` shows the function `wordCloudList`. This computes the number of occurrences of a word across all of the detected labels.

Listing 3.4 `wordCloudList` computation

```
function wordCloudList (labels) {                   The function accepts an
  let counts = {}                             ◁──┐  array of label objects.
  let wcList = []

  labels.forEach(set => {                           The label set in each label object is
    set.labels.forEach(lab => {           ◁──┐      iterated to count label occurrences.
      if (!counts[lab.Name]) {
        counts[lab.Name] = 1
      } else {
        counts[lab.Name] = counts[lab.Name] + 1
      }
    })
  })

  Object.keys(counts).forEach(key => {      ◁──┐ The map of counts is converted to an
    wcList.push([key, counts[key]])              array of word-count pairs
  })                                             represented as two-element arrays.
  return wcList
}
```

Let's go ahead and deploy the analysis service using the Serverless Framework:

```
$ cd analysis-service
$ npm install
$ serverless deploy
```

Once the deployment has completed successfully, we can re-run our system by queuing up a test message into SQS through the AWS console. Go ahead and do this, sending the same JSON message as before:

```
{
  "action": "download",
  "msg": {
    "url": "http://ai-as-a-service.s3-website-eu-west-1.amazonaws.com"
  }
}
```

This will cause the crawler service to run. Once complete, the crawler will post a message asking for an analysis of the downloaded images into the analysis SQS queue, which will trigger the analysis service. The net result will be a set of tags added to our status.json file in S3. If you go ahead and open this file, you should see something similar to the following listing.

Listing 3.5 `wordCloudList` **computation results**

```
{
  "url": "http://ai-as-a-service.s3-website-eu-west-1.amazonaws.com",
  "stat": "analyzed",
  "downloadResults": [          ←── Image download results
    {
      "url": "http://ai-as-a-service.s3-website-eu-west-1.amazonaws.com/
      cat1.png",
      "stat": "ok"
    },
    ...
  ],
  "analysisResults": [                     │ Image analysis
                                        ←─┘ results
    {
      "image": "ai-as-a-service.s3-website-eu-west-1.amazonaws.com/cat1.png",
      "labels": [
        {
          "Name": "Cat",
          "Confidence": 99.03962707519531
        }
      ]
    ...
  ],
  "wordCloudList": [          ←──┐ Word cloud
    [ "Cat", 3 ],               │ computation
    [ "Dog", 3 ],
    ....
  ]
}
```

For a more complete system, we might consider storing this information in a database or key/value store; however, for this first demonstration, S3 works just fine. This status file is used to drive the front end and UI services, and it is to these that we will now turn our attention.

3.2   *Implementing the synchronous services*

In this system, the synchronous services are comprised of the UI service and a front end. The front end renders and executes entirely in the browser, while the UI services execute as three Lambda functions.

3.2.1   *UI service*

Figure 3.2 outlines the operation of the UI service.

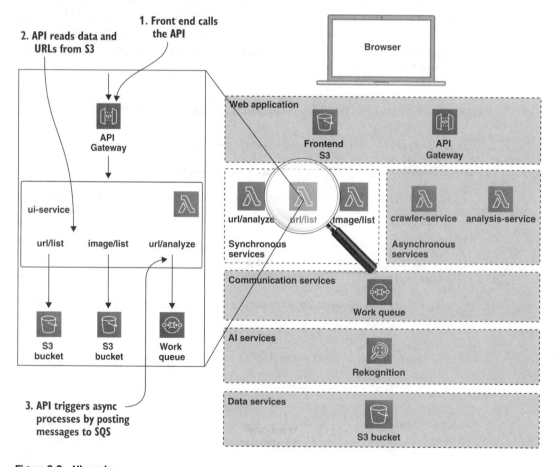

Figure 3.2   UI service

As illustrated, the UI service exposes three end points:

- `url/list` lists all URLs that have been submitted for analysis.
- `image/list` lists all images that have been analyzed for a specific URL.
- `url/analyze` submits a URL for analysis.

The Serverless Framework allows us to define multiple Lambda functions in a single configuration file, and we have used this in the configuration of the UI service. Let's take a look at the `serverless.yml` file for the UI service, shown in the next listing.

Listing 3.6   UI service `serverless.yml`

```
service: ui-service
frameworkVersion: ">=1.30.0"
plugins:                                        Domain
  - serverless-domain-manager         ◁──┘     plugin
custom:
  bucket: ${env:CHAPTER2_BUCKET}
  queue: Chap2Queue
  region: ${env:AWS_DEFAULT_REGION, 'eu-west-1'}
  domain: ${env:CHAPTER2_DOMAIN}
  accountid: ${env:AWS_ACCOUNT_ID}              Custom domain
  customDomain:                       ◁──┘      settings
    domainName: 'chapter2api.${self:custom.domain}'
    stage: dev
    basePath: api
    certificateName: '*.${self:custom.domain}'
    createRoute53Record: true
    endpointType: regional

provider:
  name: aws
  runtime: nodejs12.x
  region: ${env:AWS_DEFAULT_REGION, 'eu-west-1'}   Role
  iamRoleStatements:                     ◁──┘      permissions
  ...

functions:                          Analyze URL
  analyzeUrl:            ◁──┘        Lambda HTTP POST
    handler: handler.analyzeUrl
    environment:
      ...
    events:
      - http:
          path: url/analyze
          method: post             List URLs
  listUrls:             ◁──┘       lambda
    handler: handler.listUrls
    ...
  listImages:            ◁──┐      List images
    handler: handler.listImages    lambda
    ....
```

This configuration introduces a few new elements over and above the previous configuration files. First we are using a custom plugin—serverless-domain-manager. We are using this to help us set up a custom domain for our service. If you recall, at the start of chapter 2, we set up a domain in Route53 and created a wild card certificate. In a moment, we will use this domain for our UI service.

The permissions section in the configuration should look familiar at this point. The functions section is a little different, in that there are three entries. Note that each entry is similar, in that it is tied to an HTTP event. This tells Serverless to tie the function to API Gateway and make the function available through the given route. The custom domain entry is used to create a DNS entry for the service, and to connect this to API Gateway. We'll deploy this service in a moment, but first let's take a look at the implementation, which is in the file handler.js.

In what should now be a familiar pattern, we require the AWS SDK and then create the required objects for the service to consume, which in this case are S3 and SQS. This is shown in the following listing.

Listing 3.7 UI service `require`

```
const urlParser = require('url')        ◁──┐  The url node module is
                                               loaded for URL parsing.
const AWS = require('aws-sdk')          ◁──┐  The AWS SDK is loaded with the S3
const s3 = new AWS.S3()                        and SQS interfaces instantiated.
const sqs = new AWS.SQS({region: process.env.REGION})
```

The service defines three entry points which will be deployed as three separate Lambda functions. The listUrl function is provided in the next listing.

Listing 3.8 `listUrls` function

```
module.exports.listUrls = (event, context, cb) => {   ◁──┐  Entry
  const params = {                                          point
    Bucket: process.env.BUCKET,
    Delimiter: '/',
    MaxKeys: 1000
  }
                                                       ┐  List S3
  s3.listObjectsV2(params, (err, data) => {       ◁──┘  objects
    let promises = []
    if (err) { return respond(500, {stat: 'error', details: err}, cb) }

    data.CommonPrefixes.forEach(prefix => {
      promises.push(readStatus(prefix.Prefix))
    })
    Promise.all(promises).then(values => {
      let result = []
      values.forEach(value => {
```

```
            result.push({url: value.url, stat: value.stat})
        })
        respond(200,
            {stat: 'ok', details: result}, cb)        ◁──┐ Respond with
    })                                                    │ URL list
  })
}
```

Note that the entry point to this function is exactly the same as for all of our other services, even though in this case the function will be executed through API Gateway as a HTTP GET request. The function is quite simple in that it merely lists the set of folders at the top level in our S3 bucket and returns the list as a JSON array.

Our `listImages` function is simpler still, in that it reads the file `status.json` from S3 and returns the contents for display, so we won't cover it in much detail here. Let's instead take a look at the `analyzeUrl` function in the following code.

Listing 3.9 analyzeUrl

```
module.exports.analyzeUrl = (event, context, cb) => {
  let accountId = process.env.ACCOUNTID
  if (!accountId) {
    accountId = context.invokedFunctionArn.split(':')[4]
  }
  const queueUrl = `https://sqs.${process.env.REGION}.amazonaws.com/
    ${accountId}/
    ${process.env.QUEUE}`          ◁──┐ Build
                                       │ queue URL
  const body = JSON.parse(event.body)

  const params = {
    MessageBody: JSON.stringify({action: 'download', msg: body}),
    QueueUrl: queueUrl
  }
                                          ┐ Send
                                          │ SQS Message
  sqs.sendMessage(params, (err, data) => {  ◁──┘
      if (err) { return respond(500, {stat: 'error', details: err}, cb) }
      respond(200,
        {stat: 'ok', details: {queue: queueUrl, msgId: data.MessageId}}, cb)
  })
}
```

Again, this function is fairly straightforward. It takes a URL as the event body and posts this URL as part of the message payload to our SQS queue for the crawler service to handle.

Single responsibility principie

The *single responsibility principle* or *SRP* is a powerful idea that helps us to keep our code decoupled and well maintained. As you can hopefully see, all of the code so far adheres to the SRP. We like to think of the SRP as something that applies at several levels:

- At the architectural level, each service should have a single purpose.
- At the implementation level, each function should have a single purpose.
- At the "line of code" level, each line should do one thing only.

What do we mean by the "line of code" level? Well, the following code does multiple things on one line, in that it gets a value for `bar` and tests it against `foo`:

```
if (foo !== (bar = getBarValue())) {
```

A much clearer implementation would be to split the code into two lines, so that each line does one thing only:

```
bar = getBarValue()
if (foo !== bar) {
```

Now that we understand the UI service code, let's go ahead and deploy it. First we will need to create the custom domain entry. The `serverless.yml` file uses an environment variable `CHAPTER2_DOMAIN` as the base domain for the `ui-service` deployment. If you haven't set this variable yet, you should do so now by adding the contents of the following listing to your shell startup script.

Listing 3.10   Setting the environment variable for the base domain

```
export CHAPTER2_DOMAIN=<MY CUSTOM DOMAIN>
```

Replace `<MY CUSTOM DOMAIN>` with the domain that you created at the start of the chapter.

Next we will need to install the supporting node modules. To do this, `cd` into the `ui-service` directory and install these dependencies:

```
$ npm install
```

This will install all of the dependencies in `package.json` locally, including the `serverless-domain-manager`. To create our custom domain, run

```
$ serverless create_domain
```

This command will cause the domain manager plugin to create the domain in `Route53`. For example, if your custom domain name were `example.com`, then this would create an `A` record for `chapter2api.example.com`, as specified in the `customDomain` section of `serverless.yml`. This section is shown in the next listing.

Listing 3.11 `serverless.yml` **custom section for** `ui-service`

```
custom:
  bucket: ${env:CHAPTER2_BUCKET}
  queue: Chap2Queue
  region: ${env:AWS_DEFAULT_REGION, 'eu-west-1'}          Custom domain
  domain: ${env:CHAPTER2_DOMAIN}                          environment variable
  accountid: ${env:AWS_ACCOUNT_ID}
  customDomain:                                           Full domain
    domainName: 'chapter2api.${self:custom.domain}'       name
    stage: dev
    basePath: api                                         Certificate
    certificateName: '*.${self:custom.domain}'            reference
    createRoute53Record: true
    endpointType: regional
```

Note that you will need the `APIGatewayAdministrator` privilege for this to succeed. If you created a fresh AWS account, then this should be enabled by default. Finally we will need to deploy the service in the usual manner:

```
$ serverless deploy
```

This will deploy our UI endpoints as Lambda functions, configure API Gateway to call these functions, and tie our custom domain into API Gateway. The net result is that our functions are now available to call over HTTP as https://chapter2api.<YOUR CUSTOM DOMAIN>/api/url/list. To test this out, open a web browser and point it to that URL. You should see the following output:

```
{"stat":"ok","details":[{"url":"http://ai-as-a-service.s3-website-eu-west-
    1.amazonaws.com","stat":"analyzed"}]}
```

That's because we have so far submitted a single URL for download and analysis, and the UI service is returning a list of one element.

3.2.2 Front end service

The final part of our system is the front end service. This is a little different from the rest of the system in that it is purely a front end component and executes entirely in the user's browser. Figure 3.3 outlines the structure of the front end service.

We will deploy this service as a set of static files to S3. Let's take a look at the code first. `cd` into the `frontend-service` directory. You should see the structure shown in the next listing.

Listing 3.12 Front end structure

```
├── app
    ├── code.js
    ├── index.html
    ├── templates.js
    └── wordcloud2.js
```

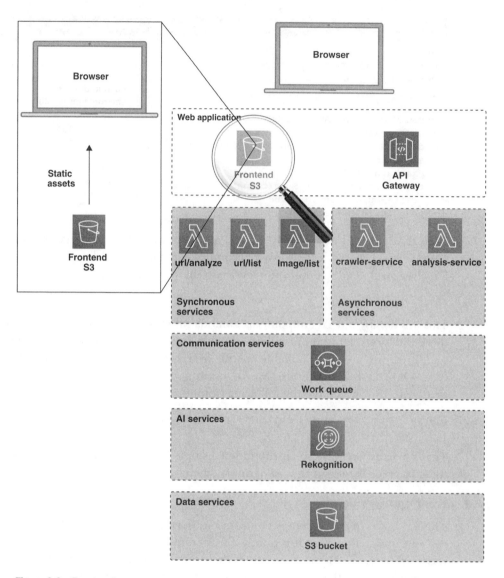

Figure 3.3   Front end

In this case we don't require a serverless.yml configuration, as we are just going to deploy our front end to an S3 bucket. The code for the front end is contained in the app directory, which holds the HTML and JavaScript for our application. Our application in this case is an example of what is known as a *single-page application (SPA)*. There are many frameworks that help with the construction of large-scale SPA applications such as Angular, React, or Vue. For our simple application, we are just using jQuery, as this provides a simple lowest common denominator, and our application is simple enough not to require the support of a front end framework.

Single-page application

The single-page application architecture is characterized by dynamically rewriting content into a single page, rather than reloading a web page in order to render new content. This approach has become increasingly popular and is used in most modern web applications. Indeed, it is the rise of this application model that has in part driven the development of many of the front end JavaScript frameworks that you may have come across, such as Angular, React, Vue, and so on.

If you are unfamiliar with this approach, we recommend this e-book as a way to brush up on this topic: https://github.com/mixu/singlepageappbook.

NOTE For this example system, we will be using S3 directly to serve up our application. To operate at scale, it is common practice to use an S3 bucket as the origin for Amazon's CloudFront CDN (content delivery network).

The code that implements the front end is fairly simple, consisting of a single HTML page and some JavaScript. Let's take a quick look at the index page, shown in the following listing.

Listing 3.13 Front end `index.html`

```html
<html>
<head>                                                          CDN libraries
  <link rel="stylesheet" href="https://stackpath.bootstrapcdn.com/
bootstrap/4.1.3/css/bootstrap.min.css">
  <script src="https://code.jquery.com/jquery-3.3.1.min.js"></script>
  <script src="https://stackpath.bootstrapcdn.com/bootstrap/4.1.3/js/
bootstrap.min.js"></script>
  <script src="/templates.js"></script>          Application
  <script src="/code.js"></script>               code
  <script src="/wordcloud2.js"></script>
</head>
<body>                                                          Define
                                                               navigation bar
<div class="navbar navbar-expand-lg navbar-light bg-light">
  ...
</div>

<div id="content"></div>          Main
                                  content area
</body>
</html>
```

In the head section of the page, we load in some standard libraries such as jQuery and Bootstrap from a shared CDN. This is just a convenience. For a production web application, we would normally redistribute these libraries ourselves in order to ensure their integrity. The main markup in this page then defines a simple navigation bar, before declaring a content area which will be populated by the application code, the bulk of which is in the file code.js.

> ### jQuery, Bootstrap, and CDN
>
> If you are unfamiliar with front end JavaScript development, you may be wondering about the links to Bootstrap and jQuery in the HTML file. As a convenience to their users, these projects both provide hosted, minified versions of major releases of their libraries on fast content-delivery networks for inclusion by external applications.

We have removed some of the detail from the code in the next listing for the sake of clarity. The full code is available in the Git repository.

Listing 3.14   Main JavaScript for front-end application

```
const BUCKET_ROOT = '<YOUR BUCKET URL>'                          Define the bucket
const API_ROOT = 'https://chapter2api.<YOUR CUSTOM DOMAIN>/api/'  URL root.

function renderUrlList () {                                      Define the
  $.getJSON(API_ROOT + 'url/list', function (body) {            UI API root.
    ...
  })                                     Fetch and
}                                        render URLs.

function renderUrlDetail (url) {
  let list = ''
  let output = ''
  let wclist = []

  $.getJSON(API_ROOT + 'image/list?url=' + url, function (data) {
    ...                     Fetch and
  })                        render images.
}


$(function () {
  renderUrlList()

  $('#submit-url-button').on('click', function (e) {
    e.preventDefault()                                Send a URL
    $.ajax({url: API_ROOT + 'url/analyze',            for analysis.
      type: 'post',
      data: JSON.stringify({url: $('#target-url').val()}),
```

```
    dataType: 'json',
    contentType: 'application/json',
    success: (data, stat) => {
    }
  })
 })
})
```

The code uses standard jQuery functions to make AJAX requests to the UI service that we just deployed. It renders the list of URLs that have been analyzed on page load, and the list of images that have been analyzed for a particular URL. Finally, it allows the user to submit a new URL for analysis. Before we deploy the front end, you should edit the file `code.js` and replace the following lines:

- `const BUCKET_ROOT = '<YOUR BUCKET URL>'` should be replaced with the URL for your specific bucket; for example, https://s3-eu-west-1.amazonaws.com /mybucket.
- `const API_ROOT = 'https://chapter2api.<YOUR CUSTOM DOMAIN>/api/'` should be replaced with your specific custom domain.

Now that's done, so we can go ahead and deploy the front end. To do this, we are going to use the AWS command line that we set up at the start of the chapter. Run the following commands:

```
$ cd frontend-service
$ aws s3 sync app/ s3://$CHAPTER2_BUCKET
```

> **NOTE** For this example we are deploying our front end into the same bucket as our scraped data. We don't advise that you do this for a production system!

We have now built and deployed a full serverless AI system; in the next section we'll give it a spin!

3.3   *Running the system*

Now that we have fully deployed our system, it's time to give it a try. To do this, open a web browser and point it to https://<YOURBUCKETNAME>.s3.amazonaws.com/ index.html. The index page should load and display a single URL that has been analyzed during our test deployments, as illustrated in figure 3.4.

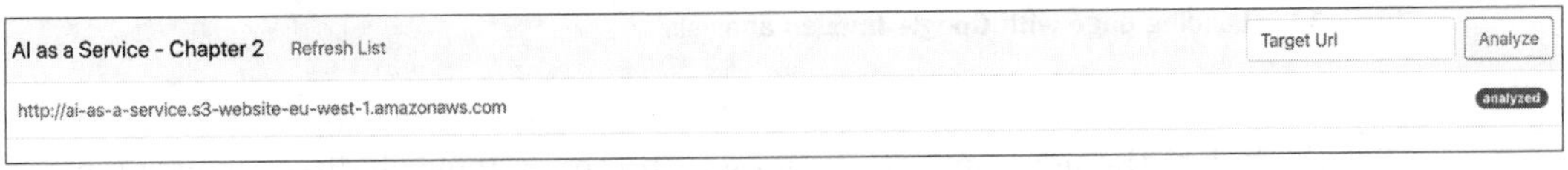

AI as a Service - Chapter 2 Refresh List	Target Url	Analyze
http://ai-as-a-service.s3-website-eu-west-1.amazonaws.com		analyzed

Figure 3.4   Default landing page with one URL

Let's see how our image analysis system gets on with some other images. Given that the internet runs on cat pictures, point your browser to Google and search for "cat pictures"—then click on the Images tab. It should look something like figure 3.5.

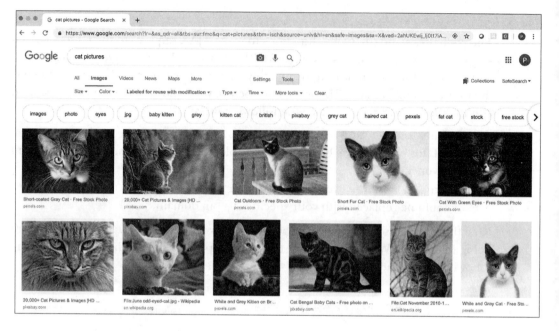

Figure 3.5   Cat pictures on Google Images

Copy the URL from the address bar, go back to the landing page, and paste it into the target URL field. Then click the Analyze button. After a few seconds, refresh the page: you should see an entry in the list for `www.google.com` with a status of analyzed, as illustrated in figure 3.6.

AI as a Service - Chapter 2	Target Url	Analyze
https://catpictures.www.google.com/search		analyzed
http://mnxvdelj.ai-as-a-service.s3-website-eu-west-1.amazonaws.com/		analyzed

Figure 3.6   Landing page with Google Images analysis

Click the link to the newly analyzed data set, and the system will display a list of images that were analyzed by Rekognition, and also a word cloud that we generated on our front end. This is shown in figure 3.7.

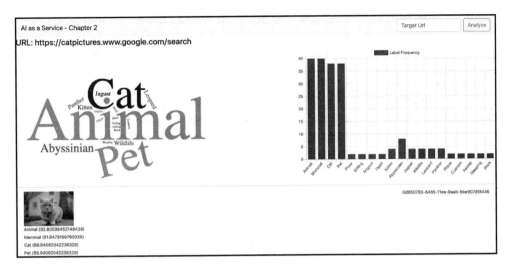

Figure 3.7   Landing page with Google Images analysis

The system has been fairly successful in recognizing our feline images; however, in some cases it failed entirely. Each image that was successfully processed will have an associated tag list. Each tag has two components: a word and a score out of 100. This number is the confidence level, and is a measure of how accurate a match the AI thinks the word is to the image. It is interesting to look at the images that failed recognition; for example, in figure 3.8. It is probably unsurprising that no accurate determination could be made on the image of the cat stretched out on its back!

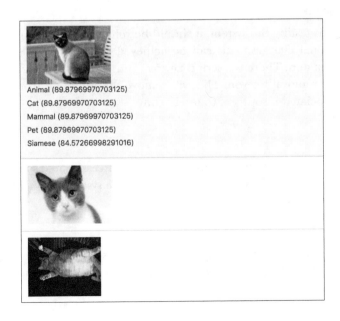

Figure 3.8   Landing page with Google Images analysis

Congratulations! You have now deployed and operated your first serverless AI system!

We covered an awful lot of ground in this chapter, from a standing start to a fully working serverless AI system that can recognize images from arbitrary web pages. While this has been a bit of a whirlwind tour, we hope that it serves to illustrate that complex AI functionality is now available to developers with no specialized knowledge.

Bear in mind that we only scratched the surface of what Rekognition and image recognition technology in general can do. Hopefully you are currently thinking of ways to use this functionality in your own work. Some use cases that we have come across include

- Extracting name and zip code information from images
- Verifying that uploaded profile pictures are of valid human faces
- Helping blind or partially sighted people by describing objects in the current field of view
- Google reverse image search, which allows one to search for visually similar images
- Identification of wine by type, price, and value through taking a picture of the label on a bottle

The possibilities are endless, and we are certain to see new businesses spring up around this technology.

Hopefully you will agree that we were able to achieve a lot of functionality with comparatively little code, allowing the cloud infrastructure to do the heavy lifting for us. We should also note that this image recognition system could be constructed with no specialized knowledge of neural networks or deep learning. We will expand upon this engineering approach to AI throughout the rest of this book.

3.4   Removing the system

Once you are done with testing the system, it should be removed entirely in order to avoid incurring additional charges. This can be achieved very simply by using the Serverless `remove` command. There is a script, `remove.sh`, in the `chapter2-3` code directory that does the removal for you. This will remove the front end from S3 and tear down all of the associated resources. To use it, run

```
$ cd chapter2-3
$ bash remove.sh
```

If you would like to redeploy the system at any time, there is an associated script called `deploy.sh` in the same folder. This will redeploy the entire system for you by automating the steps that we worked through in this chapter.

Summary

- An analysis service consumes an image recognition AI service. We use the AWS Rekognition `detectLabels` API to detect labelled objects in each image.

- A simple API was created to interact with our analysis system. We use API Gateway to provide an external endpoint for the serverless services.
- A front end single-page application can be deployed as part of a serverless application. Our single-page application is copied to a publicly accessible S3 bucket.
- All infrastructure for this system is defined as code; at no point did we need to use the AWS web console to deploy our application.
- Deployment and removal can be fully automated through a script that triggers the Serverless Framework.

WARNING   Please ensure that you fully remove all cloud resources deployed in this chapter in order to avoid additional charges!

Part 2

Tools of the trade

In chapter 4 we will create an entirely serverless to-do list application, which we will secure using AWS Cognito. We will proceed to add AI-driven interfaces to this application in chapter 5, such as speech-to-text and an interactive chatbot.

In chapter 6 we will look in more detail at the key tools and techniques that you will need to master in order to be effective with AI as a Service. These include how to create build and deployment pipelines, how to build observability into our systems, and how to effectively monitor and debug the systems that we build.

Building systems from scratch is relatively easy. Most of us in the real world are tasked with maintaining and extending preexisting platforms, so we close out this part in chapter 7 by looking at how to apply what we have learned to existing systems.

Building and securing a web application the serverless way

In this chapter we will build upon the lessons of chapters 2 and 3 to build our second, more capable serverless AI system. Most programming texts use the canonical to-do list application as a teaching example. This book is no different in that regard. However, this is certainly not your grandparents' to-do list: this is the to-do list on steroids! The to-do list application that we will build in this chapter will start out simple enough as a familiar CRUD (Create, Read, Update, Delete) type application utilizing a cloud native database. After securing the application with a login and logout screen, we will add natural language speech interfaces to record and transcribe text, and to have the system tell us our daily schedule from our to-do list. Finally, we will add a conversational interface to the system, allowing us to interact entirely through natural speech and not the keyboard.

In this chapter we will build the serverless to-do list. We will add the AI features in chapter 5, and as we will see, these can be built very rapidly by harnessing cloud AI services to do the heavy lifting.

4.1   The to-do list

Our next-generation to-do list will consume a number of AI services. As before, this will follow our canonical architectural pattern for serverless AI systems that we developed in chapter 1 and used in chapters 2 and 3. The finished product is shown in figure 4.1.

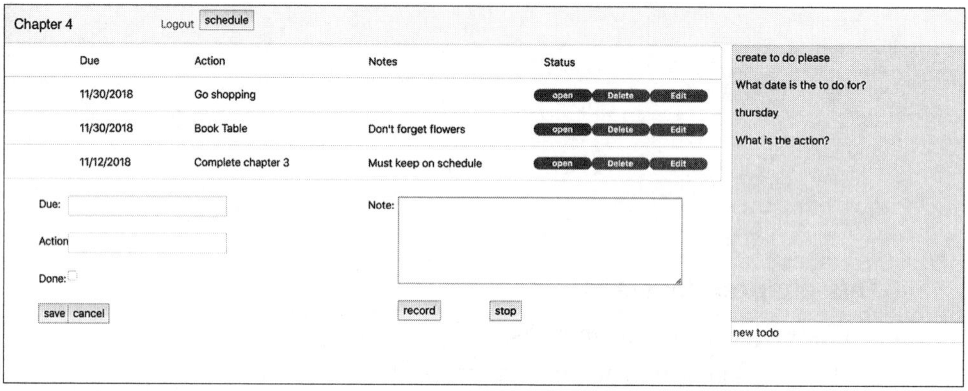

Figure 4.1   The end goal

In this image, the user is midway through creating a new to-do item through a conversation with our to-do chatbot.

4.2   Architecture

Before we get into assembling the system, let's look at the architecture and take a moment to understand how it maps back to our canonical serverless AI architecture that we developed in chapter 1. Figure 4.2 depicts the overall structure of the system.

The system architecture shows a clear separation between services. Every service has a single responsibility with a well-defined interface:

- *Web application*—Static content for the client application is served from an S3 bucket. An API Gateway provides an API that triggers event handlers in our synchronous and asynchronous services. Our web application client uses the AWS Amplify client SDK to handle the complexity of authentication.
- *Synchronous and asynchronous services*—These custom services are AWS Lambda functions that handle our API requests and perform the main business logic of our application.

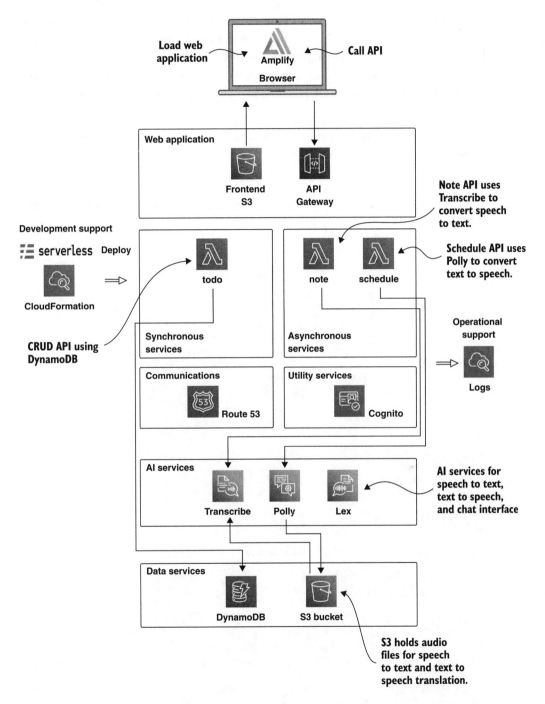

Figure 4.2 System architecture. The system is composed of custom services and managed services. Using many managed services provided by AWS allows us to quickly build and deploy scalable, production-grade applications.

- *Communication fabric*—AWS Route53 is used for DNS configuration so our services can be accessed using a custom domain name.
- *Utility services*—AWS Cognito is used for authentication and authorization.
- *AI services*—We use three managed AWS AI services: Transcribe, Polly, and Lex.
- *Data services*—DynamoDB is used as a powerful and scalable database. S3 is used for file storage.

As we work through the system, we will describe each section in more detail and explain how it is built and deployed.

4.2.1 Web application

The structure of the application is shown in figure 4.3 with the *web application* section highlighted.

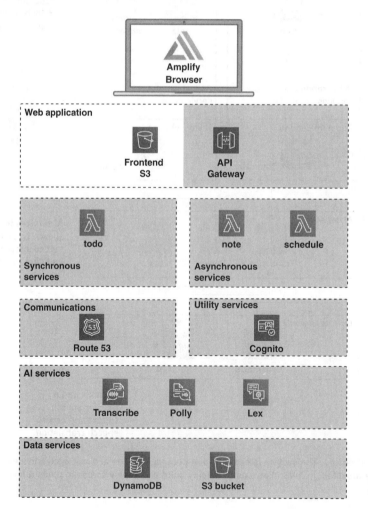

Figure 4.3
Web application

The structure shown will be familiar from our system in chapters 2 and 3. The front end of the system is a single-page application comprising HTML, CSS, and JavaScript to render the UI, deployed into an S3 bucket. We will repeat this image throughout the chapter, highlighting the relevant section as we build the complete application. As before, we are using API Gateway to provide a route into the services.

For our to-do application, we are using an additional library on the front end; AWS Amplify. Amplify is a JavaScript client library that provides secure access to nominated AWS services. In our case we are using it to provide a client interface to Cognito for login and logout, and also to access speech-to-text data stored in S3.

4.2.2 Synchronous services

Figure 4.4 shows our application architecture again, this time with the *synchronous services* section highlighted.

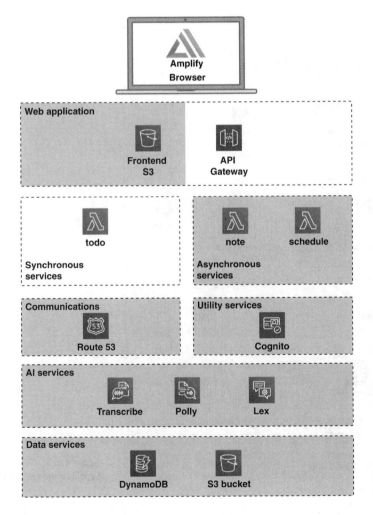

Figure 4.4
Synchronous services

There is one main synchronous service shown. This is the `to-do` service, which exposes routes for a simple CRUD interface as follows:

- `POST /todo/`—Create a new item.
- `GET /todo/{id}`—Read a specific item.
- `PUT /todo/{id}`—Update item.
- `DELETE /todo/{id}`—Delete an item.
- `GET /todo`—List all items.

4.2.3 Asynchronous services

The asynchronous services section of our application architecture is highlighted in figure 4.5.

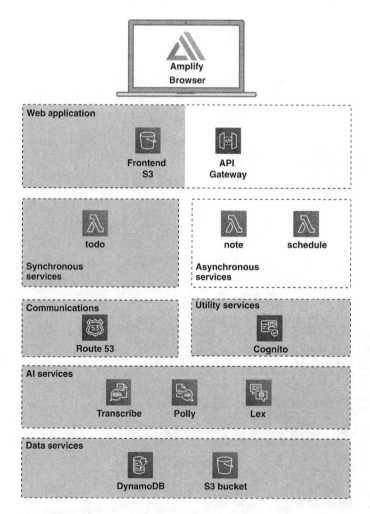

Figure 4.5
Asynchronous services

There are two asynchronous services which are concerned with speech-to-text and text-to-speech translation. These services are as follows.

NOTE SERVICE
Provides an interface to convert a voice recorded note into text:

- `POST /note`—Kick off a new asynchronous note transcription job.
- `GET /note/{id}`—Poll for information on the asynchronous transcription.

SCHEDULE SERVICE
Provides an interface to create a schedule and then convert it into a voice recording:

- `POST /schedule`—Start a new asynchronous schedule job.
- `GET /schedule/{id}`—Poll for information on the schedule.

4.2.4 Communication fabric

We have chosen to build our to-do list using a poll-based mechanism for simplicity, and have opted not to use any queue. We are primarily using HTTP and DNS as our communication fabric technologies.

4.2.5 Utility services

We are using Amazon Cognito as a mechanism for user login and authentication. User management is a "solved problem" and one that we don't want to build ourselves for each platform that we develop. For this system we use Cognito to do the heavy lifting for us.

4.2.6 AI services

The next highlighted sections of our architecture, shown in figure 4.6, cover the AI and data storage services we use in this system

Figure 4.6   AI and data services

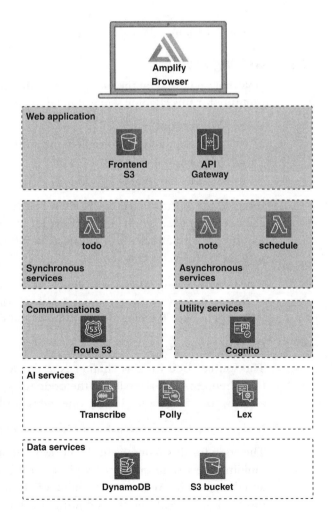

- *Transcribe* is used to provide speech-to-text conversion and reads its input from S3.
- *Polly* converts text into speech and writes its output audio files to S3.
- *Lex* is used to create interactive chatbots. We will use the Lex Web UI system to plug directly into our front-end application.

4.2.7   Data services

In the data services tier, we are using the Simple Storage Service (S3) and DynamoDB. DynamoDB is a highly scalable cloud native NoSQL database, and we are using it to store our to-do items.

4.2.8   Development support and operational support

As before, we are using the Serverless Framework as our main development support system. All logging data is collected using CloudWatch.

4.3   Getting ready

Now that we have seen the end goal, let's dive in and put the system together. As a prerequisite for this chapter, you will need to have the following:

- AWS account
- AWS command line installed and configured
- Node.js installed
- Serverless Framework installed

Instructions on how to set up Node.js and the Serverless Framework are provided in chapters 2 and 3. Setup instructions for AWS are provided in appendix A. If you haven't done so already, you will need to follow these instructions before proceeding with the code in this chapter.

> **WARNING**   Using AWS costs money! Please ensure that any cloud infrastructure is destroyed once you are finished with it. We will provide tear down instructions at the end of each chapter to help with this.

4.3.1   Getting the code

The source code for this chapter is available in the repository https://github.com/fourTheorem/ai-as-a-service in the `code/chapter4` directory. If you haven't done so already, you can go ahead and clone the repository:

```
$ git clone https://github.com/fourTheorem/ai-as-a-service.git
```

The code for this system is broken down into a number of simple steps, as we will be building the system up piece by piece. In this chapter we build the basic application and then add the AI features in chapter 5. If you look in the `chapter4` and `chapter5` directories, you will find the following breakdown:

- `chapter4/step-1-basic-todo`
- `chapter4/step-2-cognito-login`
- `chapter5/step-3-note-service`
- `chapter5/step-4-schedule-service`
- `chapter5/step-5-chat-interface`

We will be working through these directories in order. Each logical step will add additional functionality to our to-do list application. Let's get going with the first step, our basic to-do application.

4.4 Step 1: The basic application

Our basic to-do application should feel fairly familiar to most programmers, who will at some time or another have encountered the canonical to-do application. Figure 4.7 depicts the application running after deployment.

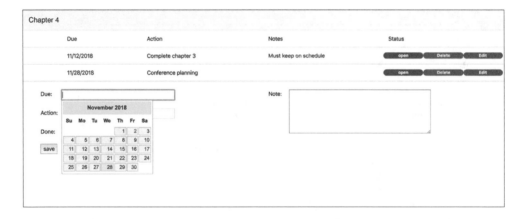

Figure 4.7   Basic to-do list

The complete application shows a list of to-dos, along with a form for adding a new to-do.

Why another to-do application?

In putting the content for this book together, we did indeed question if the world needed yet another to-do application. However on reflection we decided that it would be valuable for the following reasons:

- A to-do application needs to cover all of the basic CRUD operations.
- It is a familiar starting point for most programmers.
- Most to-do applications stop at the CRUD part; our aim is to explore how to secure and then expand the application with AI services.

At this starting point, the system is composed of a small set of components, as illustrated in figure 4.8.

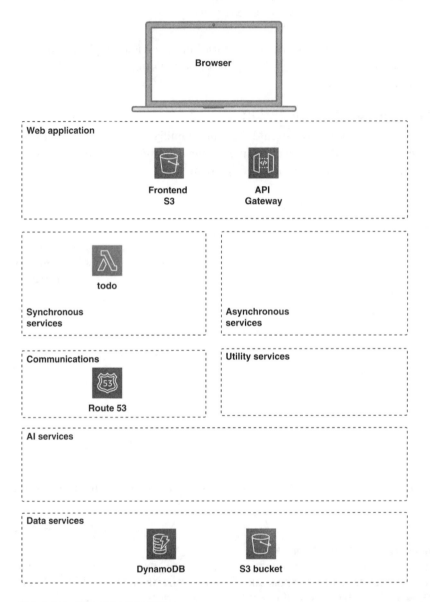

Figure 4.8   Step 1 architecture

As you can see, our system is fairly simple at this point. It uses a single API Gateway deployment, some simple Lambda functions, a DynamoDB table, and some front end code served out of S3. The source code for this first step is in the directory `chapter4/step-1-basic-todo` and has the structure shown in the next listing, which lists only the key files for the sake of clarity.

Listing 4.1   Code structure

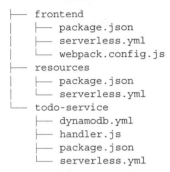

```
├── frontend
│   ├── package.json
│   ├── serverless.yml
│   └── webpack.config.js
├── resources
│   ├── package.json
│   └── serverless.yml
└── todo-service
    ├── dynamodb.yml
    ├── handler.js
    ├── package.json
    └── serverless.yml
```

Let's look at each of these components in turn.

4.4.1   Resources

As with our previous application, we define a set of global cloud resources in our `resources` directory. It is important to note that we only configure global resources here. Configuration for cloud resources that are specific to an individual service should be kept with that service. For example, the to-do service "owns" the to-do DynamoDB table; therefore this resource is configured as part of the `to-do` service definition.

> **TIP** As a rule of thumb, keep service-specific resource definitions with the service code. Only globally accessed resources should be configured outside of a service directory.

Our `serverless.yml` file for resources defines an S3 bucket for the front end, sets permissions, and enables CORS. After working through chapters 2 and 3, the format and structure of this `serverless.yml` should be very familiar, so we won't cover it here, except to note that we are using a new plugin in this configuration: `serverless-dotenv-plugin`. This reads in environment variables from a `.env` file, which contains system-specific variables such as our bucket name. We will edit this file later in this section when we deploy the system.

CORS

CORS stands for *cross-origin resource sharing*. It is a security mechanism that allows a web page to request resources from a different domain than the one from which the original web page was loaded. Using CORS, a web server may selectively allow or deny requests from different originating domains. A full explanation of CORS can be found here: https://en.wikipedia.org/wiki/Cross-origin_resource_sharing.

In our system the only shared resource is the data bucket. This will be used by services in later sections.

4.4.2   *To-do service*

For the first step, we have implemented only the basic to-do CRUD service and a minimal front end. The to-do service uses DynamoDB, Amazon's cloud-native NoSQL database. Figure 4.9 illustrates the individual routes that make up the to-do service, each of which performs a corresponding read or write operation.

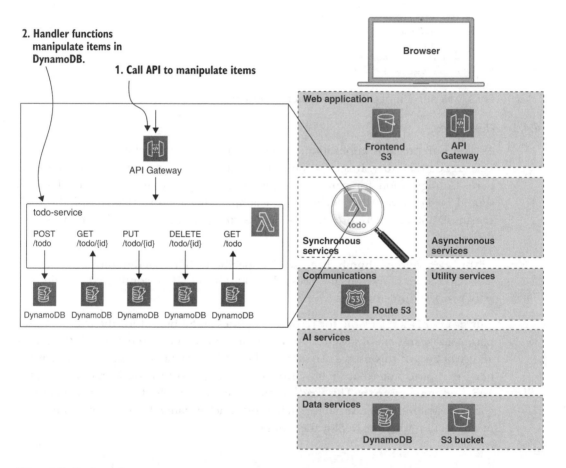

Figure 4.9   To-do service

The expanded section of the image shows the POST, PUT, and DELETE routes for adding, updating, and deleting to-do records. There are two GET routes shown: one for retrieving all to-dos, and one for retrieving a single to-do using its ID.

CRUD

If you're not familiar with the term, *CRUD* stands for *Create, Read, Update, Delete*. Sometimes you will hear the term "CRUD-based application." This term just means an application that performs these standard operations on some data store. Typically CRUD applications are implemented using a RESTful HTTP interface. This means that the following HTTP verb and routes are used:

- POST /widget—Post data to create and store a new widget.
- GET /widget/{id}—Read back the data for widget with the supplied ID.
- PUT /widget/{id}—Update the widget with the supplied ID.
- DELETE /widget/{id}—Delete the widget with the supplied ID.
- GET /widget—Get a list of all widgets.

The main section of the serverless.yml file, shown in the following listing, configures the AWS provider and defines the API Gateway routes and their associated Lambda function event handlers.

Listing 4.2 serverless.yml configuration for the to-do service

```
provider:
  name: aws
  runtime: nodejs12.x
  stage: ${opt:stage, 'dev'}
  region: ${env:AWS_DEFAULT_REGION, 'eu-west-1'}      ◁─┐ Define environment
  environment:                                           │ variable for DynamoDB
    TODO_TABLE: '${self:service}-${self:provider.stage}'
  iamRoleStatements:                                   ◁──┐ IAM access role for
    - Effect: Allow                                        │ Lambda functions to
      Action:                                              │ access DynamoDB
        - dynamodb:DescribeTable
        - dynamodb:Query
        - dynamodb:Scan
        - dynamodb:GetItem
        - dynamodb:PutItem
        - dynamodb:UpdateItem
        - dynamodb:DeleteItem
      Resource: "arn:aws:dynamodb:${self:custom.region}:${self:custom.account
      id}:*"

functions:                            ◁──┐ CRUD routes
  create:                                 │ and handlers
    handler: handler.create
    events:
      - http:
          method: POST
          path: todo
          cors: true
  ...

resources:                                         │ Include
  - ${file(./dynamodb.yml)}           ◁──┘ resources
```

Though this configuration file is a little larger than our previous examples, the structure is very much the same as for the `ui-service` in chapters 2 and 3, in that we

- Configure access to DynamoDB for our handler functions
- Define routes and handler functions

We use an environment definition in the provider section to supply our handler code with the DynamoDB table name:

```
environment:
  TODO_TABLE: '${self:service}-${self:provider.stage}'
```

This is important because we do not want to hard-code the table name into our handler functions, as this would be a violation of the DRY principle.

> **TIP** *DRY* stands for "don't repeat yourself." In the context of a software system, it means that we should strive to only have a single definition or source of truth for each piece of information in a system.

To make the serverless definition more manageable, we have chosen to place our DynamoDB table definition in a separate file and include it in our main `serverless.yml` file:

```
resources:
  - ${file(./dynamodb.yml)}
```

This can help to keep our configurations shorter and more readable. We will be using this pattern throughout the remaining chapters. Our included file, shown in the next listing, configures DynamoDB resources for the system.

Listing 4.3   Serverless DynamoDB configuration

```
Resources:
  TodosDynamoDbTable:
    Type: 'AWS::DynamoDB::Table'
    DeletionPolicy: Retain           ◁──  We specify that the table should not be deleted
    Properties:                            when the CloudFormation stack is removed. This
      AttributeDefinitions:                can help to avoid accidental data loss. The
        - AttributeName: id                CloudFormation stack is the set of resources
          AttributeType: S                 created or updated when we run serverless deploy.
      KeySchema:                       ◁──  For this table, we specify one key attribute,
        - AttributeName: id                an ID of type S (string). This attribute is a
          KeyType: HASH                    partition key, so values must be unique.
      ProvisionedThroughput:          ◁──  The capacity units for throughput are set to the
        ReadCapacityUnits: 1               lowest possible values. This will restrict the number
        WriteCapacityUnits: 1              of reads and writes that can occur but, for this
      TableName: '${self:service}-${self:provider.stage}'  application, will ensure costs are kept to a minimum.
```

This is a very simple configuration, defining a single `id` key on the DynamoDB table.

If we now look at the handler code for the `to-do` service, it should become clear how the system uses DynamoDB to store data. The code is in the file `handler.js`, shown in the following listing.

Listing 4.4   Requires and creates handler for to-do service

```
const uuid = require('uuid')
const AWS = require('aws-sdk')                                    ◁──┐ Require
const dynamoDb = new AWS.DynamoDB.DocumentClient()        ◁──┐ AWS SDK
const TABLE_NAME = {                                       ◁──┐ Create DynamoDB
  TableName: process.env.TODO_TABLE      ◁──┐                 │ client
}                                          │ Use table name
                                           │ environment variable
function respond (err, body, cb) {   ◁──┐ Respond
  ...                                   │ boilerplate
}

module.exports.create = (event, context, cb) => {       ◁──┐ Create
  const data = JSON.parse(event.body)                      │ handler
  removeEmpty(data)

  data.id = uuid.v1()
  data.modifiedTime = new Date().getTime()

  const params = { ...TABLE_NAME, Item: data }
  dynamoDb.put(params, (err, data) => {        ◁──┐ Create to-do
    respond(err, {data: data}, cb)               │ in database
  })
}
```

The handler implementation should also feel familiar if you worked through chapters 2 and 3. The pattern here is to include the AWS SDK and then create an interface into the specific service that we want to access, in this case DynamoDB. The rest of the code then uses this resource to perform operations against the service and returns a result to the caller of the service. In listing 4.4, we have shown the `create` endpoint. This maps to our `POST /to-do` route. Clients of this code will include to-do information in the `POST` request as JSON-formatted data. In this case, the JSON used is of the form shown in the following listing.

Listing 4.5   Example JSON content for the to-do POST

```
{
  dueDate: '2018/11/20',
  action: 'Shopping',
  stat: 'open',
  note: 'Do not forget cookies'
}
```

The create method adds in a `timestamp` and an `id` field before writing the to-do to the database. The rest of the methods in `handler.js` implement the other CRUD operations against the database.

4.4.3   *Front end*

Our front-end application for this first step is also fairly straightforward, and is illustrated in figure 4.10.

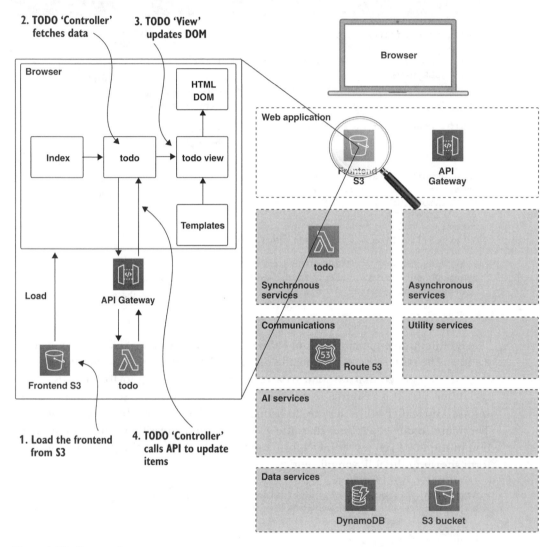

Figure 4.10   Front end

The front-end application is built and stored in S3. When a browser loads the `index.html` page, the code and other assets, such as stylesheets and images, are also loaded. Internally the front-end application is built using JQuery. As this application will do a little more than the example in chapters 2 and 3, we have introduced some structure into the code, which is illustrated in figure 4.10 and will be described shortly.

The code is in the `frontend` directory and has the structure shown in the next listing.

Listing 4.6 Front-end directory structure

```
├── assets
├── src
│   ├── index.html
│   ├── index.js
│   ├── templates.js
│   ├── todo-view.js
│   └── todo.js
├── webpack.config.js
├── package.json
└── serverless.yml
```

The root page for the application is `src/index.html`, shown in the following listing. This provides some of the initial DOM (Document Object Model) structure and loads in the main application code.

Listing 4.7 `index.html`

```
<html>
<head>
  <title>Chapter 4</title>
</head>
<body>
  <script src='main.js'></script>          ◁─┐  Load application
                                              │  code

    <nav class="navbar navbar-expand-lg navbar-light bg-light">
    .
    .                    ◁─┐  Navigation bar
    .                      │  code omitted
    </nav>

    <div id="content">        ◁─┐  Main application
    </div>                      │  content area

    <div id="footer">
        <div id="error"></div>
    </div>

</body>
</html>
```

The main code for the application lives in the `src` directory. This is composed of the following:

- index.js—Application entry point
- todo.js—To-do "model" and "controller" code
- todo-view.js—To-do DOM manipulation
- templates.js—Common rendering templates

Our index.js file, shown in the next listing, simply loads in the required resources.

Listing 4.8   index.js

```
import $ from 'jquery'
import 'bootstrap/dist/css/bootstrap.min.css'          ◁──┐ Load jquery
import 'webpack-jquery-ui/css'                             │ and styles
import {todo} from './todo'                 ◁──┐ Load
                                               │ to-do code
$(function () {
  todo.activate()        ◁──┐ Activate to-do once
})                          │ page has loaded
```

The main work is carried out in our to-do module, shown in the following listing.

Listing 4.9   todo.js

```
import $ from 'jquery'
import {view} from './todo-view'          ◁──┐ Import
                                             │ to-do view
const todo = {activate}      ◁──┐ Export activate
export {todo}                   │ function

const API_ROOT = `https://chapter4api.${process.env.CHAPTER4_DOMAIN}/api/
    todo/`

function create (cb) {       ◁──┐ Create
  $.ajax(API_ROOT, {            │ to-do
    ...
  })
}

function list (cb)
  $.get(API_ROOT, function (body) {      ◁──┐ List
    ...                                     │ to-dos
  })
}

function activate () {
  list(() => {              ◁──┐ Call list
    bindList()                 │ on load
    bindEdit()
  })
  $('#content').bind('DOMSubtreeModified', () => {
    bindList()
    bindEdit()
  })
}
```

We have omitted some of the code from listing 4.9 for clarity. Most readers will be familiar with the Model View Controller (MVC) pattern. Our to-do module can be thought of as acting as the model and controller for to-dos in our front-end application, with our view functionality handled in todo-view.js.

We are building a URL for the to-do API using an environment variable:

```
API_ROOT = `https://chapter4api.${process.env.CHAPTER4_DOMAIN}/api/todo/`
```

We will set the `CHAPTER4_DOMAIN` variable later in this section when we deploy the front end.

Why no framework?

Readers who are familiar with front-end development may be wondering why we aren't using some kind of front-end framework such as React, Vue, or Angular. The answer is that although we understand that there are a number of popular frameworks available, they take time to learn. Our aim in this book is to teach AI as a Service and not front-end frameworks, so we have opted to use a lowest common denominator approach of JQuery combined with Webpack. In this way we hope to reduce the cognitive learning load.

Our display functionality is handled in `todo-view.js` and `templates.js`. We leave it as a exercise for the reader to look through these files, which are essentially doing some very simple DOM manipulation to render the to-do list.

In the root of our `frontend` directory we have three control files: `package.json`, `webpack.config.js`, and `serverless.yml`. These files allow us to install and manage JavaScript dependencies, build a version of the front end for deployment, and create the S3 bucket to deploy the build to.

The `serverless.yml` for the front end is very similar to that in our resources directory, so we won't cover it in detail here. It simply defines an S3 bucket with the appropriate permissions to serve up our front end publicly.

We covered the structure of `package.json` in chapters 2 and 3, so this should be familiar. We should note that `webpack` itself is managed as a development dependency in `package.json`. We also define a build task under the scripts block, which runs `webpack` in order to build the application for deployment.

Webpack

Webpack is a static module bundler for modern JavaScript applications. Webpack processes JavaScript, CSS, and other source files to create a compact output JavaScript file that can be included in a web application. Webpack works by building a dependency graph rather than working on a file-by-file basis. This has several benefits:

- The dependency graph means that only the resources we need are included in the output.
- The resultant output is much more efficient, as only a single minified JavaScript file is downloaded by the web application.
- Our workflow is now clean and efficient, as we can use the `npm` module system for dependency management.

(continued)

- Webpack will also manage other static assets such as CSS, images, and so on as part of the dependency graph.

Full documentation on Webpack is available here: https://webpack.js.org/.

Our webpack configuration is listed in the following listing.

Listing 4.10   webpack.config.js

```
const Dotenv = require('dotenv-webpack')
const path = require('path')

module.exports = {
  entry: {
    main: './src/index.js'          ◁── Define dependency
  },                                     graph entry point
  devtool: 'eval-source-map',      ◁── Enable source
  devServer: {                         maps for debugging
    contentBase: './dist',
    port: 9080
  },                               Define
  output: {                   ◁── output map
    filename: '[name].js',
    path: path.resolve(__dirname, 'dist'),
    publicPath: 'dist/'
  },                              Development
  mode: 'development',        ◁── mode
  module:                  ◁── CSS and image
    rules: [{                  modules
    ...
    }]
  },                              .env file
  plugins: [                ◁── plugin
    new Dotenv({
      path: path.resolve(__dirname, '..', '.env'),
      systemvars: false,
      silent: false
    })
  ]
}
```

Our webpack configuration will build all dependencies from src/index.js into the dist folder for us. This includes all of our source code and related modules, including JQuery. We can then simply deploy the dist directory to S3 to have a functional application.

In a similar manner to the serverless-dotenv-plugin, we use the dotenv-webpack plugin here. This allows us to use a single environment configuration file across all code areas, helping to keep our system DRY.

4.4.4 Deploying step 1

Now that we understand the to-do system, let's go ahead and deploy it to AWS. If you haven't already set up an account, you will need to go to appendix A to get set up.

SET ENVIRONMENT VARIABLES

You may recall from reviewing the code that the front-end project created an S3 bucket to hold our web application and that it used an environment variable, `CHAPTER4_BUCKET`. You will need to decide on a name for your bucket that is globally unique. Remember also that we are using a custom domain for our to-do API through the environment variable `CHAPTER4_DOMAIN`.

Following the setup in appendix A, you should have the following environment variables defined in your shell:

- `AWS_ACCOUNT_ID`
- `AWS_DEFAULT_REGION`
- `AWS_ACCESS_KEY_ID`
- `AWS_SECRET_ACCESS_KEY`

These are global variables and that you should keep in just one place on your system. To deploy our to-do application, we need to provide the system-specific variables. To do this, we will use a `.env` file. Using any text editor, create a file called `.env` and place it in the `chapter4/step1-basic-todo` directory. The file should contain the contents shown in the following listing.

Listing 4.11   Environment variables for step 1

```
# environment definiton for Chapter 4
TARGET_REGION=eu-west-1
CHAPTER4_BUCKET=<your bucket name>
CHAPTER4_DATA_BUCKET=<your data bucket name>
CHAPTER4_DOMAIN=<your development domain>
```

We specify the region eu-west-l for all examples.

Specify the globally unique bucket names you have chosen.

The value for CHAPTER4_DOMAIN can be exactly as used for our chapter 2 and 3 deployment, and should refer to a domain created with AWS Route53.

Substitute your chosen names for `CHAPTER4_BUCKET`, `CHAPTER4_DATA_BUCKET`, and `CHAPTER4_DOMAIN`. Refer back to chapters 2 and 3 for full instructions on setting up a domain.

DEPLOY RESOURCES

First, we will deploy our resources project. To do this, `cd` into the `resources` directory and run

```
$ npm install
$ serverless deploy
```

This will create our S3 data bucket for later use. We can confirm creation of the bucket by using the AWS web console.

DEPLOY TODO-SERVICE

Next we will deploy the to-do service. `cd` into the `todo-service` directory and install dependencies by running

```
$ npm install
```

Before deploying, we will need to create a custom domain for our application. Our configuration for this in `serverless.yml` is shown in the next listing.

Listing 4.12   Custom domain configuration in `serverless.yml`

```
custom:
  region: ${env:AWS_DEFAULT_REGION, 'eu-west-1'}
  accountid: ${env:AWS_ACCOUNT_ID}
  domain: ${env:CHAPTER4_DOMAIN}
  customDomain:
    domainName: 'chapter4api.${self:custom.domain}'
    stage: ${self:provider.stage}
    basePath: api
    certificateName: '*.${self:custom.domain}'
    createRoute53Record: true
    endpointType: regional
  serverless-offline:
    port: 3000
```

This defines the parent domain.

The subdomain is composed of the prefix chapter4api and the parent domain.

A wildcard certificate is specified.

Our domain name for this section will be composed of our setting for `CHAPTER4_DOMAIN` and with a subdomain of `chapter4api`. That is, if we were using `example.com` for our variable `CHAPTER4_DOMAIN`, then the full custom domain for this chapter would be `chapter4api.example.com`.

Let's go ahead and create this domain

```
$ serverless create_domain
```

We can now deploy our to-do API by running

```
$ serverless deploy
```

DEPLOY THE FRONT END

Finally, in this section, we need to deploy our front end. First, to install dependencies, `cd` into the `frontend` directory and run

```
$ npm install
```

Next we need to create the bucket for our application by running

```
$ serverless deploy
```

We can now build the front end with Webpack through our npm scripts section:

```
$ source ../.env
$ npm run build
```

This will create a file `main.js` in our `dist` directory, along with an `assets` directory containing some additional images. To deploy the front end we will use the AWS command line as we did in chapters 2 and 3:

```
$ cd frontend
$ source ../.env
$ aws s3 sync dist/ s3://$CHAPTER4_BUCKET
```

This will push the contents of the `dist` directory into our chapter 4 bucket that we just created. Note that we need to `source` the contents of our environment file into the shell to provide the `CHAPTER4_BUCKET` environment variable.

TEST IT

If all of the preceding steps went well, we should now have a fully functioning system deployed to AWS. To test this out, open this URL in a browser

```
https://<CHAPTER4_BUCKET>.s3-eu-west-1.amazonaws.com/index.html
```

replacing `<CHAPTER4_BUCKET>` with your specific bucket name. You should be able to create and update to-do items through the front end in your browser.

> ### Why serve from the bucket?
> Some readers may be wondering why are we serving up content directly from the S3 bucket. Why are we not using a CDN such as CloudFront? The answer is that for a teaching system like this, CloudFront is overkill. We agree that for a full production system, the S3 bucket should be used as the origin server for a CDN; however, in development mode, CDN caching and updating will just get in the way.

We now have a working to-do system. There's just one minor problem. The system is publicly accessible, meaning that any random person on the internet can read and modify my to-do list. This is clearly not a desirable characteristic for our system, so we'd better address it quickly. Thankfully, we can use a cloud native service to handle the work here for us. In the next section we will secure our to-do list with Cognito.

4.5 *Step 2: Securing with Cognito*

User management is one of those deceptively simple problems, in that it seems like it should be easy, but usually turns out to be really hard! Many programmers have suffered long into the night rolling their own user authentication and management systems under the naive assumption that "it can't be that hard."

Fortunately, user login and management is a solved problem, so we never have to write this type of code again. We can just use a cloud native service to do the work for us. There are several options available, but for this system we will be using AWS Cognito. Cognito provides a full authentication service for us, including

- Password complexity policy
- Integration with web and mobile applications

- Multiple login strategies
- User management
- Password complexity rules
- Single sign on
- Social login via Facebook, Google, Amazon, and so on
- Security best practices and defense for the latest known security vulnerabilities

This is an awful lot of functionality for a small development effort. So, let's apply Cognito to our to-do system and secure it from the bad guys!

Figure 4.11 illustrates the system with Cognito authentication added.

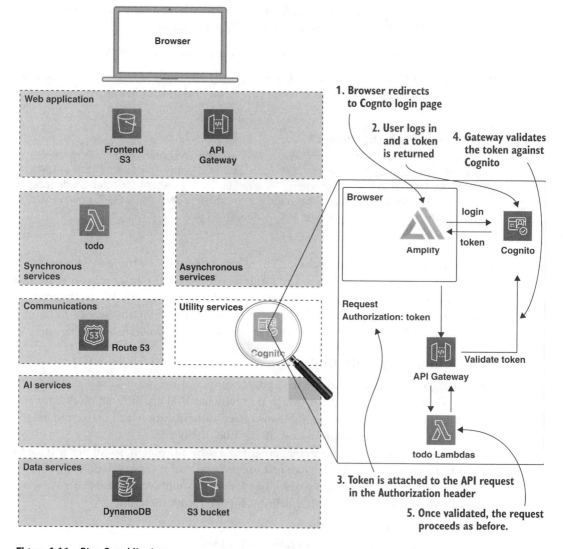

Figure 4.11   Step 2 architecture

We have added the AWS Amplify library to the front end. Amplify is a JavaScript library that provides authenticated access to various AWS services. For now, we will be using it just for authentication and access control. The token provided on successful login is passed to API calls to the API Gateway which, in turn, are handled by the AWS Lambda handler functions.

AWS Amplify

Amplify started life as a JavaScript library providing client-side access to AWS APIs. The library supports desktop browsers, as well as iOS and Android devices. A recent addition to the library is the Amplify CLI, which aims to provide a tool chain similar to the Serverless Framework that we have been using. At the time of writing, the Amplify tool chain is less mature than the Serverless Framework and lacks the plugin ecosystem support. However, this is definitely one to watch.

Full documentation on Amplify can be found here: https://aws-amplify.github.io/docs/js/start.

As illustrated in figure 4.11, we hand off the job of login to Cognito. Once a user has authenticated, they are allocated a session token, which is managed by the Amplify library. We then add an authentication step into our API Gateway setup, requiring that the user supply a valid JSON Web Token (JWT) before we allow the request to proceed. Any requests without a valid web token are rejected at this layer.

JSON Web Tokens

JSON Web Token (JWT) is an (RFC 7519) standard defining a method for securely transmitting claims as a JSON object. A JWT is comprised of three parts:

`<header>.<payload>.<signature>`

- header—Identifies the hash algorithm used by the token.
- payload—Contains a set of claims. A typical claim would be a user ID.
- signature—Is a one-way hash of the header, payload, and a secret using the algorithm defined in the header.

Typically a JWT will be issued by an authentication server on login and then used by a client to securely access resources. JWTs are typically short-lived and expire after a predefined time, forcing the client to periodically re-authenticate to generate a fresh token.

Detailed information on JWTs can be found here: https://en.wikipedia.org/wiki/JSON_Web_Token.

4.5.1 Getting the code

The code for this step is in the directory `chapter4/step-2-cognito-login` and contains the code from step 1 along with the updates for Cognito. We will walk through the updates in turn first, and then deploy the changes to secure our system.

4.5.2   User service

First up, there is a new service directory, `user-service`. This folder just contains the Serverless configuration for Cognito. There are three files:

- identity-pool.yml
- user-pool.yml
- serverless.yml

Our `serverless.yml` is short and you should be familiar with most of the boilerplate entries at this point. It imports the other two files, which contain Cognito resources. `user-pool.yml`, shown in the next listing, configures our Cognito user pool. A user pool is exactly what it sounds like, a pool of users.

Listing 4.13   Cognito user-pool configuration

```
Resources:
  CognitoUserPool:                              ◁──┐  User
    Type: AWS::Cognito::UserPool                    │  pool
    Properties:
      UserPoolName: ${self:service}${self:provider.stage}userpool
      UsernameAttributes:
        - email
      AutoVerifiedAttributes:
        - email
      EmailVerificationSubject: 'Your verification code'
      EmailVerificationMessage: 'Your verification code is {####}.'
      Schema:
        - Name: email
          AttributeDataType: String
          Mutable: true
          Required: true
      AdminCreateUserConfig:
        InviteMessageTemplate:
          EmailMessage: 'Your username is {username} and\
temporary password is {####}.'
          EmailSubject: 'Your temporary password'
        UnusedAccountValidityDays: 2
        AllowAdminCreateUserOnly: true
  CognitoUserPoolClient:                        ◁──┐  Client
    Type: AWS::Cognito::UserPoolClient              │  integration
    Properties:
      ClientName: ${self:service}${self:provider.stage}userpoolclient
      GenerateSecret: false
      UserPoolId:
        Ref: CognitoUserPool
```

Cognito provides a huge range of options. We are going to keep things simple and configure it just for email and password login. The code in listing 4.13 creates a user pool and also a user-pool client. A user pool client provides an integration bridge between a user pool and external applications. Cognito supports multiple user-pool clients against a single user pool.

To use Cognito for authorized access to AWS resources, we are going to also need an identity pool. This is configured in `identity-pool.yml`, shown in the next listing.

Listing 4.14 Cognito identity-pool configuration

```
Resources:
  CognitoIdentityPool:
    Type: AWS::Cognito::IdentityPool            ◁─┐  Define
    Properties:                                      identity pool
      IdentityPoolName: ${self:service}${self:provider.stage}identitypool
      AllowUnauthenticatedIdentities: false
      CognitoIdentityProviders:
        - ClientId:                                    Connect to
            Ref: CognitoUserPoolClient          ◁─┘   user pool
          ProviderName:
            Fn::GetAtt: [ "CognitoUserPool", "ProviderName" ]

  CognitoIdentityPoolRoles:                     ◁─┐  Attach policy to
    Type: AWS::Cognito::IdentityPoolRoleAttachment    identity pool
    Properties:
      IdentityPoolId:
        Ref: CognitoIdentityPool
      Roles:
        authenticated:
          Fn::GetAtt: [CognitoAuthRole, Arn]
```

In listing 4.14, we connected the identity pool to our user pool and also to a role, `CognitoAuthRole`. The role is also defined in `identity-pool.yml`. The key part to understand about this role is contained in the policy statement, shown in the next listing.

Listing 4.15 Identity-pool policy statements

```
Statement:
  - Effect: 'Allow'
    Action:                              ◁─┐  The policy grants all actions for Cognito,
      - 'cognito-sync:*'                      S3, Transcribe, Polly, and Lex.
      - 'cognito-identity:*'
      - 'S3:*'
      - 'transcribe:*'
      - 'polly:*'
      - 'lex:*'
    Resource: '*'
  - Effect: 'Allow'                      The policy grants access to
    Action:                         ◁─┘ invoke our API Gateway routes.
      - 'execute-api:Invoke'
    Resource:
```

This policy will be associated with all authenticated users and says that users with this role can

- Access S3
- Call the Transcribe service

- Call the Polly service
- Use the Lex service
- Execute API Gateway functions

Access to any other services will be denied for this role.

TIMEOUT!

OK, if you think all of this talk of user pools and identity pools is a little confusing, we agree! It can be overwhelming at first, so let's take some time to explain. The key concept to understand is the difference between authentication and authorization.

Authentication is the "who." In other words, can I prove that I am who I say I am? Usually this is done by proving that I know a secret piece of information—a password. A user pool deals with authentication.

Authorization is the "what." Given that I have proved who I am, what resources am I allowed to access? Typically this is achieved through some type of permissions model. For example, in a file system there are user- and group-level access controls that implement a basic permissions model. The AWS policy that we just created is a permissions model for our logged-in user. An identity pool deals with authorization.

Identity pools are also referred to as *federated identities*. This is because an identity pool can have multiple sources of identity. This is illustrated in figure 4.12.

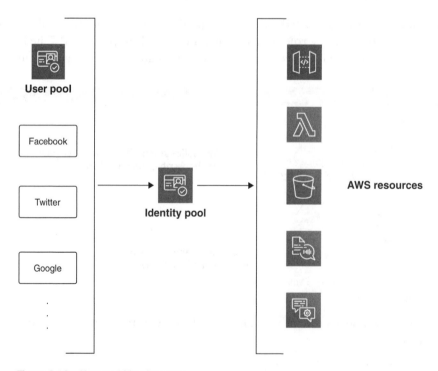

Figure 4.12   User and identity pools

As illustrated, a user pool can be thought of as one source of validated identities. Other sources include Facebook, Google, Twitter, and so on. An identity pool can be configured to use multiple sources of identity. For each validated identity, the identity pool allows us to configure a policy for authorized access to our AWS resources.

For this system, we will just use a Cognito user pool as our source of authenticated users; we won't enable social logins.

4.5.3   *To-do service*

Now that we have a source of authenticated users, we need to update our service to ensure that we have locked it down against unauthorized access. This is very simple to implement, and requires a small update to our `serverless.yml` for our to-do service, shown in the following listing.

Listing 4.16   Changes to to-do `serverless.yml`

```
custom:
  poolArn: ${env:CHAPTER4_POOL_ARN}          ⟵─┐ Include user
                                                │ pool ARN
functions:
  create:
    handler: handler.create
    events:
      - http:
          method: POST
          path: todo
          cors: true
          authorizer:                          ┐ Declare
            arn: '${self:custom.poolArn}'    ⟵─┘ authorizer
  list:
    handler: handler.list
    events:
      - http:
          method: GET
          path: todo
          cors: true
          authorizer:                          ┐ Declare
            arn: '${self:custom.poolArn}'    ⟵─┘ authorizer
```

We simply declare an authorizer against each endpoint that we wish to secure. We will also need to update our environment to include the user pool identifier `CHAPTER4_POOL_ARN`.

4.5.4   *Front-end service*

The final set of changes to our front end provides login, logout, and token management. We have added AWS Amplify to our front-end `package.json` as a dependency. Amplify requires that we supply it with some configuration parameters. This is done in `index.js`, shown in the next listing.

Listing 4.17   Amplify configuration in `index.js`

```
const oauth = {
  domain: process.env.CHAPTER4_COGNITO_DOMAIN,        ◁─┐ Configure
  scope: ['email'],                                      │ OAuth flow.
  redirectSignIn: `https://s3-${process.env.TARGET_REGION}.amazonaws.com/
    ${process.env.CHAPTER4_BUCKET}/index.html`,
  redirectSignOut: `https://s3-${process.env.TARGET_REGION}.amazonaws.com/
    ${process.env.CHAPTER4_BUCKET}/index.html`,
  responseType: 'token'
}
                                         ┌─ Configure
Amplify.configure({                  ◁──┘ Amplify.
  Auth: {
    region: process.env.TARGET_REGION,
    userPoolId: process.env.CHAPTER4_POOL_ID,
    userPoolWebClientId: process.env.CHAPTER4_POOL_CLIENT_ID,
    identityPoolId: process.env.CHAPTER4_IDPOOL,
    mandatorySignIn: false,
    oauth: oauth
  }
})
```

Our configuration is broken into two separate parts. First, we configure OAuth by providing a domain name and redirect URLs. These must match our Cognito configuration, which we will set up shortly when we deploy these changes. Second, we configure Amplify with our pool identifiers; we will grab these IDs during deployment and adjust our environment file accordingly in the next section.

The login implementation is handled by `auth.js` and `auth-view.js`. The code for `auth.js` is shown in the following listing.

Listing 4.18   `auth.js`

```
...
function bindLinks () {
  ...
  $('#login').on('click', e => {
    const config = Auth.configure()
    const { domain, redirectSignIn, responseType } = config.oauth
    const clientId = config.userPoolWebClientId
    const url = 'https://' + domain              ◁─┐ Redirect to Cognito
      + '/login?redirect_uri='                     │ login page
      + redirectSignIn
      + '&response_type='
      + responseType
      + '&client_id='
      + clientId
    window.location.assign(url)
  })
}

function activate () {
```

```
    return new Promise((resolve, reject) => {
      Auth.currentAuthenticatedUser()
        .then(user => {
          view.renderLink(true)
          bindLinks()
          resolve(user)
        })
        .catch(() => {
          view.renderLink(false)
          bindLinks()
          resolve(null)
        })
    })
}
```

◁─┐ **Check if logged in** (points to `Auth.currentAuthenticatedUser()`)

◁─┐ **Render logout link** (points to `view.renderLink(true)`)

◁─┐ **Else render login link** (points to `view.renderLink(false)`)

auth.js hands off most of the work to Amplify. In the activate function, it checks to see if the user is already logged in, and then calls the view to render either a login or logout link. It also provides a login handler that redirects to the Cognito login page.

Finally, in the front end, we need to update our calls to the to-do API to include our authorization token; otherwise, we will be denied access. This is shown in listing 4.19.

Listing 4.19 Updated `create` method

```
function create (cb) {
  auth.session().then(session => {
    $.ajax(API_ROOT, {
      data: JSON.stringify(gather()),
      contentType: 'application/json',
      type: 'POST',
      headers: {
        Authorization: session.idToken.jwtToken
      },
      success: function (body) {
        ...
      }
    })
  }).catch(err => view.renderError(err))
}
```

◁─┐ **Get the session.** (points to `auth.session().then(session => {`)

◁─┐ **Supply JWT through an Authorization header** (points to `Authorization: session.idToken.jwtToken`)

We have updated each of the functions in to-do.js to include an Authorization header, which is used to pass the JWT obtained from Cognito to our API.

4.5.5 Deploying step 2

Now that we understand Cognito, let's get the changes deployed and our application secured.

DEPLOYING COGNITO POOLS

First, cd into step-2-cognito-login/user-service and deploy the pools by running

```
$ serverless deploy
```

This will create a user and identity pool. We will need to supply some additional configuration through the AWS console. Open up a browser, log in to the AWS console, and go to the Cognito section. Select the option to Manage User Pools and select the pool `chapter4usersdevuserpool`. We need to provide a domain name to our user pool. Select the Domain Name option from the App Integration section, and provide a new domain name as illustrated in figure 4.13.

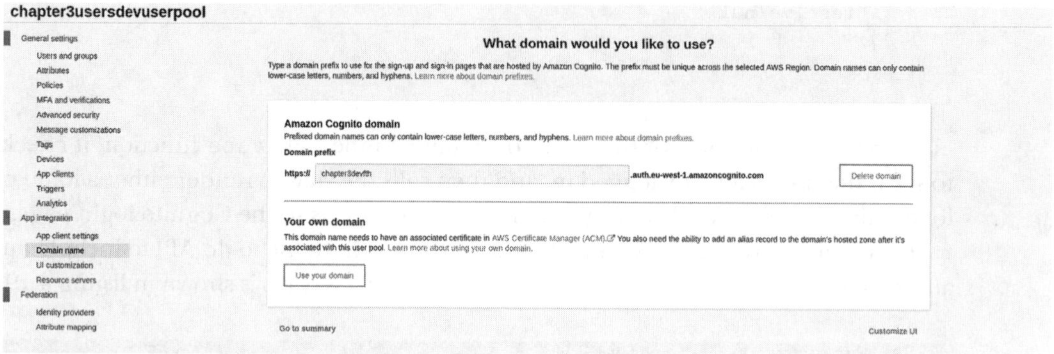

Figure 4.13   User and identity pools

For our user pool, we have used the domain name `chapter4devfth`. You can use any unique domain name that is available.

Next we need to configure our OAuth flows. Select the option App Client Settings and provide settings as illustrated in figure 4.14.

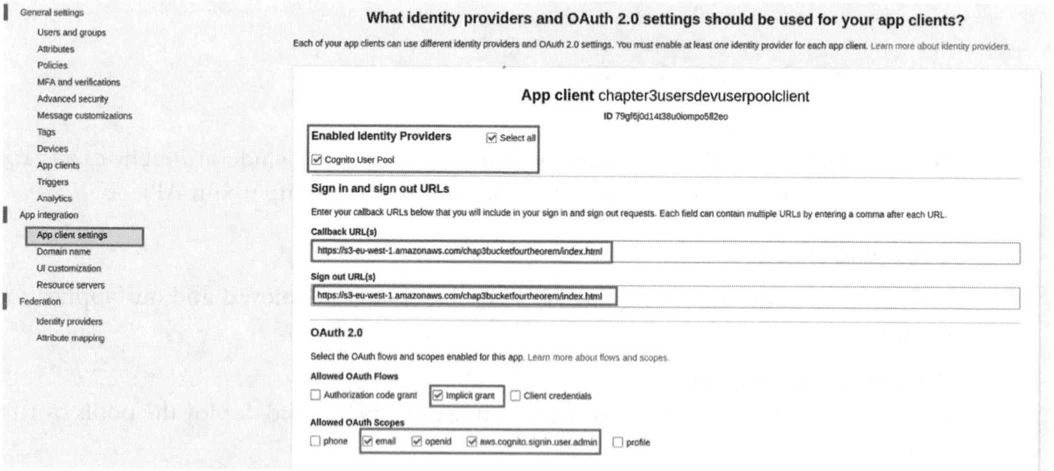

Figure 4.14   OAuth flow configuration

For the login and logout callback URLs, you should provide the URL to your front-end bucket using the custom domain that we created in step 1. These should be provided in this form: https://s3-eu-west-1.amazonaws.com/<YOUR BUCKET NAME>/ index.html.

> ## OAuth
>
> OAuth is a standard protocol for authentication and authorization which is widely implemented. A full discussion of the OAuth 2.0 protocol would require an entire book of its own. In fact, we would refer readers who are interested in this to the Manning publication, *OAuth 2 in Action*, by Justin Richer and Antonio Sanso (https://www.manning.com/books/oauth-2-in-action).
>
> More details on the OAuth 2.0 protocol can be found here: https://oauth.net/2/.

Finally, for the user pool we will need to create an account to log in with. To do this, select Users and Groups and click on the Create User button. Here, you can use your email address as the username and pick a temporary password. Enter your email address in the email field too. There is no need to enter a phone number, so deselect Mark Phone Number as Verified. The default selection for all other fields can be kept.

UPDATING THE ENVIRONMENT

Now that we have configured our pools, we need to update our `.env` file. `cd` into the `chapter4/step-2-cognito-login` directory and edit the file `.env` to match the following listing.

Listing 4.20 Updated `.env` file

```
# environment definition for Chapter 4
TARGET_REGION=eu-west-1                              The first block of environment variables
CHAPTER4_BUCKET=<your bucket name>                  is retained from listing 4.II.
CHAPTER4_DATA_BUCKET=<Your data bucket name>
CHAPTER4_DOMAIN=<your development domain>
CHAPTER4_COGNITO_BASE_DOMAIN=<your cognito domain>
CHAPTER4_COGNITO_DOMAIN=<your cognito domain>.auth.eu-west-
    1.amazoncognito.com                              The new environment variables reference the
CHAPTER4_POOL_ARN=<your user pool ARN>              AWS Cognito resources we have created.
CHAPTER4_POOL_ID=<your user pool ID>
CHAPTER4_POOL_CLIENT_ID=<your app integration client ID>
CHAPTER4_IDPOOL=<your identity pool ID>
```

You can find these IDs in the Cognito section of the AWS Management Console. The user-pool ID is located in the user-pool view, shown in figure 4.15.

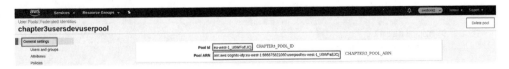

Figure 4.15   User pool ID and ARN

The client ID can be located in the *App client settings* section of the Cognito user-pools view. This is shown in figure 4.16.

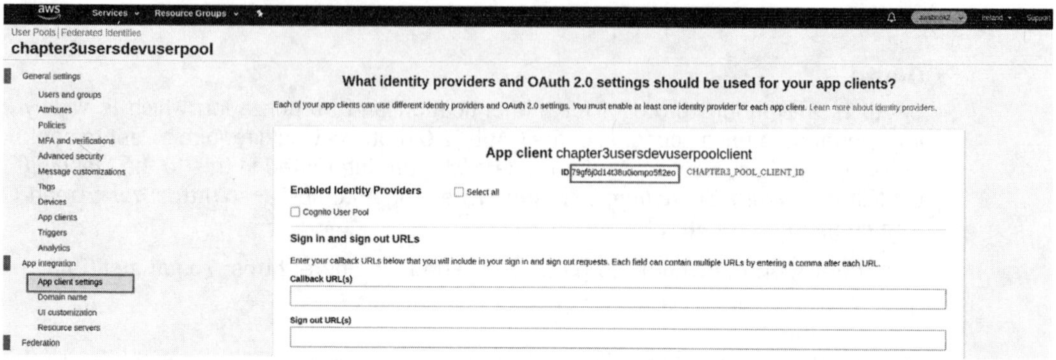

Figure 4.16   Pool client ID

The identity-pool ID can be located in the *Federated Identities* view. Simply select the identity pool that has been created and select Edit Identity Pool at the top right. The edit view is shown in figure 4.17. From here, you can view and copy the identity-pool ID.

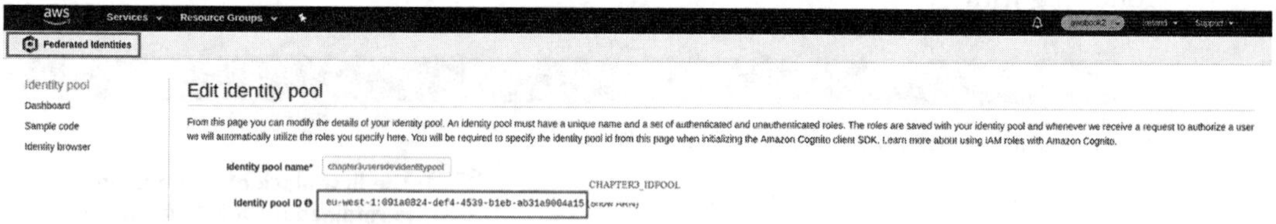

Figure 4.17   Identity-pool ID

Note that you may see a warning stating that no unauthenticated role has been specified. This can be ignored, as all users must be authenticated for our application.

Once you have located the required values in the AWS Console, populate the .env file with the relevant values.

UPDATING THE TO-DO API

Now that we have updated our environment, we can deploy the changes to our to-do service. cd into the step-2-cognito-login/todo-service directory and run

```
$ npm install
$ serverless deploy
```

This will push a new version of the API, which will include our Cognito authorizer.

UPDATING THE FRONT END

Now that our API is safely secured, we need to update our front end to allow access. To do this, `cd` into the `step-2-cognito-login/frontend` directory and run

```
$ source ../.env
$ npm install
$ npm run build
$ aws s3 sync dist/ s3://$CHAPTER4_BUCKET
```

This will build a new version of our application, including the authentication code, and deploy it to our bucket. If you point a browser at our application, you should see a blank page and a Login link at the top of the page. Click this link to bring up a Cognito login dialog. Once logged in, the application should function as before.

Though it takes a little effort to set up Cognito, the benefits far outweigh the costs. Let's review what you get with this service:

- User registration
- Secure JWT login
- Integration into the AWS IAM security model
- Password reset
- Federated identities both enterprise and social (such as Facebook, Google, Twitter...)
- Password policy control

Those of you who have had to deal with these issues before will appreciate the large overhead that can come with implementing these features, even when using a third-party library. The key reason for using Cognito is that the responsibility for much of the work of keeping user accounts secure can be offloaded onto this service. Of course, we still have to be mindful of the security of our applications; however, it is comforting to know that the Cognito service is being actively managed and updated for us.

We covered a lot of ground to get our secured serverless application up and running. The important point to note about this is that we were able to rapidly deploy our application in a secure manner with very little work. In the next chapter we will add some AI services to our to-do list.

Summary

- An end-to-end serverless platform, from client to database, can be defined in code and deployed using the Serverless Framework.
- A DynamoDB table can be created as part of the resources section of the `serverless.yml` file.
- The AWS SDK is used in our Lambda functions to pass data from events to our database read and write invocations.
- Authentication and authorization are configured with AWS Cognito. We configure a user pool, identity pool, and custom domain along with a policy to protect specific resources.

- AWS Amplify is used with Cognito to create a login interface with Cognito. Amplify is an easy-to-use client SDK from AWS that integrates with Cognito to enable powerful security features.
- API Gateway CRUD routes can be created to trigger Lambda functions. API Gateway routes are created through the events we define in the `serverless.yml`, linked to the associated Lambda function or *handler.*

WARNING Chapter 5 continues to build on this system and we provide instructions on how to remove the deployed resources at the end of chapter 5. If you are not planning on working on chapter 5 for some time, please ensure that you fully remove all cloud resources deployed in this chapter in order to avoid additional charges!

Adding AI interfaces
to a web application

This chapter covers

- Speaking a note with Transcribe
- Reading back a schedule with Polly
- Adding a chatbot interface with Lex

In this chapter we will build upon the to-do list application from chapter 4, adding off-the-shelf AI capability to the system. We will add natural language speech interfaces to record and transcribe text and to have the system tell us our daily schedule from our to-do list. Finally, we will add a conversational interface to the system, allowing us to interact entirely through a natural language interface. As we will see, this can be built very rapidly by harnessing cloud AI services to do the heavy lifting.

If you haven't worked through chapter 4, you should go back and do so now before proceeding with this chapter, as we will be building directly on top of the to-do list application that we deployed at the end of that chapter. If you're good with the content from chapter 4, we can dive right in and add our note service. We will pick up where we left off, starting with step 3.

5.1 Step 3: Adding a speech-to-text interface

Now that we have a basic serverless application deployed and secured, it's time to add in some AI features. In this section we are going to add a speech-to-text interface to allow us to dictate a note into the system rather than typing. We will use AWS Transcribe to do this. As we will see, adding in speech-to-text is actually not too hard for such an advanced feature.

Figure 5.1 shows how this feature will be implemented.

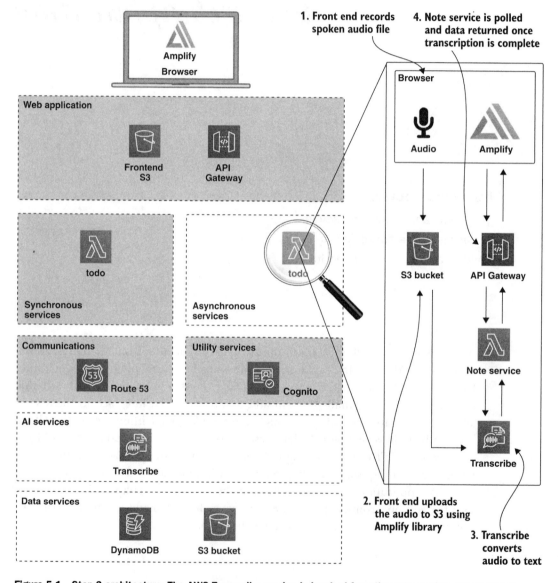

Figure 5.1   Step 3 architecture. The AWS Transcribe service is invoked from the note service. The front-end application uses Amplify to upload the file processed by Transcribe to S3.

The system will use the browser to capture spoken audio and save it to S3 using the Amplify library. Once the audio file is uploaded, the note service is called. This will kick off a Transcribe job to convert the audio to text. The client will poll the note service periodically to determine when the conversion has been completed. Finally, the front end will populate the note field with the converted text.

5.1.1 Getting the code

The code for this step is in the directory `chapter5/step-3-note-service`. This directory contains all of the code from step 2, along with our audio transcription changes. As before, we will walk through the updates in turn first, and then deploy the changes.

5.1.2 Note service

Our note service follows what should by now be a familiar pattern: the code is in the `note-service` directory and contains a `serverless.yml` configuration file along with the implementation. Most of this is boilerplate: the main difference is that we configure the service to have access to an S3 data bucket and also access to the Transcribe service. This is in the `iamRoleStatements` section of our configuration, shown in the following listing.

Listing 5.1 Role statements for note service

```
provider:
  ...
  iamRoleStatements:
    - Effect: Allow             Data bucket
      Action:               ◁─┘ for audio files
        - s3:PutObject
        - s3:GetObject
      Resource: "arn:aws:s3:::${self:custom.dataBucket}/*"
    - Effect: Allow
      Action:                   Allow this service to
        - transcribe:*       ◁─ access transcribe.
      Resource: "*"
```

The note service defines two routes: `POST /note` and `GET /note/{id}` to create and fetch a note respectively. As with the to-do CRUD routes, we are using our Cognito pool to lock down access to our note APIs, and we are using the same custom domain structure, just with a different base path of `noteapi`. Our handler code uses the AWS SDK to create transcription jobs, shown in the next listing.

Listing 5.2 Note service handler

```
const AWS = require('aws-sdk')
var trans = new AWS.TranscribeService()    ◁─┐ Create the transcription
                                              │ service object.
module.exports.transcribe = (event, context, cb) => {
  const body = JSON.parse(event.body)
```

```
const params = {
  LanguageCode: body.noteLang,
  Media: { MediaFileUri: body.noteUri },
  MediaFormat: body.noteFormat,
  TranscriptionJobName: body.noteName,
  MediaSampleRateHertz: body.noteSampleRate,
  Settings: {
    ChannelIdentification: false,
    MaxSpeakerLabels: 4,
    ShowSpeakerLabels: true
  }
}

trans.startTranscriptionJob(params, (err, data) => {        ⟵┐ Start an asynchronous
  respond(err, data, cb)                                       │ transcription job.
})
}
```

As you can see from the listing, the code is fairly simple in that it just calls a single API to kick the job off, passing in a link to our audio file. The code responds back to the client with a transcription job ID, which is used in the `poll` function. Check the code in detail to see the implementation of `poll`, which uses the `getTranscriptionJob` API to check the status of our running job.

5.1.3   *Front-end updates*

To provide the transcription functionality, we made a few updates to the front end. First, we have added some configuration to the Amplify library in `index.js`. This is shown in the next listing.

Listing 5.3   Updated Amplify configuration

```
Amplify.configure({
  Auth: {
    region: process.env.TARGET_REGION,
    userPoolId: process.env.CHAPTER4_POOL_ID,
    userPoolWebClientId: process.env.CHAPTER4_POOL_CLIENT_ID,
    identityPoolId: process.env.CHAPTER4_IDPOOL,
    mandatorySignIn: false,
    oauth: oauth
  },                                                │ Configure the S3 bucket used by
  Storage: {                               ⟵──────┘ the Amplify storage interface.
    bucket: process.env.CHAPTER4_DATA_BUCKET,
    region: process.env.TARGET_REGION,
    identityPoolId: process.env.CHAPTER4_IDPOOL,
    level: 'public'
  }
})
```

This configuration tells Amplify to use our data bucket that we set up in step 1. Because we have already configured Amplify with our Cognito settings, we can access this bucket from the client once we are logged in.

We have added some code for audio handling in the directory `frontend/src/`
`audio`. This uses the browser Media Stream Recording API to record audio into a buffer. We'll treat this code as a black box for the purpose of this book.

NOTE More information on the Media Stream Recording API can be found here: http://mng.bz/X0AE.

The main note handling code is in `note.js` and `note-view.js`. The view code adds two buttons to the UI: one to start recording and one to stop recording. These map to the functions `startRecord` and `stopRecord` in `note.js`. The `stopRecord` function is shown in the following listing.

Listing 5.4 `stopRecord` **function**

```
import {Storage} from 'aws-amplify'
...
function stopRecord () {
  const noteId = uuid()

  view.renderNote('Thinking')
  ac.stopRecording()
  ac.exportWAV((blob, recordedSampleRate) => {        ⟵┐ Export recorded
    Storage.put(noteId + '.wav', blob)                   │ buffer to WAV format
      .then(result => {                               ⟵─┐ Save WAV file to
        submitNote(noteId, recordedSampleRate)        ⟵  │ S3 using Amplify
      })                                                 Submit the WAV
      .catch(err => {                                    file for processing.
        console.log(err)
      })
    ac.close()
  })
}
```

`stopRecord` uses the `Storage` object from Amplify to write a WAV (Wave Audio file format) file directly to S3. It then calls the `submitNote` function, which calls our note service API `/noteapi/note` to kick off the transcription job. The `submitNote` code is shown in the next listing.

Listing 5.5 `submitNote` **function**

```
const API_ROOT = `https://chapter4api.${process.env.CHAPTER4_DOMAIN}
/noteapi/note/`
...
function submitNote (noteId, recordedSampleRate) {
  const body = {
    noteLang: 'en-US',
    noteUri: DATA_BUCKET_ROOT + noteId + '.wav',
    noteFormat: 'wav',
    noteName: noteId,
    noteSampleRate: recordedSampleRate
```

```
    }
    auth.session().then(session => {                    Call the
      $.ajax(API_ROOT, {                          ◁──┘  note service.
        data: JSON.stringify(body),
        contentType: 'application/json',
        type: 'POST',
        headers: {
          Authorization: session.idToken.jwtToken
        },
        success: function (body) {
          if (body.stat === 'ok') {               Enter
            pollNote(noteId)                 ◁──┘ polling
          } else {
            $('#error').html(body.err)
          }
        }
      })
    }).catch(err => view.renderError(err))
}
```

Our poll function calls the note service on the back end to check the transcription job
progress. The poll function code is shown in the following listing.

Listing 5.6   note.js pollNote function

```
function pollNote (noteId) {
  let count = 0
  itv = setInterval(() => {                        Obtain the authenticated
    auth.session().then(session => {          ◁──┘ session with Cognito.
      $.ajax(API_ROOT + noteId, {            ◁──┐ Invoke the API to
        type: 'GET',                              check the note status.
        headers: {
          Authorization: session.idToken.jwtToken
        },
        success: function (body) {
          if (body.transcribeStatus === 'COMPLETED') {
            clearInterval(itv)
            view.renderNote(body.results.transcripts[0].transcript)   ◁──┐
          } else if (body.transcribeStatus === 'FAILED') {
            clearInterval(itv)
            view.renderNote('FAILED')                If the transcription is
          } else {                                   complete, render the
            count++                                   transcribed note.
            ...
          }
        }
      })
    }).catch(err => view.renderError(err))
  }, 3000)
}
```

Once the job is complete, the resulting text will be rendered into the note input field on the page.

> **Polling**
>
> Polling is generally an inefficient way to handle events, and certainly does not scale up well. Our use of polling here does expose a drawback with AWS Lambda, in that functions are generally expected to execute for a short period of time. This makes them unsuitable for applications that may require a long-lived connection. A better way to receive an update when a job has completed would be to establish a web socket connection and then push an update down to the browser. This is much more efficient and will scale well.
>
> There are several better options that could be used here instead of polling, such as
>
> - Using AWS API Gateway with WebSockets—http://mng.bz/yr2e.
> - Using a third-party service such as Fanout—https://fanout.io/.
>
> The best approach to use would, of course, depend on the specific system. Description of these methods is outside the scope of this book, which is why we have used a simple poll-based approach for our note service.

5.1.4　Deploying step 3

Let's deploy our note functionality. First we will need to set up our environment. To do this simply copy your `.env` file from `step-2-cognito-login` to `step-3-note-service`.

　Next we will deploy our new note service. `cd` into the `step-3-note-service/note-service` directory and run

```
$ npm install
$ serverless deploy
```

This will create our note service endpoint in API Gateway and install our two Lambda functions. Next, deploy updates to the front end. `cd` in to the `step-3-note-service/frontend` directory and run

```
$ source ../.env
$ npm install
$ npm run build
$ aws s3 sync dist/ s3://$CHAPTER4_BUCKET
```

5.1.5　Testing step 3

Let's try out our new speech-to-text functionality. Open up the to-do application in a browser and log in as before. Hit the button to create a new to-do, and put in an action and a date. You should see two additional buttons as shown in figure 5.2: a Record button and a Stop button.

Figure 5.2 Record note

Hit the Record button and start talking! Once you've finished, hit the Stop button. A few seconds later, you should see that the note you just dictated is rendered as text into the note field, allowing you to go ahead and save the new to-do, complete with transcribed note.

The time to transcribe audio to text is variable, depending on the current global number of transcription jobs in progress. At worst, it may take up to 20 to 30 seconds for the transcription to complete. While a note on a to-do is a way to demonstrate AWS Transcribe, bear in mind that the API we are using is optimized for batch processing and can transcribe large audio files with multiple speakers—for example, a board meeting or an interview. We will introduce a faster conversational interface in step 5 later in the chapter. However, we should point out that in a recent update to the service, AWS Transcribe now supports real-time processing as well as batch mode.

5.2 Step 4: Adding text-to-speech

The next AI feature that we are going to add to our to-do list is the reverse of the note service. Our schedule service will build a daily schedule from our to-do list and then read it out to us. We will be using AWS Polly to achieve this. Polly is the AWS speech-to-text service. We can plug this into our system in a similar manner to our note service, through the use of an API. Figure 5.3 depicts the architectural structure for the schedule service.

When a user of our system requests a schedule, a call is made to our schedule service that creates a schedule as text and then submits it to Amazon Polly. Polly interprets the text and converts it to audio. The audio file is written to our S3 data bucket, and once available, we play this back to our user. Again, we would note that this is a small amount of work for an advanced feature!

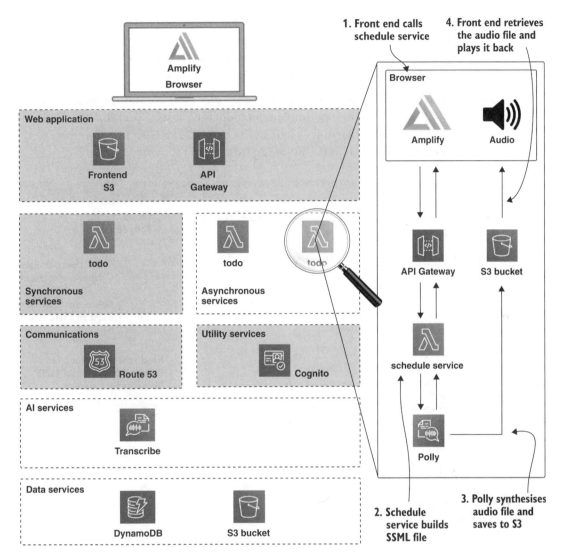

Figure 5.3   Record note

5.2.1   Getting the code

The code for this step is in the directory `chapter5/step-4-schedule-service`. This directory contains all of the code from step 3 along with our schedule service. As before, we will walk through the updates in turn and then deploy the changes.

5.2.2   Schedule service

Our schedule service is similar to the note service, in that it provides two API endpoints using the same domain manager structure as before:

- /schedule/day—Creates a schedule for today and submits a text-to-speech job to Polly
- /schedule/poll—Checks on the status of the job and returns a reference to the audio file once completed

This structure is reflected in the serverless.yml configuration, which should be very familiar at this stage. The implementation for these two endpoints, day and poll, is in handler.js. First, let's look at the buildSchedule function used by the day handler. This is shown in the following listing.

Listing 5.7   buildSchedule function in the schedule service day handler

```
const dynamoDb = new AWS.DynamoDB.DocumentClient()          Create the SDK
const polly = new AWS.Polly()                               Polly object.
const s3 = new AWS.S3()
const TABLE_NAME = { TableName: process.env.TODO_TABLE }    Get the to-do table
...                                                         from environment
function buildSchedule (date, speakDate, cb) {
  let speech = '<s>Your schedule for ' + speakDate + '</s>'  Define the function to
  let added = false                                          build an SSML schedule.
  const params = TABLE_NAME

  dynamoDb.scan(params, (err, data) => {                     Read schedule items from
    data.Items.forEach((item) => {                           DynamoDB and create SSML
      if (item.dueDate === date) {                           for items that are due.
        added = true
        speech += '<s>' + item.action + '</s>'
        speech += '<s>' + item.note + '</s>'
      }
    })
    if (!added) {
      speech += '<s>You have no scheduled actions</s>'
    }
    const ssml = `<speak><p>${speech}</p></speak>`
    cb(err, {ssml: ssml})
  })
}
```

We have seen how the buildSchedule function reads to-do items for a given day and creates SSML. This is used by the day handler in the schedule service. The code for this handler is shown in the next listing.

Listing 5.8   day handler for the schedule service

```
module.exports.day = (event, context, cb) => {
  let date = moment().format('MM/DD/YYYY')
  let speakDate = moment().format('dddd, MMMM Do YYYY')
  buildSchedule(date, speakDate, (err, schedule) => {
    if (err) { return respond(err, null, cb) }
```

```
  const params = {
    OutputFormat: 'mp3',              ⊲──┐  Configure the voice and output
    SampleRate: '8000',                  │  bucket parameters for Polly.
    Text: schedule.ssml,
    LanguageCode: 'en-GB',
    TextType: 'ssml',
    VoiceId: 'Joanna',
    OutputS3BucketName: process.env.CHAPTER4_DATA_BUCKET,
    OutputS3KeyPrefix: 'schedule'
  }

  polly.startSpeechSynthesisTask(params, (err, data) => {   ⊲──┐  Start the
    ...                                                         │  Polly speech
    respond(err, result, cb)                                    │  synthesis task.
  })
  })
}
```

The `buildSchedule` function created a block of SSML to pass to Polly, which will convert this into an output `mp3` file. Our `day` function sets up a parameter block that specifies the output format, and the S3 bucket that Polly should place its output into. The code in the next listing shows the `poll` handler.

Listing 5.9   `poll` handler for the schedule service

```
module.exports.poll = (event, context, cb) => {
  polly.getSpeechSynthesisTask({TaskId: event.pathParameters.id},
    (err, data) => {                                      ⊲──┐  Check the status
    // Create result object from data                        │  of the task.
    ...
    respond(err, result, cb)          ⊲──┐  Provide the task
  })                                     │  status to the API caller.
}
```

The poll-handler code shows the Lambda function invoking the Polly service to retrieve the speech synthesis task. This is provided in the API response.

SSML

Speech Synthesis Markup Language (SSML) is an XML dialect used for text-to-speech tasks. Whereas Polly can handle plain text, SSML can be used to provide additional context to speech synthesis tasks. For example, the following SSML uses the whisper effect:

```
<speak>
  I want to tell you a secret.
  <amazon:effect name="whispered">I am not a real human.</amazon:effect>.
  Can you believe it?
</speak>
```

More detail on SSML can be found here: http://mng.bz/MoW8.

Once our speech-to-text task had been initiated, we use the `poll` handler to check on the status. This calls `polly.getSpeechSynthesisTask` to determine the status of the task. Once our task is complete, we use `s3.getSignedUrl` to generate a temporary URL to access the resulting mp3 file.

5.2.3   Front-end updates

To access our schedule service, we place a "schedule" button in the applications navigation bar, as illustrated in figure 5.4

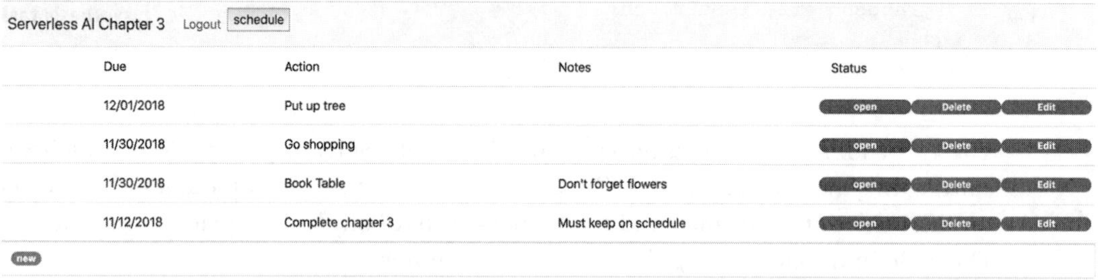

Figure 5.4   Updated UI

This is connected to a front end handler in the file `frontend/src/schedule.js`, shown in the following listing.

Listing 5.10   schedule.js

```
import $ from 'jquery'
import {view} from './schedule-view'
...
const API_ROOT = `https://chapter4api.${process.env.CHAPTER4_DOMAIN}
/schedule/day/`
let itv
let auth

function playSchedule (url) {                        ◁─┐ Play the
  let audio = document.createElement('audio')           │ schedule file.
  audio.src = url
  audio.play()
}

function pollSchedule (taskId) {          ◁─┐
  itv = setInterval(() => {                 │  Poll for
    ...                                     │  schedule
    $.ajax(API_ROOT + taskId, {          ◁─┘  status.
      ...
      playSchedule(body.signedUrl)       ◁─┐ Pass the signed
      ...                                   │ URL to the player.
```

```
  }, 3000)
}

function buildSchedule (date) {
  const body = { date: date }

  auth.session().then(session => {
    $.ajax(API_ROOT, {                    ◁──┐ Start the
      ...                                      │ schedule job.
      pollSchedule(body.taskId)
      ...
    })
  }).catch(err => view.renderError(err))
}
```

Using a temporary signed URL from S3 allows the front-end code to use a standard audio element to play the schedule without compromising the security of our data bucket.

5.2.4 Deploying step 4

Deployment of this step should be very familiar by now. First, we need to copy our environment across from the previous step. Copy the file `step-3-note-service/ .env` to `step-4-schedule-service`.

Next, deploy the schedule service by executing the following commands:

```
$ cd step-4-schedule-service/schedule-service
$ npm install
$ serverless deploy
```

Finally, deploy the front end updates as before:

```
$ cd step-4-schedule-service/frontend
$ source ../.env
$ npm install
$ npm run build
$ aws s3 sync dist/ s3://$CHAPTER4_BUCKET
```

5.2.5 Testing step 4

Let's now get our to-do list to read out our schedule for the day. Open the application in a browser, log in, and then create some to-do entries for today's date. Once you have entered one or two items, click the schedule button. This will trigger the schedule service to build and send our schedule to Polly. After a few seconds, the application will read out our schedule for us!

We now have a to-do system that we can talk to, and that can talk back to us. Our to-dos are stored in a database, and the system is secured through a username and password. All of this without ever needing to boot up a server or get into the details of text/speech conversion!

In our final update to the to-do system, we will add a more conversational interface to the system by building a chatbot.

5.3 Step 5: Adding a conversational chatbot interface

In our final update to the to-do application, we will implement a chatbot. The chatbot will allow us to interact with the system via a text-based interface or through speech. We will use Amazon Lex to build our bot. Lex uses the same AI technology as Amazon Alexa. This means that we can use Lex to create a more natural human interface to our system. For example, we can ask our application to schedule a to-do for "tomorrow" or "next Wednesday." While this is a natural way for a human to express dates, it is actually very complex for a computer to understand these ambiguous commands. Of course, by using Lex, we get all of this for free. Figure 5.5 illustrates how our chatbot integrates into our system.

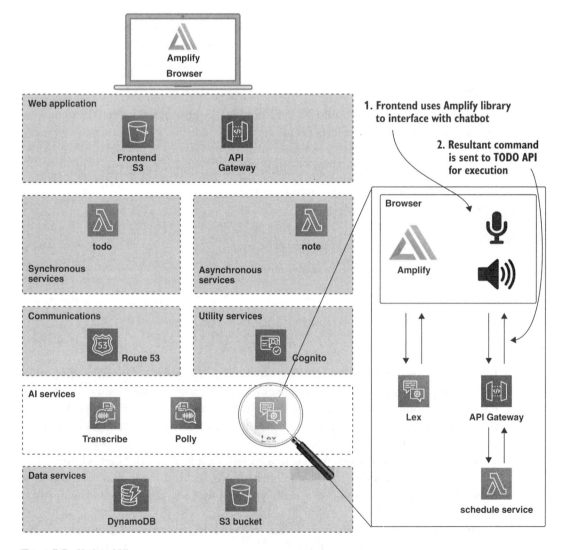

Figure 5.5 Updated UI

Users can supply commands either through a chat window or by speaking. These commands are sent to our chatbot which is hosted by Lex, and a response is returned. At the end of the conversation, the bot will have gathered all of the information required to create or update a to-do item. The front end will then take this information and post it to the to-do API as before.

It's important to note at this point that we do not have to change our underlying to-do API in order to add a conversational interface to it. This can be layered on top with minimal disruption to existing code.

5.3.1   Getting the code

The code for this step is in the directory `chapter5/step-5-chat-bot`. This directory contains all of the code from step 4 along with code to interface with our chatbot.

5.3.2   Creating the bot

We have created a command-line script to create our `todo` bot. The code for this is in the directory `chapter5/step-5-chat-bot/bot`. The file `create.sh` uses the AWS command line to set up the bot, as shown in the following listing.

Listing 5.11   Chatbot creation script

```
#!/bin/bash
ROLE_EXISTS=`aws iam get-role \
--role-name AWSServiceRoleForLexBots \
| jq '.Role.RoleName == "AWSServiceRoleForLexBots"'`

if [ ! $ROLE_EXISTS ]                        ⟵┐  Create service
then                                              │  role if needed
   aws iam create-service-linked-role --aws-service-name lex.amazonaws.com
fi
                                             ┌─  Define the
aws lex-models put-intent \                  ⟵┘  CreateTodo intent.
--name=CreateTodo \
--cli-input-json=file://create-todo-intent.json
                                             ┌─  Define the
aws lex-models put-intent \                  ⟵┘  MarkDone intent.
--name=MarkDone \
--cli-input-json=file://mark-done-intent.json

aws lex-models create-intent-version --name=CreateTodo
aws lex-models create-intent-version --name=MarkDone

aws lex-models put-bot --name=todo \         ⟵┐  Define
--locale=en-US --no-child-directed \              │  the bot.
--cli-input-json=file://todo-bot.json
```

NOTE The `create.sh` script uses the `jq` command, which is a command-line utility for handling JSON data. If this is not on your development environment, you will need to install it using your system's package manager.

This script uses some JSON files to define the characteristics of our chatbot. Go ahead and run the `create.sh` script. It will take several seconds for our bot to be created; we can check on progress by running the command

```
$ aws lex-models get-bot --name=todo --version-or-alias="\$LATEST"
```

Once the output from this command contains the output `"status": "READY"`, our bot is good to go. Open the AWS console in a web browser and select Lex from the list of services. Click on the link to the `todo` bot.

> **NOTE** You may initially see an error message when first creating the bot of the form: `The role with name AWSServiceRoleForLexBots cannot be found`. This is because Lex creates this service role the first time that a bot is created in an account.

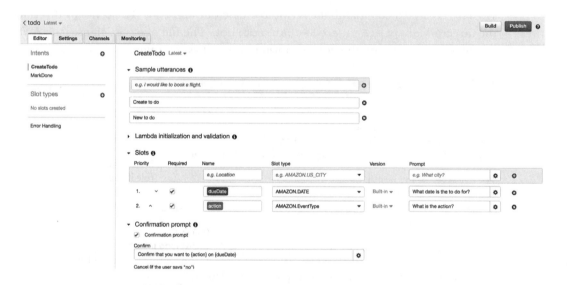

Figure 5.6   Updated UI

Your console should look like figure 5.6. This might look a little complex to begin with, but the configuration is really quite straightforward once we understand three key concepts: intents, utterances, and slots.

INTENTS

An *intent* is a goal that we want to achieve; for example, "order pizza" or "book appointment." Think of an intent as an overall task for the bot, for which it will need to gather additional data to fulfill. A bot can have multiple intents, but usually these are related to some central concept. For example, a pizza-ordering bot might have the intents "order pizza," "check delivery time," "cancel order," "update order," and so on.

In the case of the `todo` bot, we have two intents: `CreateTodo` and `MarkDone`.

UTTERANCES

An *utterance* is a phrase that is used to identify an intent. For our `CreateTodo` intent, we have defined the utterances `Create to-do` and `New to-do`. It is important to understand that an utterance is not a set of key words that must be provided exactly. Lex uses several AI techniques to match an utterance to an intent. For example, our create intent could be identified by any of the following:

- "Initialize to-do"
- "Get a to-do"
- "I'd like a new to-do, please"
- "Make me a to-do"

An utterance provides sample language to Lex, not keywords that need exact matching.

SLOTS

A *slot* can be thought of as an output variable from a Lex conversation. Lex will use the conversation to elicit slot information. For our `CreateTodo` intent, we have defined two slots: `dueDate` and `action`. We have used built-in slot types of `AMAZON.DATE` and `AMAZON.EventType` for these slots. In most cases, the built-in slot types provide enough context; however, it is possible to define custom slot types as required by the bot.

Lex will use the slot type as a means to help understand the response. For example, when Lex prompts us for a date, it can handle most reasonable responses such as

- Tomorrow
- Thursday
- Next Wednesday
- Christmas day
- Labour day 2019
- A month from today

This allows for a flexible conversational interface via text or speech

TRYING IT OUT

Let's test out our bot! Click the Build button on the top right and wait for the build to complete. Then select the Test Chatbot link to bring up a message panel on the right side, and try creating some to-dos. Figure 5.7 shows a sample session.

In addition to typing commands to the bot, you can also use the microphone button

Figure 5.7   Updated UI

to speak voice commands to the bot and have it reply with audio. The key point to notice is that Lex has extracted structured information from a loosely structured conversation. We can then use the extracted, structured data in our code.

5.3.3 Front-end updates

Now that we have a working bot, it's time to integrate it into our application. Code for the updated front end is in the directory chapter5/step-5-chat-bot/frontend. The main bot integration is in src/bot.js. First, let's look at the activate function shown in the following listing.

> **Listing 5.12   bot.js activate function**

```
import $ from 'jquery'
import * as LexRuntime from 'aws-sdk/clients/lexruntime'      ◁─┐ Import
import moment from 'moment'                                      │ Lex API
import view from 'bot-view'

const bot = {activate}
export {bot}

let ac
let auth
let todo
let lexruntime
let lexUserId = 'chatbot-demo' + Date.now()
let sessionAttributes = {}
let recording = false

...

function activate (authObj, todoObj) {                              Configure Lex
  auth = authObj                                                   with region and
  todo = todoObj                                                      credentials
  auth.credentials().then(creds => {
    lexruntime = new LexRuntime({region: process.env.TARGET_REGION,
      credentials: creds})                                          ◁─
    $('#chat-input').keypress(function (e) {      ◁─┐ Get typed
      if (e.which === 13) {                          │ input.
        pushChat()             ◁─┐ Invoke pushChat
        e.preventDefault()        │ with the entered text.
        return false
      }
    })
    bindRecord()
  })
}
```

LexRuntime is the AWS SDK service interface for dealing with the Lex chatbot service. It has two methods for sending user input to Lex. One method, postContent, supports audio and text streams. The simpler method, postText, supports sending user input as text only. In this application, we will use `postText`. The next listing shows the code for passing the entered text captured in the front end to Lex.

Listing 5.13 `bot.js` `pushChat` **function**

```
function pushChat () {
  var chatInput = document.getElementById('chat-input')

  if (chatInput && chatInput.value && chatInput.value.trim().length > 0) {
    var input = chatInput.value.trim()
    chatInput.value = '...'
    chatInput.locked = true

    var params = {                          ⟵┐ Configure
      botAlias: '$LATEST',                    │ parameters
      botName: 'todo',
      inputText: input,
      userId: lexUserId,
      sessionAttributes: sessionAttributes
    }

    view.showRequest(input)                        ┐ Send text
    lexruntime.postText(params, function (err, data) {  ⟵┘ to bot
      if (err) {
        console.log(err, err.stack)
        view.showError('Error:  ' + err.message + ' (see console for details)
')
      }
      if (data) {
        sessionAttributes = data.sessionAttributes
        if (data.dialogState === 'ReadyForFulfillment') {  ┐ Create
          todo.createTodo({                             ⟵┘ new to-do
            id: '',
            note: '',
            dueDate: moment(data.slots.dueDate).format('MM/DD/YYYY'),
            action: data.slots.action,
            stat: 'open'
          }, function () {})
        }
        view.showResponse(data)
      }
      chatInput.value = ''
      chatInput.locked = false
    })
  }
  return false
}
```

`bot.js`, along with some display functions in `bot-view.js`, implements a simple text-messaging interface to our bot through the API `postText`. This sends our user's text input to Lex and elicits a response. Lex will set the response data `dialogState` to `ReadyForFulfillment` once our two slots, `dueDate` and `action`, have been populated. At this point, we can then read the slot data from the Lex response, create a JSON structure for our to-do item, and post it to our to-do API.

There is also a function pushVoice that we have wired into the browser audio system. This works in a similar manner to the pushChat function, except that it will push audio to the bot. In the case that we push audio (i.e. a spoken command) to the bot, it will respond with text as before, but will also include an audio response in the field audioStream that is attached to the response data object. The function play-Response takes this audio stream and simply plays it back, allowing us to have a voice-activated conversation with the bot.

5.3.4 Deploying step 5

As we have already deployed our bot, we only need to update the front end. As before, copy the .env file from step 4 into the step 5 directory and run the commands in the following listing to deploy a new version.

Listing 5.14 Deploy commands to update the front end

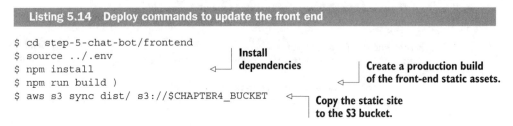

```
$ cd step-5-chat-bot/frontend
$ source ../.env
$ npm install
$ npm run build )
$ aws s3 sync dist/ s3://$CHAPTER4_BUCKET
```

Install dependencies

Create a production build of the front-end static assets.

Copy the static site to the S3 bucket.

The updated front end has now been deployed.

5.3.5 Testing step 5

Open up a browser and load up the latest changes. After logging in, you should see the chatbot interface on the right side of the page, as in figure 5.8.

Figure 5.8 Updated UI

You should now be able to go ahead and interact with the bot in the context of the to-do application. Once the conversation is complete, a new to-do item will be created in the to-do list!

Though we wrote a bunch of code to achieve this, the code was fairly simple to implement. Most of the time we were really just calling external APIs, a job that is familiar to most working programmers. By calling these APIs, we were able to add advanced AI functionality to our to-do list without needing to understand any of the science of natural language processing or speech-to-text translation.

Voice and chatbot interfaces are becoming increasingly common, particularly with mobile applications. Some great use cases that we have come across recently include

- Web-integrated first line customer support and sales inquiries
- Personal assistants for meeting schedules
- Travel assistance to help with booking flights and hotels
- Personal shopping assistants for e-commerce sites
- Healthcare and motivational bots to promote lifestyle changes

Hopefully this chapter will have inspired you to apply this technology to your own work!

5.4 Removing the system

Once you are done with testing the system, it should be removed entirely in order to avoid incurring additional charges. This can be done manually with the `serverless remove` command. We have also provided a script to remove all of the deployed resources in chapters 4 and 5 in the `chapter5/step-5-chat-bot` directory. There is also a separate `remove.sh` script in the `bot` subdirectory. To use these scripts, execute the following commands:

```
$ cd chapter5/step-5-chat-bot
$ bash ./remove.sh
$ cd bot
$ bash ./remove.sh
```

If you would like to redeploy the system at any time, there is an associated script called `deploy.sh` in the same folder. This will redeploy the entire system for you by automating the steps that we worked through in chapter 4 and this chapter.

Summary

- AWS Transcribe is used to convert speech to text. Transcribe allows us to specify a file, a file format, and language parameters, and start a transcription job.
- Use AWS Amplify to upload data to an S3 bucket. We can save audio captured from the browser to a WAV file by using the Amplify `Storage` interface.
- Speech Synthesis Markup Language (SSML) is used to define conversational speech.

- AWS Polly converts text to speech.
- AWS Lex is used to create powerful chatbots.
- Lex utterances, intents, and slots are the components used to construct Lex chatbots.

WARNING   Please ensure that you fully remove all cloud resources deployed in this chapter in order to avoid additional charges!

How to be effective with
AI as a Service

This chapter covers

- Structuring a serverless project for rapid and effective development
- Building a serverless continuous deployment pipeline
- Achieving observability with centralized, structured logs
- Monitoring serverless project metrics in production
- Understanding application behavior through distributed tracing

So far, we have built some very compelling AI-based serverless applications. With very little code, these systems have an extraordinary amount of capability. You might have observed, however, that our serverless AI applications have many moving parts. We have adhered to the single responsibility principle, ensuring that each application is composed of many small units, each with a dedicated purpose. This chapter is about *effective* AI as a Service. By this, we mean that we move beyond simple application prototypes to production-grade applications that are capable of serving real users. For this, we need to think not just about how to get the basics working, but also about when things might stop working.

We have been clear about the advantages of small units of code and off-the-shelf, managed services. Let's take a step back and think about the pros and cons of this approach from the perspective of architects and developers moving from more traditional software development.

We will outline how the primary challenges relate to structuring, monitoring, and deploying your application in ways that ensure you continue to deliver quickly without compromising on quality and reliability. This includes having a clear project layout, a working continuous delivery pipeline, and the ability to quickly gain insight into the application's behavior when things go wrong.

This chapter will present practical solutions for overcoming each challenge and help you to establish effective serverless development practices.

6.1   *Addressing the new challenges of Serverless*

Given our success with deploying great serverless AI applications so far in this book, it's easy to be deceived and think it will always be smooth sailing! As with any way of developing software, there are drawbacks and pitfalls to be aware of. Often, you don't encounter these until you have built and brought systems into production. To help you foresee potential issues and solve problems in advance, we will list the benefits and challenges of serverless development. Then, we will present a template project that you can use as a basis for your own private projects. The aim is to save you the time and frustration that might be spent stumbling over these issues as they arise.

6.1.1   *Benefits and challenges of Serverless*

Table 6.1 lists the primary benefits and challenges of developing serverless applications using managed AI services.

Table 6.1   The benefits and challenges of Serverless

Benefits	Challenges
On-demand computing allows you to get started and scale quickly with no infrastructure to manage.	You rely on the cloud vendor's environment to accurately run your code.
Smaller units of deployment allow you to adhere to a single-responsibility principle. These units are fast to develop and relatively easy to maintain, since they have a clear purpose and interface. The teams maintaining such components do not have to consider the subtle details of the rest of the system.	There is a significant learning curve to becoming truly serverless. It takes time to understand effective serverless architecture, learn the available managed services, and establish an effective project structure.
Managed services for computation, communication, storage, and machine learning give you a huge leap in capability with minimal design and programming effort. At the same time, you are relieved of the maintenance and infrastructure burden you would have if you had to build this capability in your own organization.	The distributed and fragmented nature of a serverless-microservice architecture makes it harder to visualize or reason about the behavior of the system as a whole.

Table 6.1 The benefits and challenges of Serverless

Benefits	Challenges
In serverless systems, you pay only for what you use, eliminating waste and allowing you to scale in line with business success.	Though serverless reduces the number of systems you need to consider in your security responsibility, it is quite different from a traditional approach. For instance, a malicious attack gaining access to an AWS Lambda execution environment using an over-privileged IAM policy might allow the attacker to access your resources and data as well as consume potentially unlimited AWS resources, like more Lambda executions, EC2 instances, or databases. It could incur a significant bill from your cloud vendor.
A serverless approach allows you to select multiple managed database services, ensuring the right tool for any job. This "polyglot persistence" is quite different from past experiences of trying to pick one database for the majority of cases, resulting in a heavy maintenance burden and a poor fit for some data access requirements.	Dealing with multiple databases can be a challenge when your team is required to have the skills and understanding to use them correctly. Though it is easy to get started with something like DynamoDB, managing changes and ensuring optimal performance is a new skill that must be acquired through study and experience.
Serverless projects are cheap to create, so they can be recreated many times for different environments.	Dynamically-created cloud resources are typically given generated names. Allowing services to be discovered by other components is something that must be addressed to ensure the right balance of loose coupling, service availability, and ease of deployment.

These challenges and benefits are presented to give a clear and honest picture of the reality of serverless software in production. Now that you are aware of the pitfalls as well as the potential gains, we are ready to discuss how to avoid the pitfalls and maximise the effectiveness of your projects. We will do this with the help of a reference project that comes with many solutions to these problems out of the box.

6.1.2 A production-grade serverless template

The authors of this book have spent plenty of time building serverless applications and experiencing all the benefits and challenges. As a result, we have built up a set of best practices. We decided to put all of those practices into a template that we can use to start new serverless projects extremely rapidly. We also made the decision to open source this project and make it available to anyone building production-grade serverless applications. It is intended as a learning resource, and allows us to gather ideas and feedback from a much wider community.

The project, called *SLIC Starter*, is free to use and open to contributions. SLIC stands for Serverless, Lean, Intelligent, and Continuous. You can find it on GitHub at https://github.com/fourTheorem/slic-starter. Creating production-ready serverless applications from scratch can be daunting. There are many choices and decisions to be made. SLIC Starter is intended to answer 80% of those questions so we can start building meaningful business functionality as quickly as possible. The areas where decisions need to be made are shown in figure 6.1.

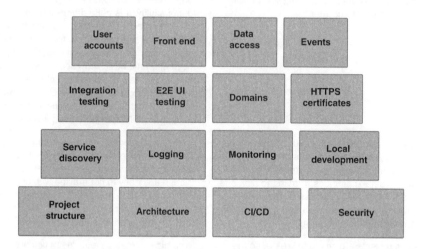

Figure 6.1   Aspects of a serverless project requiring decision-making. SLIC Starter aims to provide a template for each of these topics so adopters are freed up and get to production faster.

SLIC Starter is a template that can be applied to any application within any industry. It comes with a sample application for managing checklists. The application, called *SLIC Lists*, is deliberately simple, but has enough requirements to allow us to apply many serverless best practices. Once you have become familiar with SLIC Starter, you can replace the SLIC Lists application with the features for your own application. The sample SLIC Lists application has the following capabilities:

- Users can sign up and log in.
- Users can create, edit, and delete checklists.
- Users can create entries in the checklist and mark them as done.
- Any checklist can be shared with another user by providing their email address. The recipient must accept the invitation and log in or create an account to view and edit the list.
- When a user creates a checklist, they are sent a "welcome email" to notify them that they have created the list.

The components of our system are shown in figure 6.2. The primary components or *services* shown are as follows:

- The *checklist service* is responsible for storing and retrieving lists and their entries. It is backed by a database and provides a public API to authorized users.

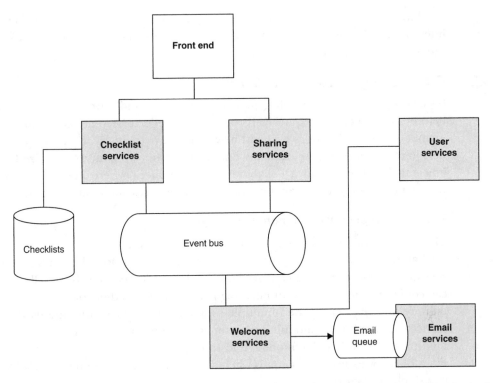

Figure 6.2 SLIC Starter services for the SLIC Lists application. The application is composed of five back-end services. There is also a front-end component as well as additional services to deal with certificates and domains.

- The *email service* is responsible for sending emails. Emails are passed to this service through an inbound queue.
- The *user service* manages users and accounts. It also provides an internal API for access to user data.
- The *welcome service* sends welcome notification messages to users when they create a checklist.
- The *sharing service* handles invitations to share lists with new collaborators.
- The *front end* handles the front-end web application build, deployment, and distribution. It is linked by configuration to the public, back-end services.

In addition, we have supporting services for certificate deployment and creating a public-facing API domain.

What this application does is unlikely to be relevant to your application, but *how* this application is built should be very relevant. Figure 6.1 already illustrated the foundational considerations that you will eventually need to consider as you build a mature, production-grade software application. The checklist application provides a template for each of these considerations, and acts as a learning resource, helping you to address the challenges without taking too much time to stop and perform research into all possible solutions. The first consideration we start with is how you structure the project codebase and repository.

6.2   *Establishing a project structure*

It's a good idea to establish clear practices for project and source repository structure before the project scales quickly. If you don't do this, it becomes confusing for team members to make changes and add new features, particularly when new team members join a project. There are many options here, but we want to optimize for rapid, efficient development in a collaborative environment where many developers are working together to build, deploy, and run new features and modifications.

6.2.1   *The source repository—monorepo or polyrepo*

The way you organise your teams' code seems like a trivial topic. But as we have discovered after many projects, simple decisions on how this is done have a big impact on how quickly you can make changes and get them released, and how well developers can communicate and collaborate. A big part of this is whether you go for polyrepo or monorepo. A *polyrepo* is when multiple source control repositories are used for each service, component, or module within an application. In a microservices project with multiple front ends (web, mobile, and so on), this can result in hundreds or thousands of repositories. A *monorepo* is when all services and front end codebases are kept in a single repository.

Google, Facebook, and Twitter are well known for using a monorepo at ridiculously large scale. Of course, it's never a good idea to go with an approach just because Google/Facebook/Twitter said so. Instead, as with everything, measure how this impacts you and make the decision that works well for your organization. Figure 6.3 illustrates the difference between the two approaches.

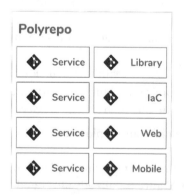

Figure 6.3   Monorepo versus polyrepo. A monorepo includes multiple services, supporting libraries, and Infrastructure as Code (IaC) in one repository. A polyrepo favours a separate repository for each individual component.

The polyrepo approach has certain benefits. For example, each module can be separately versioned and can have fine-grained access control. However, in our experience, too much time is spent managing the coordination across multiple repositories. The overhead can quickly get out of hand as you add more services, libraries, and dependencies. Often, polyrepos must be managed with custom tooling to manage cross-repository dependencies. A new developer should be able to start working on your product as quickly as possible. Avoid unnecessary ceremony and any learning curve that is unique to your team or company.

With a monorepo, when a bug fix or feature affects multiple modules/microservices, all changes are made in the same repository. There is just one branch on a single repository. No more tracking across multiple repositories. Each feature gets a single pull request. There is no risk that the feature is going to be partially merged.

By sticking with a single repository, your external tests (end-to-end or API tests) also belong with the code under test. The same goes for Infrastructure as Code. Any changes required in your infrastructure are captured together with the application code. If you have common code, utilities, and libraries that are consumed by your microservices, keeping them in the same repository makes it quite easy to share.

6.2.2 *Project folder structure*

The SLIC Starter repository follows the monorepo approach. The application is laid out in a similar way to many of the applications we have already described in this book. Each service has its own folder containing a `serverless.yml`. The project folder structure in the SLIC Starter monorepo repository is shown in the next listing.

Listing 6.1 SLIC Starter project structure

```
├── certs/                   Hosted zone and HTTPS Certificates (ACM)
├── api-service/             API Gateway custom domain
├── checklist-service/       API Gateway for checklists, DynamoDB
├── welcome-service/         Event handler to send emails on checklist creation
├── sharing-service/         API Gateway list sharing invitations
├── email-service/           SQS, SES for email sending
├── user-service/            Internal API Gateway and Cognito for user accounts
├── frontend/                S3, CloudFront, ACM for front-end distribution
├── cicd/                    Dynamic pipelines and cross account roles
├── e2e-tests/               End-to-end tests using TestCafe
└── integration-tests/       API tests
```

6.2.3 *Get the code*

To explore this repository with its project structure and to prepare for the rest of this chapter, fetch the code from the SLIC Starter GitHub repository. If you want to build and deploy the application automatically later in the chapter, you will need this code to be in a repository you control. To achieve this, fork the SLIC Starter repository (https://github.com/fourTheorem/slic-starter) before cloning it:

```
$ git clone https://github.com/<your_user_or_organization>/slic-starter.git
```

You should now have a solid understanding of what it means to have an effective project structure. You also have access to a template project that exemplifies this structure. Our next consideration deals with automating deployment of the project components.

6.3   *Continuous deployment*

So far, all of our serverless applications have been deployed manually. We have relied on the Serverless Framework's `serverless deploy` command to deploy each service into a specific target environment. This is fine for early development and prototyping, especially when our applications are small. But when real users depend on our applications and feature development is expected to be frequent and rapid, manual deployment is far too slow and error-prone.

Can you imagine manual deployment of your application when it is composed of hundreds of independently-deployable components? Real-world serverless applications are, by their nature, complex distributed systems. You can't and shouldn't rely on having a clear mental model of how they all fit together. Instead, you rely on the power of automation for deployment and testing.

Effective serverless applications require continuous deployment. *Continuous deployment* means that changes in our source code repository are automatically delivered to target production environments. When continuous deployment is triggered, any components affected by a code change are built and tested. There is also a system in place for integration testing our changed components as part of the entire system. A proper continuous deployment solution gives us confidence to make changes quickly. The principles of continuous deployment are equally valid for the deployment of data sets and machine learning models.

Let's look at the design of a serverless continuous deployment system from a high level.

6.3.1   *Continuous deployment design*

We have already discussed how our approach for serverless applications favors source code stored in a monorepo. This has an impact on how the continuous deployment process is triggered. If each module or service were stored in its own individual repository, changes to that repository could trigger that service's build. The challenge would then become how to coordinate builds across multiple repositories. For the monorepo approach, we want to avoid building everything when a small number of commits have been made, affecting one or two modules. Take a look at the high-level continuous deployment flow illustrated in figure 6.4.

The phases of the deployment pipeline are as follows:

1 A change-detection job determines which modules are affected by source code commits.
2 The pipeline then triggers parallel builds of each module. These build jobs will also run unit tests for the relevant modules.

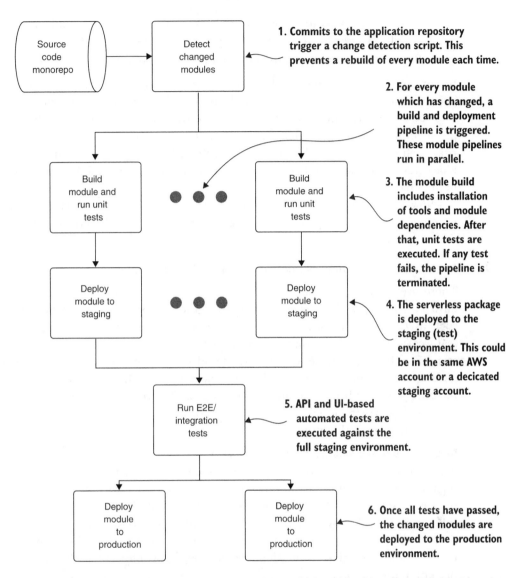

Figure 6.4 Our monorepo approach requires us to detect which modules have changed before triggering parallel build and unit test jobs for each affected module. Once that is successful, modules are deployed to a staging environment where integration tests can be run. Successful test execution triggers a deployment to production.

3 When all builds are successful, the modules are deployed to the staging environment. The staging environment is a replica of the production environment, not exposed to real users.

4 We run a set of automated, end-to-end tests that give confidence that the new changes do not break basic features in the system under predictable test

conditions. Of course, breaking changes under less-predictable production conditions are always possible, and you should prepare for that.

5 If all tests are successful, the new modules are deployed to production.

In our pipeline, we assume two target environments—a staging environment for testing new changes before they go live, and a production environment for our end users. The staging environment is entirely optional. In fact, it is ideal to get changes into production as soon as possible and have effective measures in place to mitigate the risk. Such measures include the ability to roll back quickly, deployment patterns like blue/green or canary,[1] and good observability practices. Observability is covered later in this chapter.

Now that we have an understanding of the continuous deployment flow, let's examine how we can implement it using managed cloud build services that are themselves serverless!

6.3.2 *Implementing continuous deployment with AWS services*

There are many great options for hosting your continuous build and deployment environment. These include everything from the immortal Jenkins, to SaaS offerings such as CircleCI (https://circleci.com) and GitHub Actions (https://github.com/features/actions). The choice depends on what is most efficient for you and your team. For this chapter, we will use AWS build services in keeping with the theme of picking cloud-managed services. The neat advantage of this approach is that we will be using the same Infrastructure-as-Code approach as our application itself. The continuous deployment pipeline will be built using CloudFormation and reside in the same monorepo as the other services in SLIC Starter.

MULTI-ACCOUNT AND SINGLE-ACCOUNT DEPLOYMENT

SLIC Starter supports multi-account deployment out of the box. This allows us to use separate AWS accounts for our staging and production environments, affording us increased isolation and security. We can also use a separate "tooling" account where the continuous deployment pipeline and artifacts will reside. This approach takes time to set up, and creating multiple accounts may not be feasible for many users. For these reasons, a single-account deployment is also possible. This is the option we will present in this chapter.

BUILDING THE CONTINUOUS DEPLOYMENT PIPELINE

The AWS services we will use for the pipeline are AWS CodeBuild and AWS CodePipeline. CodeBuild allows us to perform build steps like install, compile, and test. A build artifact is usually produced as its output. CodePipeline allows us to combine multiple actions together into stages. Actions can include source fetching, CodeBuild

---

[1] For more on these and other deployment strategies, see "Six Strategies for Application Deployment," an article by Etienne Tremel, 21 November 2017, thenewstack.io, https://thenewstack.io/deployment-strategies/.

executions, deployment, and manual approval steps. Actions can be run in sequence or in parallel.

On each commit or merge to the `master` branch of our repository, we will build and deploy affected modules in parallel. To accomplish this, we will create a separate pipeline per module. These pipelines will be executed and monitored by a single, overall *orchestrator pipeline*. This can all be seen in figure 6.5.

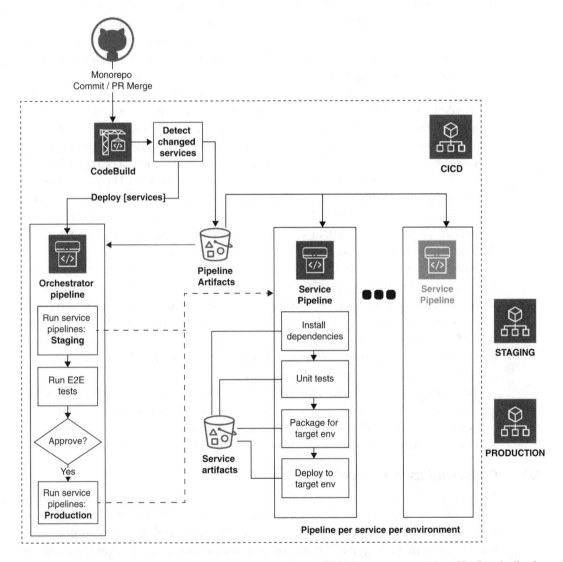

Figure 6.5 The canonical serverless CI/CD architecture is part of SLIC Starter. It uses a CodePipeline pipeline for each module. The execution of these pipelines in parallel is coordinated by an orchestrator pipeline. The build, deployment, and test phases are implemented as CodeBuild projects.

Since we are using AWS services for the build pipeline, we will deploy using CloudFormation stacks, just as with our serverless applications. So far, we have used the Serverless Framework to construct these stacks. For the deployment stacks, we will use the AWS Cloud Development Kit (CDK) instead.

CDK provides a programmatic way to construct CloudFormation templates. There are pros and cons to using standard programming languages for Infrastructure as Code. We prefer it, as it mirrors how we build the application itself but, for many people, infrastructure is better defined using a configuration language like JSON or YAML. In this case, it allows us to dynamically create projects and pipelines rather than rely on a static configuration. As we add new modules to the application, CDK will generate new resources automatically. CDK supports JavaScript, Python, Java, and TypeScript. We are using TypeScript, a superset of JavaScript that gives us type safety. Type safety is a powerful aid when creating resources with complex configuration syntax. It allows us to leverage auto-completion and get immediate documentation hints. Detailed coverage of CDK and TypeScript are beyond the scope of this book. If you are interested in exploring how the pipelines are built, explore the CDK TypeScript code in the `cicd` folder. We will jump straight in and deploy our CI/CD pipelines!

The latest documentation on deploying and running the CI/CD pipeline is in the `QUICK_START.md` document in the SLIC Starter repository. Once you have run all of the steps, your pipeline is ready. Every commit to the repository will trigger the source CodeBuild project and result in execution of the orchestrator pipeline. Figure 6.6 shows how this pipeline looks in the AWS CodePipeline Console.

Here, we can clearly see the steps of the pipeline that have run. The current execution is in the "Approval" stage. This is a special stage that requires the user to review and click Approve in order to advance the pipeline. This gives us the chance to check and cancel any production deployment. The execution shown has successfully deployed to staging, and our test jobs have completed successfully. In the SLIC Starter, automated API integration tests and user interface end-to-end (E2E) tests are run in parallel against the public API and front end.

Once our system has been deployed to production, we need to understand what's going on there. When things go wrong, we need to be able to troubleshoot and answer many questions about the state of the application. This brings us to *observability*, arguably the most important part of an effective production serverless deployment!

6.4   *Observability and monitoring*

At the start of this chapter, one of the challenges we described was the fragmented nature of serverless systems. This is a common problem with distributed systems composed of many small parts. It can lead to a lack of understanding of the running behavior of the system, making it difficult to solve problems and make changes. The problem has become better-understood as microservice architecture is more widely adopted. With serverless applications utilizing third-party managed services, the problem is especially prevalent. These managed services are, to some degree, black boxes.

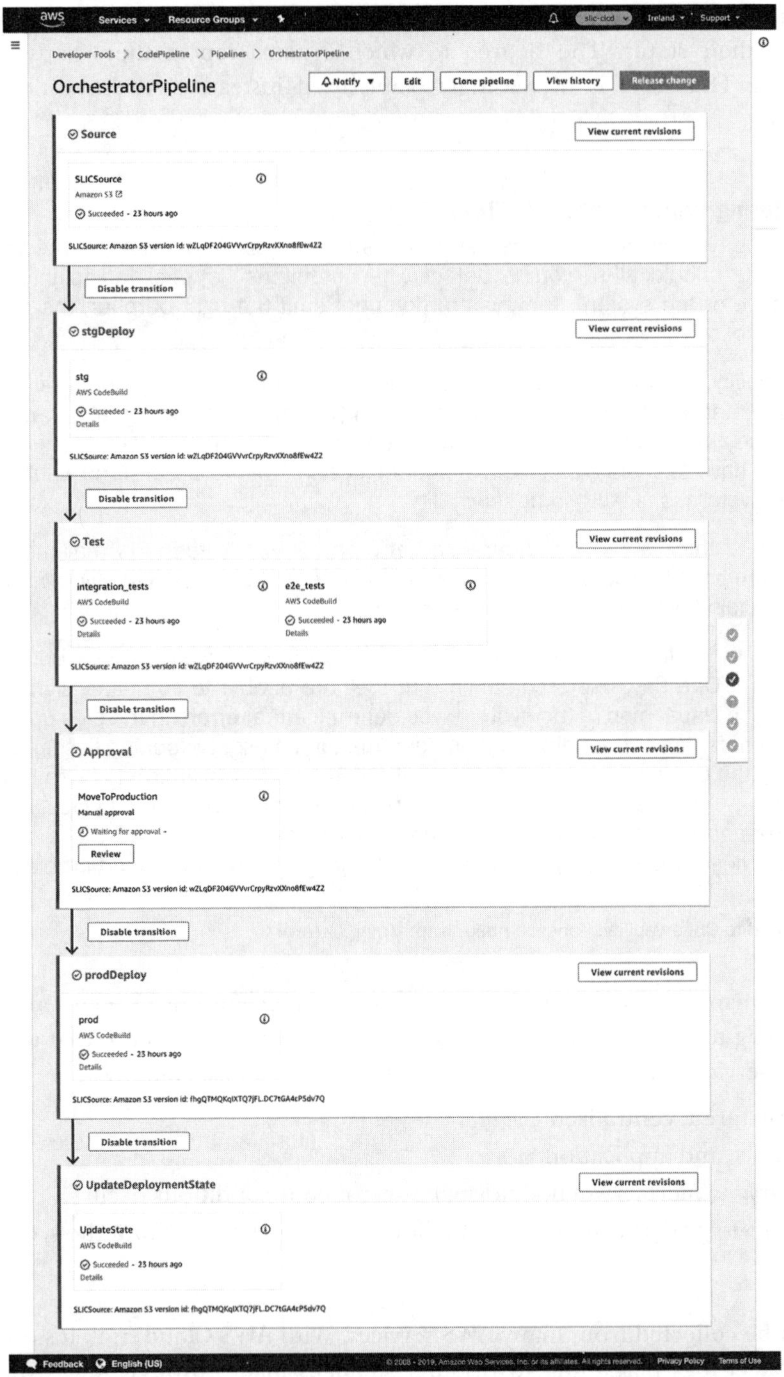

Figure 6.6 **The canonical serverless CI/CD architecture is part of SLIC Starter. It uses a CodePipeline pipeline for each module. The execution of these pipelines in parallel is coordinated by an orchestrator pipeline. The build, deployment, and test phases are implemented as CodeBuild projects.**

How much we can understand them depends on the interfaces those services provide to report their status. The degree to which systems report their status is called *observability*. This term is increasingly being used instead of the traditional term, monitoring.

Monitoring versus observability

Monitoring typically refers to the use of tools to inspect known metrics of a system. Monitoring should allow you to detect when problems happen and to infer *some* knowledge of the system. If a system does not emit the right outputs, the effect of monitoring is limited.

Observability,[a] a term from control theory, is the property of a system that allows you to understand what's going on inside by looking at its outputs. The goal of observability is to be able to understand any given problem by inspecting its outputs. For example, if we have to change a system and redeploy it in order to understand what's going on, the system is lacking in observability.

One way to think about the difference between these two terms is that monitoring allows you to detect when known problems occur, and observability aims to provide understanding when unknown problems occur.

As an example, let us suppose that your application has a well-tested, working sign-up feature. One day, users complain that they are unable to complete sign-ups. By looking at a visual map of the system, you determine that errors in the sign-up module result from failures in sending sign-up confirmation emails. By looking further into the errors in the email service, you notice that an email sending limit has been reached, preventing the emails from being sent. The visual map of dependencies between modules and errors led you to the email service logs, which gives the root cause details. These observability features helped to resolve an unexpected problem.

[a] Introduction to Observability, honeycomb.io, http://mng.bz/aw4X.

There are many approaches to achieving observability. For our checklist application, we are going to look at what we want to observe and how to achieve that using AWS-managed services. We will look at four practical areas of observability:

- Structured, centralized *logging*
- Service and application *metrics*
- *Alarms* to alert us when abnormal or erroneous conditions occur
- *Traces* to give us visibility into the flow of messages throughout the system

6.5   *Logs*

Logs can be collected from many AWS services. With AWS CloudTrail, it's even possible to collect logs pertaining to resource changes made through the AWS SDK or Management Console. Here, we will focus on our application logs, those created by our Lambda functions. Our goal is to create log entries for meaningful events in our application, including information logs, warnings, and errors. Current trends lead us to a *structured logging* approach, and with good reason. Unstructured, plain text logs can be difficult to search through. They are also difficult for log analysis tools to parse. Structured, JSON-based logs can be parsed, filtered, and searched easily. Structured logs can be considered *operational data* for your application.

In a traditional, non-serverless environment, logs were often collected in files or using a log agent. With Lambda, those aren't really options, so the approach becomes much simpler. Any console output (to *standard output* or *standard error*) from our Lambda functions appears as logging output. AWS Lambda automatically collects this output and stores it in CloudWatch logs. These logs are stored in a log group named according to the Lambda function name. For example, if our Lambda function is called `checklist-service-dev-get`, its logs will be collected in a CloudWatch log group named `/aws/lambda/checklist-service-dev-get`.

CloudWatch log concepts

CloudWatch logs are organized into *log groups*. A log group is a grouping of related logs, typically relating to a specific service. Within each log group is a set of *log streams*. A stream is a set of logs from the same source. For Lambda functions, each provisioned *container* has a single log stream. A log stream is made up of a series of *log events*. A log event is simply a record logged to the stream and associated with a timestamp.

Logs can be stored in CloudWatch logs for inspection using the APIs or the AWS Management Console. Log groups can be configured with a *retention period* to govern how long they are persisted. By default, logs are kept forever. This is usually not the right choice, since log storage in CloudWatch is significantly more expensive than archiving or deleting them.

Logs can be forwarded to other services using a *subscription filter*. One subscription filter may be set per log group, allowing a filter pattern and destination to be set. The filter pattern can be optionally used to extract only messages that match a string. The destination can be any of the following:

- A Lambda function.
- A Kinesis data stream.
- A Kinesis Data Firehose delivery stream. A delivery stream can be used to collect logs in S3, Elasticsearch, or Splunk.

There are many third-party options for storing centralized logs, including the popular combination of Elasticsearch, Logstash, and Kibana, commonly referred to as the *ELK Stack*. An ELK solution is tried and tested and very powerful in its ability to execute complex queries and generate visualizations of log data. For simplicity, and also because it is an adequate solution for many applications, we will retain logs in Cloud-Watch and use CloudWatch Logs Insights to view and query them. Setting it up requires a lot less work than an Elasticsearch-based solution. First, let's deal with how we generate structured logs.

6.5.1   *Writing structured logs*

When choosing how to write logs, the goals should be to make it as easy as possible for developers and to minimize the performance impact on the application. In Node.js applications, the Pino logger (https://getpino.io) fits the bill perfectly. Other options include Bunyan (https://www.npmjs.com/package/bunyan) and Winston (https://www.npmjs.com/package/winston). We use Pino since it is specifically designed for high performance and minimum overhead. To install it in your serverless modules, add it as a dependency as follows:

```
npm install pino --save
```

It's also worth installing `pino-pretty`, a companion module that takes structured log output from Pino and makes it human-readable. This is ideal when viewing logs on the command line:

```
npm install pino-pretty -g
```

To generate structured logs in our code, we create a new Pino logger and invoke a logging function for the desired log level—any of `trace`, `debug`, `info`, `warning`, `error`, or `fatal`. The following listing demonstrates how the Pino logger is used to generate structured logs.

Listing 6.2   Pino log messages with contextual, structured data

```
const pino = require('pino')
const log = pino({ name: 'pino-logging-example' })    ⟵  A logger is created with a specific
                                                           name to identify the source of logs

log.info({ a: 1, b: 2 }, 'Hello world')    ⟵  An information message is logged along
const err = new Error('Something failed')       with some data. The data is passed as
log.error({ err })    ⟵                         an object in the first argument.
```

An error is logged using the property err. This is a special property that results in the error being serialized as an object. The object includes the error type and the stack trace as a string.

The JSON logs for the first log record look like this:

```
{"level":30,"time":1575753091452,"pid":88157,"hostname":"eoinmac","name":"pin
    o-logging-example","a":1,"b":2,"msg":"Hello world","v":1}
```

The error log is difficult to read as JSON. If we pipe the output to `pino-pretty`, the result is easier to understand. This is shown in the next listing.

Listing 6.3   Structured JSON logs are made human-readable using `pino-pretty`

```
[1575753551571] INFO  (pino-logging-example/90677 on eoinmac): Hello world
    a: 1
    b: 2
```

```
[1575753551572] ERROR (pino-logging-example/90677 on eoinmac):
    err: {
      "type": "Error",
      "message": "Something failed",
      "stack":
          Error: Something failed
              at Object.<anonymous> (/Users/eoin/code/chapter5/
                pino-logging-example/index.js:9:13)
              at Module._compile (internal/modules/cjs/loader.js:689:30)
              at Object.Module._extensions..js (internal/modules/cjs/
                loader.js:700:10)
              at Module.load (internal/modules/cjs/loader.js:599:32)
              at tryModuleLoad (internal/modules/cjs/loader.js:538:12)
              at Function.Module._load (internal/modules/cjs/loader.js:530:3)
              at Function.Module.runMain (internal/modules/cjs/
                loader.js:742:12)
              at startup (internal/bootstrap/node.js:283:19)
              at bootstrapNodeJSCore (internal/bootstrap/node.js:743:3)
    }
```

6.5.2 Inspecting log output

We can trigger some log output by using the SLIC Starter application. Go to the URL of the deployed SLIC Lists front end. If you followed the Quick Start guide for SLIC Starter, you should have this at hand. In this example, we will use the staging environment for the continuously-deployed open source repository, https://stg.sliclists.com.

You will need to sign up and create an account. From there, you can log in and create a checklist. You are first presented with a login screen, as shown in figure 6.7. Follow the link on that screen to sign up and create your account before logging in.

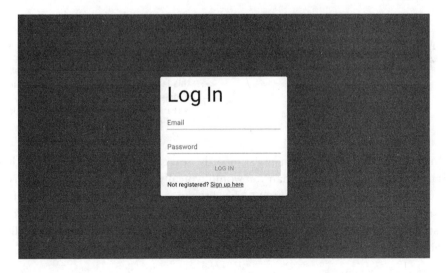

Figure 6.7 When you launch SLIC Lists for the first time, you can sign up to create an account and log in.

Once you have logged in, you can create a list, as shown in figure 6.8.

Figure 6.8   SLIC Lists allows you to create and manage checklists. Here, we create a checklist by entering a title and, optionally, a description. In the serverless backend, this creates a DynamoDB item. It also triggers an event-driven workflow, resulting in a welcome message being sent by email to the list creator.

Finally, you can add some entries to the checklist. This is shown in figure 6.9.

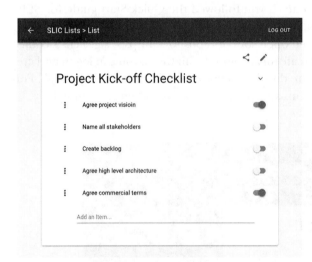

Figure 6.9   Here, we add some items to the checklist. This step adds entries to the checklist item we just created. If you are interested in how this is achieved with DynamoDB data modelling, check out `services/checklists/` `entries/entries.js` in the checklist-service folder.

Once you have created the checklist records, you can inspect the logs. Note that SLIC Starter produces more logs than you would typically expect in a system like this. In particular, information is logged at `INFO` level that you would reasonably expect in `DEBUG`-level logs. The cost of CloudWatch logs is a real consideration here. In a real production system, you should consider reducing the log output, redacting any personally-identifiable user information, and implementing sampling[2] for debug logs.

---

[2] "You need to sample debug logs in production," Yan Cui, 28 April 2018, https://hackernoon.com/you-need-to-sample-debug-logs-in-production-171d44087749.

Our first way to inspect the CloudWatch logs is with the Serverless Framework CLI. Here, we'll use `serverless logs` to see the latest logs for the `create` function. The output is again piped to `pino-pretty` for readability:

```
cd checklist-service
serverless logs -f create --stage <STAGE> | pino-pretty
  # STAGE is one of dev, stg or prod
```

The log output showing the `INFO`-level logs can be seen in the next listing.

> **Listing 6.4** `serverless logs` **fetches log events and prints them to the console**

```
[1576318523847] INFO  (checklist-service/7 on 169.254.50.213): Result received
    result: {
      "entId": "4dc54f8e-e28b-4de2-9456-f30caef781e4",
      "title": "Entry 2"
    }
END RequestId: fa02f8b1-2a42-46a8-83b4-a8834483fa0a
REPORT RequestId: fa02f8b1-2a42-46a8-83b4-a8834483fa0a  Duration: 74.44 ms
    Billed Duration: 100 ms Memory Size: 1024 MB
  Max Memory Used: 160 MB

START RequestId: 0e56603b-50f1-4581-b208-18139e85d597 Version: $LATEST
[1576318524826] INFO
  (checklist-service/7 on 169.254.50.213): Result received
    result: {
      "entId": "279f106f-469d-4e2d-9443-6896bc70a2d5",
      "title": "Entry 4"
    }
END RequestId: 0e56603b-50f1-4581-b208-18139e85d597
REPORT RequestId: 0e56603b-50f1-4581-b208-18139e85d597  Duration: 25.08 ms
    Billed Duration: 100 ms Memory Size: 1024 MB
  Max Memory Used: 160 MB
```

In addition to the structured JSON logs, formatted for readability by `pino-pretty`, we see the log entries generated by the Lambda container itself. These include the `START`, `END`, and `REPORT` records. The `REPORT` record prints useful records concerning the memory used and the function duration. Both are important when it comes to optimizing the memory configuration for performance and cost.

CHOOSING THE OPTIMAL LAMBDA MEMORY CONFIGURATION Lambda functions are billed per request and per GB-second. As with many services, there is a free tier—1 million requests and 400,000 GB-seconds per month at the time of writing. This means you can do quite a lot of computation before you are charged at all. Once you have used up the free tier in a production application, choosing the correct size for each function is important in terms of cost and performance.

When you configure a Lambda function, you can choose how much memory is allocated to it. Doubling the memory will double the cost per second of execution. However, allocating more memory also increases the vCPU allocation to the function linearly.

Suppose you have a function that takes 212ms to execute in a Lambda function with 960MB of memory, but 190ms to execute in a function with 1024MB of memory. The GB-second pricing of the higher memory configuration will be about 6% higher but, since executions are billed in 100ms units, the lower memory configuration will use 50% more units (3 instead of 2). Counterintuitively, the higher memory configuration will be significantly cheaper and deliver better performance.

Similarly, if you have a function that typically executes in 10ms and latency is not that critical, you might be better off using a lower memory configuration with decreased CPU allocation and letting it execute in a time closer to 100ms.

6.5.3   *Searching logs using CloudWatch Logs Insights*

We have seen how to inspect logs for a single function on the command line. It's also possible to view individual log streams in the AWS Management Console. This is useful during development, but less so when you have many functions deployed and frequently executed in a production system. For that, you need large-scale, centralized logging capable of searching terabytes of log data. CloudWatch Logs Insights is a convenient service for this job, and it requires no setup in advance. It can be found under the Insights section of the CloudWatch service in the AWS Management Console. Figure 6.10 shows a query for logs relating to checklists with the phrase "Kick-off" in the title.

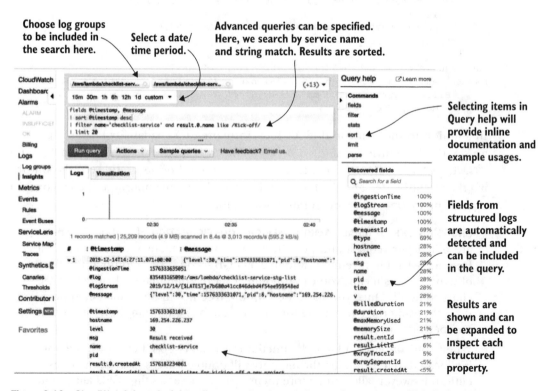

Figure 6.10   CloudWatch Logs Insights allows you to run complex queries across multiple log groups.

The query shown here is a simple example. The query syntax supports many functions and operations. You can perform arithmetic and statistical operations as well as extract fields, sort, and filter. Figure 6.11 shows how we can use statistical functions to analyze the memory usage and duration of the Lambda by extracting data from the REPORT logs for each execution.

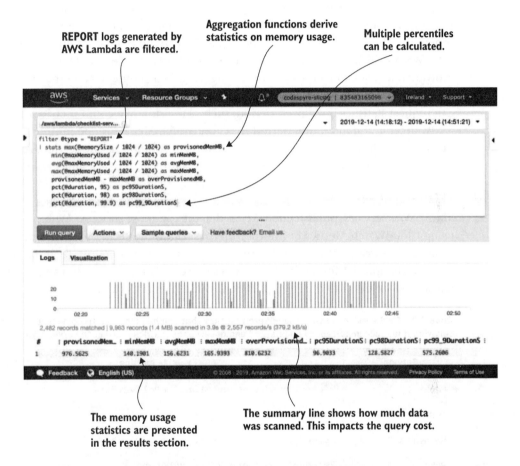

Figure 6.11 Statistical and arithmetic operations can be used with Lambda REPORT logs to analyze whether functions are configured with the optimal memory amount for cost and performance. Here, we show memory usage and compare the maximum memory used to the provisioned memory capacity. We also show the 95, 98, and 99.9 percentiles for function duration to get a sense of performance.

In the example shown, we have provisioned much more memory than is required. This might justify reducing the memory size for the container to 256MB. Since the function being analyzed simply invokes a DynamoDB write operation, it is more I/O-bound than CPU-bound. As a result, reducing its memory and CPU allocation is unlikely to have a significant impact on the duration of executions.

You should now have a good understanding of how centralized, structured logs together with CloudWatch Logs Insights can be used to add observability to your application. Next, we'll look at metrics you can observe and create to gain further knowledge of your application's behavior.

6.6   *Monitoring service and application metrics*

As part of the goal of achieving observability, we want to be able to create and view metrics. Metrics can be service-specific, like the number of concurrently-executing Lambda functions. They can also be application-specific, like the number of entries in a checklist. AWS provides a metrics repository called CloudWatch Metrics. This service collects individual metrics and allows you to view aggregations on them. Note that it is not possible to view individual metric data points once they have been collected. Instead, you can request statistics for a given period, such as the sum of a count metric per minute.

By default, the minimum period for CloudWatch Metrics is one minute. It is possible to add high-resolution custom metrics with a resolution of one second. After three hours of retention, high-resolution metrics are aggregated to one-minute intervals.

6.6.1   *Service metrics*

Many AWS services publish metrics by default for most services. Whether you are using CloudWatch Metrics or another metrics solution, it is important to be aware of what metrics are published and which ones you should monitor. Table 6.2 lists just some of the metrics for a sample of AWS services. We have chosen examples that are particularly relevant to the AI applications built in chapters 2-5.

Table 6.2   **AWS services publish CloudWatch Metrics that can be monitored to gain insight into system behavior. It is really important to understand and observe the metrics relevant to services you are using.**

Service	Example metrics
Lex[a]	`MissedUtteranceCount`, `RuntimePollyErrors`
Textract[b]	`UserErrorCount`, `ResponseTime`
Rekognition[c]	`DetectedFaceCount`, `DetectedLabelCount`
Polly[d]	`RequestCharacters`, `ResponseLatency`
DynamoDB[e]	`ReturnedBytes`, `ConsumedWriteCapacityUnits`
Lambda[f]	`Invocations`, `Errors`, `IteratorAge`, `ConcurrentExecutions`

[a]   See *Monitoring Amazon Lex with Amazon CloudWatch*, http://mng.bz/emRq.
[b]   See *CloudWatch Metrics for Amazon Textract*, http://mng.bz/pzEw.
[c]   See *CloudWatch Metrics for Rekognition*, http://mng.bz/OvAa.
[d]   See *Integrating CloudWatch with Amazon Polly*, http://mng.bz/YxOa.
[e]   See *DynamoDB Metrics and Dimensions*, http://mng.bz/Gd2J.
[f]   See *AWS Lambda Metrics*, http://mng.bz/zrgA.

Thorough coverage of all metrics for the services we have used is beyond the scope of this book. We recommend that you explore the CloudWatch Metrics section of the AWS Management Console with the applications you have built so far while reading the book. A comprehensive list of services and their metrics can be found in the AWS documentation.[3]

6.6.2 Application metrics

CloudWatch Metrics can be used as a repository for custom application metrics in addition to the built-in metrics published by AWS services. In this section, we'll explore what it takes to add a metric. Let's revisit the checklist application in the SLIC Starter project. We might want to gather application-specific metrics that inform us how the product is developed further. Let's suppose we are thinking about developing an Alexa skill for the application. An *Alexa skill* is a serverless application in AWS that allows users to interact with a service using a smart speaker device. This would be a very similar endeavor to the Lex-driven to-do chatbot from chapter 5! In order to design this skill, our User Experience department wants to gather statistics on how users are currently using *SLIC Lists*. Specifically, we want to understand the following:

- How many entries are users putting into checklists?
- How many words are in a typical checklist entry?

With CloudWatch Metrics, there are two ways we could add these metrics:

- Using the AWS SDK and a call to the `putMetricData` API[4]
- Using logs specially formatted according to the *Embedded Metric Format*

Using the `putMetricData` API has a disadvantage. Making an SDK call like this will result in an underlying HTTP request. This adds unwanted latency to our code. We will instead use the Embedded Metric Format log. This method requires us to create a specially formatted log message that has all the details of the metric we want to produce. Since we are using CloudWatch logs, CloudWatch will automatically detect, parse, and convert this log message into a CloudWatch metric. The overhead of writing this log message will have a negligible impact on the performance of our code. In addition, the raw metrics will be available for as long as we retain the logs.

Let's take a look at how we produce these metric logs and what the result looks like. An outline of the log message format is shown in the following listing.

Listing 6.5 The structure of Embedded Metric Format logs

```
{
  "_aws": {              ◁——┐  The _aws property defines
    "Timestamp": 1576354561802,   the metadata for our metrics.
```

---

[3] AWS Services That Publish CloudWatch Metrics, http://mng.bz/0Z5v.
[4] AWS JavaScript SDK, putMetricData, https://docs.aws.amazon.com/AWSJavaScriptSDK/latest/AWS/CloudWatch.html#putMetricData-property.

```
"CloudWatchMetrics": [
  {
    "Namespace": "namespace"          ◁──┐  A namespace for the metric is the
    "Dimensions": [["stagej"]]            │  grouping under which this metric falls.
    "Metrics": [                    ◁───────
      {                                          Each metric can be given up to ten
        "Name": "Duration",    ◁───┐            dimensions. A dimension is a name-
        "Unit": "Milliseconds"      │            value pair that categorizes the metric.
      }                             │
    ],                              │  A single metric is defined here, giving it a name
    ...                             │  and its unit. There is a defined list of supported
  }                                 │  metric units in the AWS documentation.[5]
  ]
},                              ┌─  The value for dimensions named
"stage": "prod",          ◁─────┘   in the metadata is given here.
"Duration": 1        ◁───┐
}                         │  The value for metrics named in
                          │  the metadata is provided here.
```

These JSON structured log messages are automatically recognized by CloudWatch and result in CloudWatch Metrics being created with minimal performance overhead. It is possible to create this JSON structure and log it to CloudWatch logs in our Lambda function code using `console.log`. Another way is to use the `aws-embedded-metrics` Node.js module.[6] This module gives us a number of functions for logging metrics. In this case, we'll use the `createMetricsLogger` function. We are going to add the metric logging code in `checklist-service/services/checklists/entries/entries.js`. See the following listing for the relevant extract from the `addEntry` function.

Listing 6.6 Structured logging compliant with the Embedded Metric Format

createMetricsLogger creates a logger that we can call explicitly. The aws-embedded-metrics module also provides a wrapper or "decorator" function that avoids the explicit flush call.

The number of entries in the checklist is recorded as a count metric.

```
const metrics = createMetricsLogger()                                    ◁──┐
metrics.putMetric('NumEntries', Object.keys(entries).length, Unit.Count) ◁──
metrics.putMetric('EntryWords', title.trim().split(/s/).length, Unit.Count) ◁──
await metrics.flush()      ◁──┐
```

We flush the metrics to ensure they are written to the console output.

The number of words in the checklist entry is recorded.

To generate some metrics, we need to invoke this function with varying inputs. The SLIC Starter end-to-end integration tests include a test that creates a checklist with an

---

[5] Supported units for CloudWatch Metrics are covered in MetricDatum, http://mng.bz/9Azr.

[6] `aws-embedded-metrics` on GitHub, https://github.com/awslabs/aws-embedded-metrics-node.

entry count and word counts according to a realistic distribution. We can run this test a number of times to get some reasonable metrics in CloudWatch.

There are some setup steps in SLIC Starter's integration tests. Check out the `README.md` file in the `integration-tests` folder. Once you have prepared the tests and verified that you can run them once, we can proceed to running a batch of integration tests to simulate some load:

```
cd integration-tests
./load.sh
```

The `load.sh` script runs a random number of integration test executions in parallel, and repeats that process until it has been done 100 times. Now, we can proceed to the CloudWatch Metrics section of the AWS Management Console to visualize statistics on the checklist entries that were created.

When you select CloudWatch Metrics in the console, the view should look something like figure 6.12.

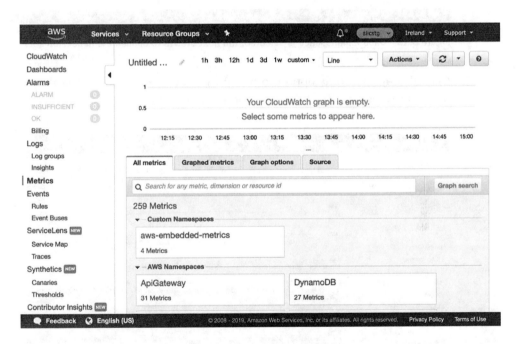

Figure 6.12   Browsing to the CloudWatch Metrics view in the AWS Management Console allows you to select from custom namespaces and namespaces for AWS services.

From here, select the *aws-embedded-metrics* namespace. This brings you to a table where you can see the sets of dimensions within the selected namespace. This is shown in figure 6.13.

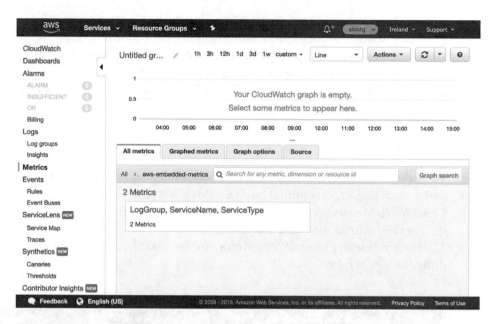

Figure 6.13   Once a namespace is selected, the next step is to choose the dimension sets.

Click through the only option to reveal the viewable metrics. Select the two metrics from the `addEntry` function, as shown in figure 6.14.

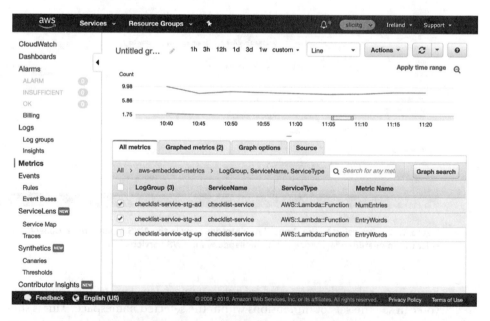

Figure 6.14   The CloudWatch Metrics console presents all metrics within the selected namespace and dimensions. Clicking the checkbox next to each one adds the metric to the graph displayed.

We now want to customize the presentation of these metrics. First, let's add to the default average statistic. This can be done by switching to the Graphed Metrics tab. Select the Duplicate icon next to each metric. Do this twice for both the NumEntries and EntryWords metrics. This will create copies of the average metric. Change one copy of each to use the Maximum and p95 statistics. Lastly, change the graph type from Line to Number. The resulting view should look like figure 6.15.

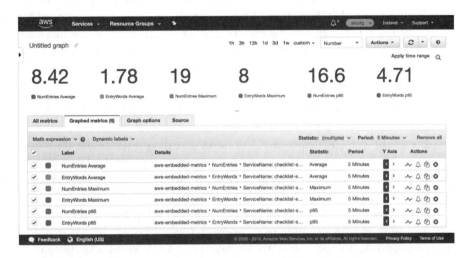

Figure 6.15 Switching to the Graphed Metrics tab allows you to customize and copy metrics. Here, we select new statistics for the same two metrics. Switching the graph from Line to Number also gives us a plain and simple view of the statistics we need.

Using the Number visualization instead of Line is more useful in this case, as the change in values over time as viewed on a line graph is not interesting for these metrics. We have ended up with some simple numbers that can help our User Experience team design an Alexa skill! We know that most entries have fewer than five words, with the average being two words. The average list has around 8 entries and 95% have 16.6 or fewer.

6.6.3   Using metrics to create alarms

At this point, you have seen the value of understanding and monitoring AWS service metrics and custom application metrics. When you have unexplained system behavior, this knowledge should help you to start revealing some of the unknowns. It's not a great idea, however, to wait until something goes wrong to start digging for answers. It's preferable to think about what the normal system behavior is and to create alarms for when the system behavior deviates from this norm. An *alarm* is a notification to system operators when a specified condition is reached. Typically, we would set up alarms for deviations such as the following:

1 A metric that counts the number of errors within an AWS service, and is triggered when the value is greater than a given number. For example, we might

like to be alerted when the number of Lambda invocations across all our functions exceeds 10 in a five-minute period.

2   The level of service to our end users is reaching an unacceptable level. An example of this is when the 99th percentile for the API Gateway Latency metric for a critical API endpoint exceeds 500ms.

3   Business metrics are really valuable for creating alarms. It is often easier to create thresholds relating to interactions from an end-user perspective. For example, in our SLIC Starter application, we might know that it's typical for between 50 and 60 checklists to be created every hour. If the number falls wildly outside this threshold, we can receive an alarm and investigate. This might be just a spurious change in activity, or indicative of some underlying technical problem we might not have otherwise detected.

In the context of AWS, alerts like these are possible using CloudWatch Alarms. Alarms are always based on CloudWatch Metrics. It is possible to define the period and statistic used (e.g., the *average* latency over *5 minutes*). The threshold for the alarm can be based on a numeric value or based on anomaly detection using standard deviation bands. The alerting mechanism for CloudWatch Alarms is through SNS Topics. *SNS* (or *Simple Notification Service*) is a Pub/Sub for sending events. SNS allows alerts to be delivered via email, SMS or webhook, or to another service, including SQS and Lambda.

A comprehensive example of creating alarms is beyond the scope of this chapter. It is worthwhile to use the AWS Management Console to experiment and create some alarms. Once you are familiar with the configuration options for CloudWatch Alarms, you can proceed to create them as resources in the `serverless.yml` file for your application. The following resources also allow us to create alarms with less configuration:

- The *Serverless Application Repository* provides hosted CloudFormation stacks that can be included as nested applications within your own application. Other organizations have published stacks that simplify the process of creating a reasonable set of alarms for serverless applications. One example is the *SAR-cloudwatch-alarms-macro* application.[7] It creates alarms for common errors in AWS Lambda, API Gateway, AWS Step Functions, and SQS.
- Plugins for the Serverless Framework such as the AWS Alerts Plugin (http://mng.bz/jVre) make the process of creating alarms easier.

6.7   *Using traces to make sense of distributed applications*

At the start of the chapter, we said that one of the challenges in serverless development is the distributed and fragmented nature of systems. This aspect makes it harder to visualize or reason about the behavior of the system as a whole. The practices of centralized logging, metrics, and alarms can help with that. Distributed tracing is an

---

[7]   SAR-cloudwatch-alarms-macro from Lumigo, http://mng.bz/WqeW.

additional tool that makes understanding the flow of data through a serverless system possible. Within the AWS ecosystem, distributed tracing is provided by X-Ray and CloudWatch ServiceLens. X-Ray is the underlying tracing service, and ServiceLens is the area of the CloudWatch console that provides tracing visualization integrated with logs and metrics. There are commercial alternatives such as Datadog, Lumigo, and Epsagon. Though these are certainly worth exploring, we will use the managed AWS services, as they are sufficient to demonstrate and learn the concepts of observability and tracing.

6.7.1 Enabling X-Ray tracing

The purpose of distributed tracing is to both monitor and profile performance of requests as they propagate through many services in a system. The best way to illustrate this is with a visual example. Consider the scenario of creating a checklist in the SLIC Starter application. From the point when a user clicks the Save button in the front end, the sequence shown in figure 6.16 occurs.

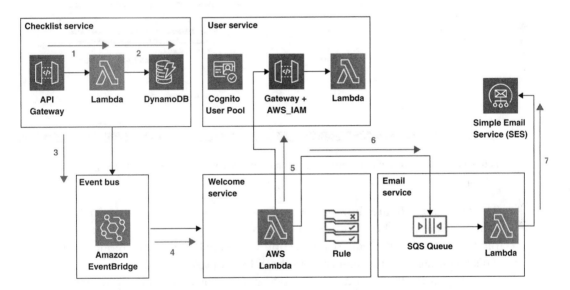

Figure 6.16 A typical request to a serverless system results in multiple messages across many services.

1 The request goes through API Gateway to a Lambda in the checklist service.
2 This Lambda calls DynamoDB.
3 The Lambda publishes a "list created" event to Amazon EventBridge.
4 The event is picked up by the welcome service.
5 The welcome service calls the user service API to look up the checklist owner's email address.
6 The welcome service puts an SQS message on the email service's queue.

7 The email service accepts incoming SQS messages and send an email using the Simple Email Service (SES).

This is a relatively simple distributed workflow, but it's already easy to see how this chain-reaction of events can be difficult to comprehend for developers. Imagine what it's like in a system with hundreds or thousands of services! By capturing traces for the entire flow, we can view the sequence and timings in ServiceLens. Part of this sequence is shown in figure 6.17.

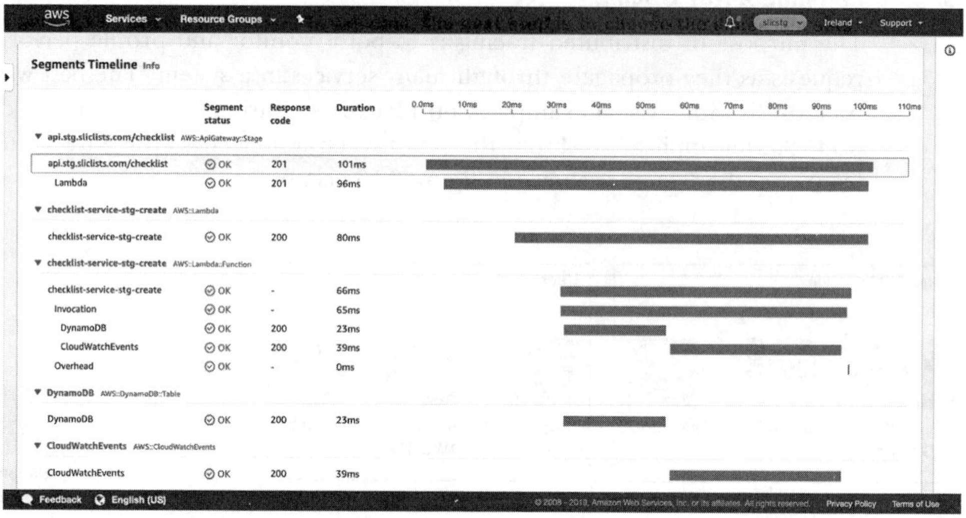

Figure 6.17   CloudWatch ServiceLens shows individual traces with times for each segment.

The trace in the figure shows the segments of the distributed request, including their timings. Note that this picture relates to a single request. With X-Ray, traces are sampled. By default, one request per second is sampled, and 5% of requests thereafter. This is configurable through rules in the X-Ray console.

X-Ray works by generating trace IDs and propagating these from one service to another as the request is fulfilled. In order to enable this behavior, developers can use the AWS X-Ray SDK to add automatic tracing instrumentation of AWS SDK calls. The effect of this is that tracing headers containing trace and segment identifiers are added to requests. Request data, including timings, are also sent by the X-Ray SDK to a daemon that collects tracing samples. The following code shows how we initialize the X-Ray SDK in our Node.js Lambda function code:

```
const awsXray = require('aws-xray-sdk')
const AWS = awsXray.captureAWS(require('aws-sdk'))
```

This snippet, taken from `slic-tools/aws.js` in SLIC Starter, loads the X-Ray SDK before loading the standard AWS SDK. The X-Ray SDK's `captureAWS` function is invoked to intercept all SDK requests and create new segments as part of the trace.[8] The other change required to enable X-Ray traces is to turn them on in API Gateway and Lambda configuration. When using the Serverless Framework, this involves an addition to the `serverless.ymlprovider` section, shown in the following code:

```
tracing:
    apiGateway: true
    lambda: true
```

This is done for all services in SLIC Starter, so you already have everything required to view distributed tracing results.

6.7.2 *Exploring traces and maps*

In addition to the individual trace timeline we already saw, the X-Ray console and the newer CloudWatch ServiceLens console have the capability to show a full map of your services. This is an extremely powerful visualization tool. An example of the SLIC Starter service map is shown in figure 6.18.

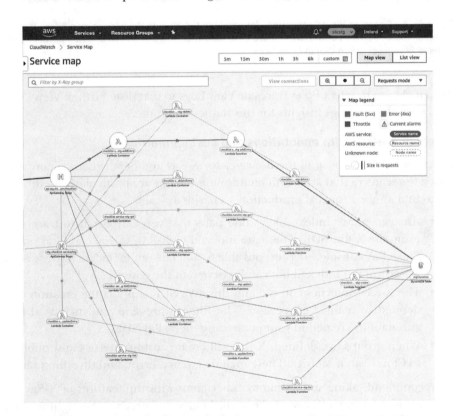

Figure 6.18 A map showing the request propagation between services can be shown in CloudWatch ServiceLens. Although this diagram shows so many services that it becomes hard to read, you have the option to zoom in and filter out when using the AWS Console.

---

[8] See Tracing AWS SDK Calls with the X-Ray SDK for Node.js, http://mng.bz/8GyD.

All visualisations, including maps and traces, show any errors captured. The map view shows an error percentage per node. Selecting any node in the map will show the request rate, latency, and number of errors. Figure 6.19 shows a selection of the service map for the `deleteEntry` function in the checklist service with a 50% error rate.

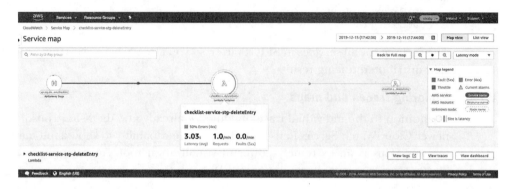

Figure 6.19   Choosing View Connections for any selected node in the service map filters the view to show connected services only. Here, we see error incidents that can be investigated further by using the correlating request IDs in CloudWatch Logs.

We can choose to select View Traces or View Logs to diagnose further. View Logs takes us to CloudWatch Logs Insights for this request and time.

6.7.3   *Advanced tracing with annotations and custom metrics*

We are not able to cover all the use cases for X-Ray and ServiceLens. There are, however, a few features that are worth mentioning, as they are particularly useful when trying to find answers for real production scenarios at scale:

- *Annotations* are indexed key-value pairs that you can assign to trace segments using the X-Ray SDK. These are indexed by X-Ray, so you can filter on them in the X-Ray console.[9] It's also possible to add custom metadata to trace segments. These are not indexed but can be viewed in the console.
- The X-Ray Analytics console and the AWS SDK support the creation of *groups*, defined by a filter expression. The filter expression can include the custom annotations created in your code using the X-Ray SDK.
- When groups are defined, X-Ray will create custom metrics and publish them to CloudWatch Metrics. These include latency, error, and throttling rates.

We recommend taking some time to experiment with the features of X-Ray through the AWS Management Console. This will help you to create the right annotations, metadata, and groups for your own serverless applications.

---

[9]   Add Annotations and Metadata to Segments with the X-Ray SDK for Node.js, http://mng.bz/EEeR.

Summary

- CodePipeline and CodeBuild can be used to create a serverless continuous deployment pipeline.
- The monorepo approach is an effective strategy for structuring a scalable serverless application.
- There are challenges with distributed serverless application architectures that can be addressed using observability best practices.
- Centralized logging can be implemented using structured JSON logs and AWS CloudWatch logs.
- CloudWatch Logs Insights is used to view and drill down into logs.
- Service metrics can be viewed using CloudWatch.
- It is possible to create application-specific custom metrics.
- Distributed tracing using X-Ray and ServiceLens allows us to make sense of a highly-distributed serverless system.

In the next chapter, we will continue to look at real-world AI as a Service, focusing on integration into existing systems built on vastly different technologies.

WARNING   Please ensure that you fully remove all cloud resources deployed in this chapter in order to avoid additional charges!

Applying AI to existing platforms

7

This chapter covers

- Integration patterns for serverless AI
- Improving identity verification with Textract
- An AI-enabled data processing pipeline with Kinesis
- On-the-fly translation with Translate
- Sentiment analysis with Comprehend
- Training a custom document classifier with Comprehend

In chapters 2–5 we created systems from scratch and applied AI services from the start. Of course, the real world is not always this clean and simple. Almost all of us have to deal with legacy systems and technical debt. In this chapter we are going to examine some strategies for applying AI services to existing systems. We will start by looking at some architectural patterns for this, and from there we will develop some specific examples drawn from real world experience.

7.1   *Integration patterns for serverless AI*

There is no escaping the fact that real world enterprise computing is "messy." For a medium to large enterprise, the technology estate is typically large, sprawling, and has often grown organically over time.

An organization's compute infrastructure can be broken down along domain lines such as finance, HR, marketing, line-of-business systems, and so on. Each of these domains may be composed of many systems from various vendors, along with home-grown software, and will usually mix legacy with more modern Software as a Service (SaaS) delivered applications.

Concomitant to this, the various systems are typically operated in a hybrid model mixing on-premise, co-location, and cloud-based deployment. Furthermore, each of these operational elements must typically integrate with other systems both in and outside of the domain. These integrations can be by way of batch ETL jobs, point-to-point connections, or through some form of enterprise service bus (ESB)

ETL, point-to-point, and ESB

Enterprise system integration is a large topic which we won't cover here, except to note that there are a number of ways in which systems can be connected together. For example, a company may need to export records from its HR database to match up with an expense tracking system. *Extract, transform, and load (ETL)* refers to the process of exporting records from one database (typically in CSV format), transforming, and then loading into another database.

Another method of connecting systems is to use a point-to-point integration. For example, some code can be created to call the API of one system and push data to another system's API. This does, of course, depend on the provision of a suitable API. Over time, the use of ETL and point-to-point integration can accumulate into a very complex and difficult-to-manage system.

An *enterprise service bus (ESB)* is an attempt to manage this complexity by providing a central system over which these connections can take place. The ESB approach suffers from its own particular pathologies, and has often caused as many problems as it has solved.

Figure 7.1 illustrates a typical mid-size organization's technology estate. In this example, separate domains are connected together through a central bus. Within each domain, there are separate ETL and batch processes connecting systems together.

Needless to say, a description of all of this complexity is outside the scope of this book. The question we will concern ourselves with is how we can adopt and leverage serverless AI in this environment. Fortunately there are some simple patterns that we can follow to achieve our goals, but first let's simplify the problem.

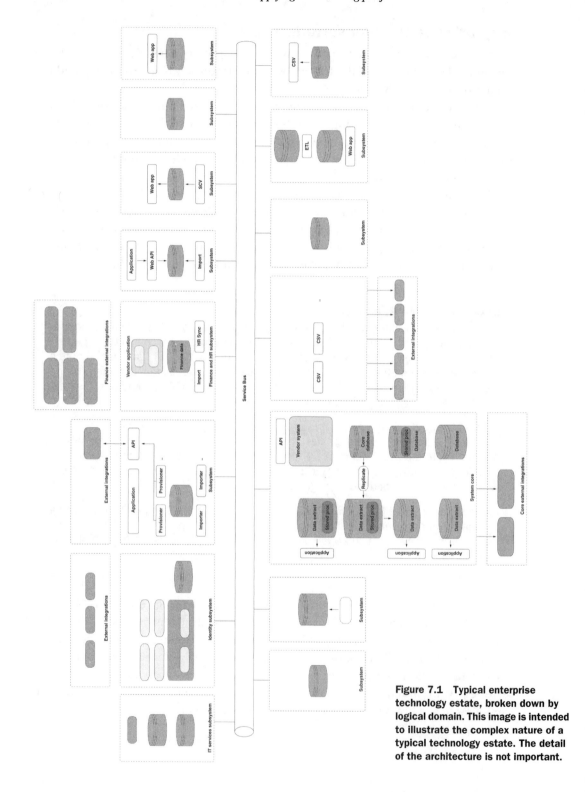

Figure 7.1   Typical enterprise technology estate, broken down by logical domain. This image is intended to illustrate the complex nature of a typical technology estate. The detail of the architecture is not important.

We will use figure 7.2 to represent our "enterprise estate" in the following discussion, to allow us to treat the rest of our infrastructure as a black box. In the next section we will examine four common patterns for connecting AI services. We will then build some concrete examples to show how AI services can be used to augment or replace existing business flows within an enterprise.

For example, if part of a company's business workflow requires proof of identity via a utility bill or passport, that can be provided as an AI-enabled service, reducing the manual workload.

Another example is that of forecasting. Many organizations need to plan ahead to predict their required levels of inventory or staff over a given period of time. AI services could be integrated into this process to build more sophisticated and accurate models, saving the company money or opportunity costs.

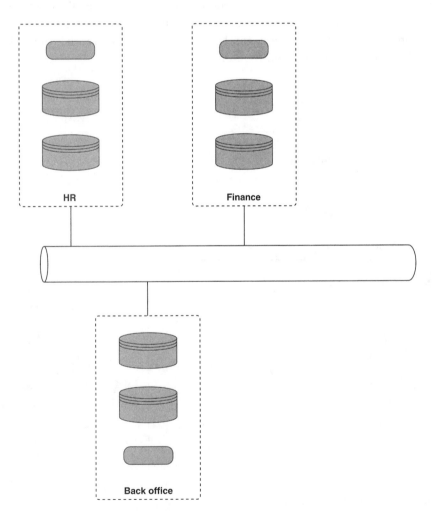

Figure 7.2 Simplified enterprise representation

We will examine four approaches:

- Synchronous API
- Asynchronous API
- VPN Stream In
- VPN Fully connected streaming

Bear in mind that these approaches simply represent ways of getting the appropriate data into the required location to enable us to execute AI services to achieve a business goal.

7.1.1   Pattern 1: Synchronous API

The first and simplest approach is to create a small system, much like we did in the first few chapters, in isolation from the rest of the enterprise. Functionality is exposed through a secured API and accessed over the public internet. If a higher lever of security is required, a VPN connection can be established, through which the API can be called. This simple pattern is illustrated in figure 7.3.

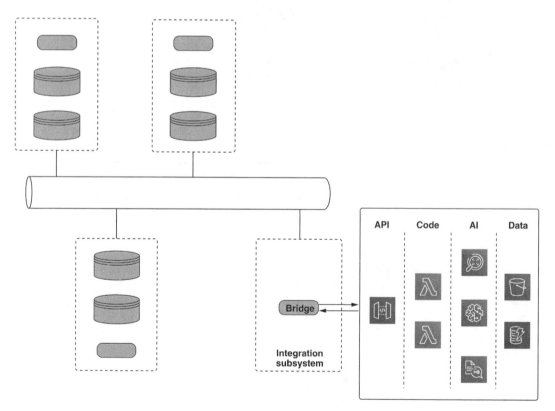

Figure 7.3   Integration Pattern 1: Synchronous API

In order to consume the service, a small piece of bridging code must be created to call the API and consume the results of the service. This pattern is appropriate when results can be obtained quickly and the API is called in a request/response manner.

7.1.2 *Pattern 2: Asynchronous API*

Our second pattern is very similar, in that we expose functionality through an API; however, in this case the API acts asynchronously. This pattern, which is appropriate for longer-running AI services, is illustrated in figure 7.4.

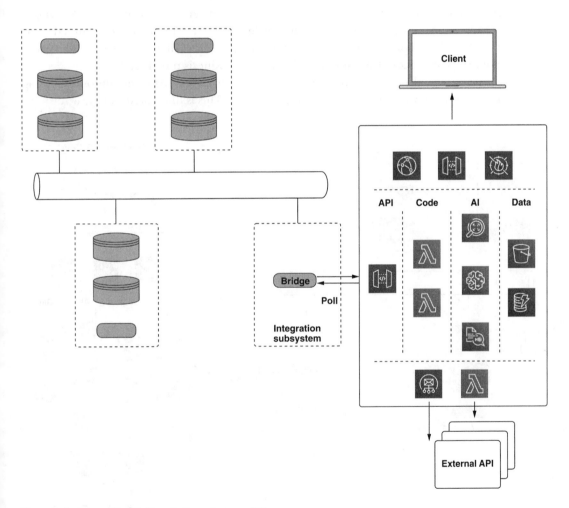

Figure 7.4   Integration Pattern 2: Asynchronous API

Under this "fire and forget" model, the bridge code calls the API but does not receive results immediately, apart from status information. An example of this might be a document classification system that processes a large volume of text. The outputs of the system can potentially be consumed by the wider enterprise in a number of ways:

- By constructing a web application that users can interact with to see results
- By the system messaging the results through email or other channels
- By the system calling an external API to forward details of any analysis
- By the bridge code polling the API for results

7.1.3   *Pattern 3: VPN Stream In*

A third approach is to connect the estate to cloud services through a VPN. Once a secure connection is established, the bridge code can interact more directly with cloud services. For example, rather than using an API Gateway to access the system, the bridge code could stream data directly into a Kinesis pipeline.

Results can be accessed in a number of ways: though an API, via outbound messaging, through a web GUI, or via an output stream. This is illustrated in figure 7.5.

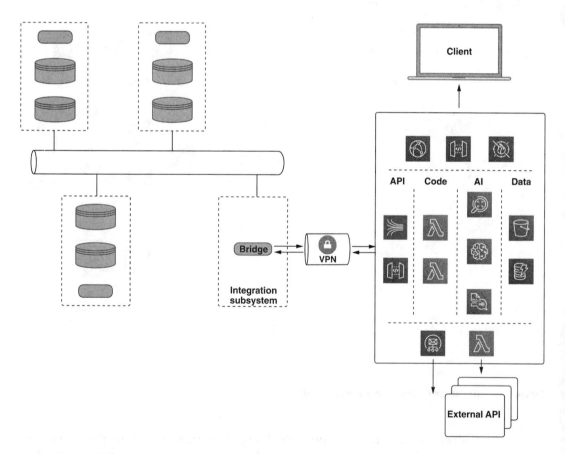

Figure 7.5   Integration Pattern 3: Stream In

> ### VPN
>
> A *virtual private network (VPN)* can be used to provide a secure network connection between devices or networks. VPNs typically use the IPSec protocol suite to provide authentication, authorization, and secure encrypted communications. Using IPSec lets you use insecure protocols, such as those used for file sharing between remote nodes.
>
> A VPN can be used to provide secure access into a corporate network for remote workers, or to securely connect a corporate network into the cloud. Though there are a number of ways to set up and configure a VPN, we would recommend a serverless approach using the AWS VPN service.

7.1.4 *Pattern 4 VPN: Fully connected streaming*

Our final pattern involves a much deeper connection between the estate and cloud AI services. Under this model, we establish a VPN connection as before, and use it to stream data in both directions. Though there are several streaming technologies available, we have had good results using Apache Kafka. This is illustrated in figure 7.6

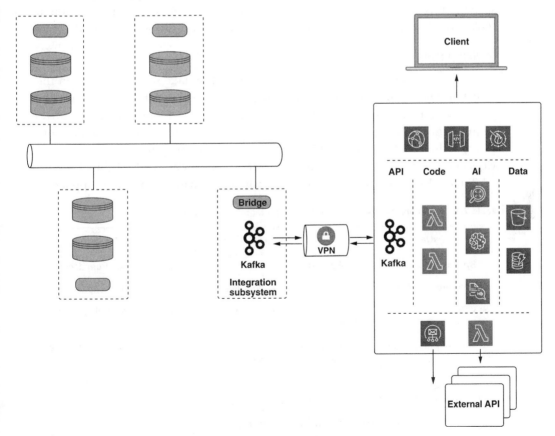

Figure 7.6   Integration Pattern 4: Full Streaming

This approach involves operating a Kafka cluster on both ends of the VPN, and replicating data between the clusters. Within the cloud environment, services consume data by pulling from the appropriate Kafka topics and place results back onto a different topic for consumption by the wider enterprise.

> ### Kafka
>
> Apache Kafka is an open source, distributed streaming platform. Kafka was originally developed at LinkedIn, and later donated to the Apache Foundation. Though there are other streaming technologies available, Kafka's design is unique in that it is implemented as a distributed commit log.
>
> Kafka is increasingly being adopted in high-throughput data streaming scenarios by companies such as Netflix and Uber. It is, of course, possible to install, run, and manage your own Kafka cluster; however, we would recommend that you take the serverless approach and adopt a system such as AWS Managed Streaming for Kafka (MSK).

A full discussion of the merits of this approach and Kafka in general is outside the scope of this book. If you are not familiar with Kafka, we recommend that you take a look at the Manning book *Kafka in Action* by Dylan Scott to get up to speed.

7.1.5   *Which pattern?*

As with all architectural decisions, which approach to take really depends on the use case. Our guiding principle is to keep things as simple as possible. If a simple API integration will achieve your goal, then go with that. If over time the external API set begins to grow, then consider changing the integration model to a streaming solution to avoid the proliferation of APIs. The key point is to keep the integration to AI services under constant review and be prepared to refactor as needs dictate.

Table 7.1 summarizes the context and when each pattern should be applied.

Table 7.1   Applicability of AI as Service legacy integration patterns

Pattern	Context	Example
1: Synchronous API	Single service, fast response	Text extraction from document
2: Asynchronous API	Single service, longer running	Document transcription
3: VPN Stream In	Multiple services, results for human consumption	Sentiment analysis pipeline
4: VPN Fully Connected	Multiple services, results for machine consumption	Batch translation of documents

In this chapter we will build two example systems:

- Pattern 1: Synchronous API approach
- Pattern 2: Asynchronous API

Though we won't look at the streaming approach in detail, bear in mind that both of our example systems could also be connected to an enterprise through this method by replacing the API layer with an appropriate technology such as Apache Kafka.

7.2   *Improving identity verification with Textract*

For our first example, we will extend an existing platform by creating a small, self-contained API that can be called directly. Let's imagine that an organization needs to validate identities. Most of us have had to go through this process at one time or another; for example, when applying for a mortgage or car loan.

This typically requires a scan of several pieces of documentation in order to prove your identity and address to the lender. Though a human will need to see these scans, extracting the information from them and manually entering the information into the lender's system is time-consuming and error-prone. This is something that we can now achieve through the application of AI.

Our small, self-contained service is illustrated in figure 7.7. It uses AWS Textract to grab the details from a scanned-in document. For this example, we will be using a passport, but other identifying documents would work just as well, such as utility bills or bank statements.

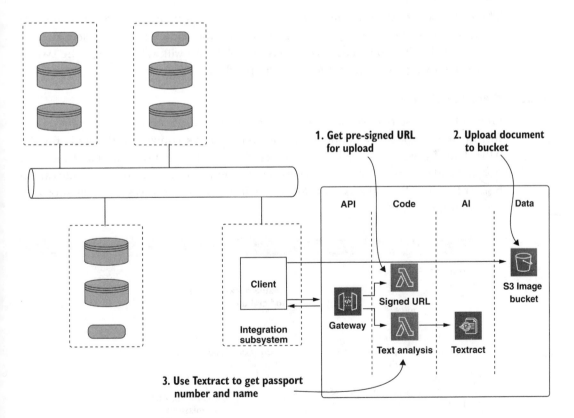

Figure 7.7   Document recognition API

Our API has two parts. First we will need to upload a scanned image to S3. The simplest way to do this is by using a pre-signed S3 URL, and our API provides a function to generate one of these and return it to the client. Once we have our image in S3, we will use a Lambda function to call Textract, which will analyze our scanned-in image, returning the data in a text format. Our API will return this data to the client for further processing.

> ### Personally identifiable information
>
> It goes without saying that any personally identifiable information must be handled with the utmost care. Whenever a system must deal with user-supplied information, particularly identification documents, it must comply with all of the statutory legal requirements for the territory in which the information is gathered.
>
> In the European Union, this means that the system must comply with the General Data Protection Regulation (GDPR). As developers and system architects, we need to be aware of these regulations and ensure compliance.

7.2.1   Get the code

The code for the API is in the directory `chapter7/text-analysis`. This contains two directories: `text-analysis-api`, which has the code for our API service, and `client`, which has some code to exercise the API. We will walk through the system before deploying and testing with some sample data.

7.2.2   Text Analysis API

Our API codebase consists of a `serverless.yml` configuration file, `package.json` for our node module dependencies, and `handler.js` containing the logic for the API. The `serverless.yml` is fairly standard, defining two Lambda functions: `upload` and `analyze`, which are accessible through API Gateway. It also defines an S3 bucket for the API, and sets up IAM permissions for the analysis service, as shown in the following listing.

Listing 7.1   Textract permissions

```
iamRoleStatements:
    - Effect: Allow                          ◁─┐  Enable bucket access
      Action:                                   │  to Lambda
        - s3:GetObject
        - s3:PutObject
        - s3:ListBucket
      Resource: "arn:aws:s3:::${self:custom.imagebucket}/*"
    - Effect: Allow
      Action:
        - textract:AnalyzeDocument           ◁─┐  Enable Textract
      Resource: "*"                             │  permissions
```

Bucket permissions are required for our Lambda functions to generate a valid pre-signed URL, in addition to enabling access for Textract to the uploaded documents.

The next listing shows the call to the S3 API to generate a pre-signed URL. The URL along with the bucket key is returned to the client, which performs a PUT request to upload the document in question.

Listing 7.2   Get signed URL

```
const params = {
    Bucket: process.env.CHAPTER7_IMAGE_BUCKET,
    Key: key,                                      Set expiry time
    Expires: 300                                   of five minutes
}
s3.getSignedUrl('putObject', params, function (err, url) {
    respond(err, {key: key, url: url}, cb)
})
```

The pre-signed URL is restricted to a specific action for that given key and file only—in this case, a PUT request. Note also that we have set an expiry time of 300 seconds on the URL. This means that if the file transfer is not initiated within five minutes, the signed URL will become invalid, and no transfer will be possible without generating a fresh URL.

Once the document is uploaded to the bucket, we can initiate the call to Textract to perform the analysis. The next listing shows how this is done in `handler.js`.

Listing 7.3   Calling Textract

```
const params = {
    Document: {                               Point to uploaded
        S3Object: {                           document
            Bucket: process.env.CHAPTER7_IMAGE_BUCKET,
            Name: data.imageKey
        }
    },
    FeatureTypes: ['TABLES', 'FORMS']         Set feature
}                                             types
                                              Call
txt.analyzeDocument(params, (err, data) => {  Textract
    respond(err, data, cb)
})
```

Textract can perform two types of analysis, TABLES and FORMS. The TABLES analysis type tells Textract to preserve tabular information in its analysis, whereas the FORMS type requests that Textract extract information as key-value pairs if possible. Both analysis types can be preformed in the same call if required.

```
{
 Blocks: [
  {
   BlockType: 'PAGE'
   Id:
   Relationships: [{
    Type: CHILD
    Ids: [
     ...
    ]
   }]
  },
  {
   BlockType: 'LINE'
   Confidence: 99.8,
   Geometry: {
    BoundingBox: {
     Width: 0.09791304916143417,
     Height: 0.025393398478627205,
     Left: 0.12474661320447922,
     Top: 0.036540355533361435
    }
   }
   Id:
    Relationships: [{
     Type: CHILD
     Ids: [
      ...
     ]
    }]
  },
  {
   BlockType:: 'WORD'
   Confidence: 96.2
   Geometry: {
    ...
   }
   Id:
    Relationships: [{
     Type: CHILD
     Ids: [
      ...
     ]
    }]
   }
  ]}
```

Links to

Links to

Figure 7.8   Textract output JSON

On completion of the analysis, Textract returns a block of JSON containing the results. The result structure is illustrated in figure 7.8.

The structure should be fairly self-explanatory, in that it consists of a root PAGE element that links to child LINE elements, each of which links to a number of child WORD elements. Each WORD and LINE element has an associated confidence interval: a number between 0 and 100 indicating how accurate Textract thinks the analysis was for each element. Each LINE and WORD element also has a Geometry section; this contains coordinate information on the bounding box around the element. This can be useful for applications where some additional human verification is required. For example, a UI could display the scanned-in documents with an overlaid bounding box in order to confirm that the extracted text matches the expected document area.

7.2.3   Client code

Code to exercise the API is in the client directory. The main API calling code is in client.js. There are three functions: getSignedUrl, uploadImage, and analyze. These functions map one-to-one with the API, as already described.

The following listing shows the analyze function.

Listing 7.4   Calling the API

```
function analyze (key, cb) {
    req({
        method: 'POST',
        url: env.CHAPTER7_ANALYZE_URL,
        body: JSON.stringify({imageKey: key})
    }, (err, res, body) => {
```

Make POST request to the API

```
      if (err || res.statusCode !== 200) {
        return cb({statusCode: res.statusCode,
          err: err,
          body: body.toString()})
      }
      cb(null, JSON.parse(body))                    ◁──┐ Return
   })                                                   │ results
}
```

The code uses the `request` module to execute a `POST` request to the analyze API, which returns the Textract results block to the client.

7.2.4 *Deploy the API*

Before we deploy the API, we need to configure some environment variables. Both the API and the client read their configuration from an `.env` file in the `chapter7/text-analysis` directory. Open up your favorite editor and create this file with the contents, as shown in the next listing.

Listing 7.5 `.env` file for Textract example

```
TARGET_REGION=eu-west-1
CHAPTER7_IMAGE_BUCKET=<your bucket name>
```

Replace `<your bucket name>` with a globally unique bucket name of your choice.

To deploy the API, we need to use the Serverless Framework as before. Open a command shell, `cd` to the `chapter7/text-analysis/text-analysis-api` directory, and run

```
$ npm install
$ serverless deploy
```

This will create the document image bucket, set up API Gateway, and deploy our two Lambda functions. Once deployed, Serverless will output the Gateway URLs to our two functions, which will look similar to the output illustrated in the next listing.

Listing 7.6 Endpoint URLs

Upload URL

```
endpoints:
GET - https://63tat1jze6.execute-api.eu-west-1.amazonaws.com/dev/upload    ◁──┘
POST - https://63tat1jze6.execute-api.eu-west-1.amazonaws.com/dev/analyze  ◁──┐
functions:
upload: c7textanalysis-dev-upload
analyze: c7textanalysis-dev-analyze
```

Analyze URL

We will use these URLs to call our text analysis API.

7.2.5 Test the API

Figure 7.9 Sample passport

Now that we have deployed our API, it's time to test it with some real data. The service that we have just deployed is able to read and identify text fields in documents such as utility bills or passports. We have provided some sample passport images in the data sub directory, one of which is shown in figure 7.9. These are, of course, composed from dummy data.

To test the API, we first need to update our .env file. Open the file in a text editor and add the two URLs and bucket name, as shown in the next listing, using your specific names.

Listing 7.7 Environment file

```
TARGET_REGION=eu-west-1
CHAPTER7_IMAGE_BUCKET=<your bucket name>
CHAPTER7_ANALYZE_URL=<your analyze url>        Replace with the
                                               analyze URL
CHAPTER7_GETUPLOAD_URL=<your upload url>                    Replace with the
                                                           upload URL
```

Next, cd into the chapter7/text-analysis/client directory. There are some sample images in the data sub directory. Code to exercise the client is in index.js. To run the code, open a command shell and execute

```
$ npm install
$ node index.js
```

The client code will use the API to upload an example document to the image bucket, and then call our analyze API. The analyze API will call Textract to analyze the image and return the results back to our client. Finally, the client code will parse through the output JSON structure and pick out a few key fields, displaying them to the console. You should see output similar to the following listing.

Listing 7.8 Client output

```
{
  "passportNumber": "340020013 (confidence: 99.8329086303711)",
  "surname": "TRAVELER (confidence: 75.3625717163086)",
  "givenNames": "HAPPY (confidence: 96.09229278564453)",
  "nationality": "UNITED STATES OF AMERICA (confidence: 82.67759704589844)",
  "dob": "01 Jan 1980 (confidence: 88.6818618774414)",
  "placeOfBirth": "WASHINGTON D.C. U.S.A. (confidence: 84.47944641113281)",
  "dateOfIssue": "06 May 2099 (confidence: 88.30438995361328)",
  "dateOfExpiration": "05 May 2019 (confidence: 88.60911560058594)"
}
```

It is important to note that Textract is applying multiple techniques in order to extract this information for us. First it performs an *optical character recognition (OCR)* analysis to recognize the text in the image. As part of this analysis, it retains the coordinate information for the recognized characters, grouping them into blocks and lines. It then uses the coordinate information to associate form fields as name-value pairs.

To be accurate, we need to supply Textract with good-quality images: the better the quality, the better the result we will get from the analysis. You can test this by creating or downloading your own low-quality images and passing these to the API. You should find that Textract will struggle to identify the same fields in a low-quality image.

Listing 7.8 shows the fields that Textract has identified, and also a confidence level. Most AI services will return some associated confidence level, and it is up to us, as consumers of the service, to figure out how we should deal with this number. For example, if our use case is highly sensitive to errors, then perhaps it is correct to only accept a 99% or better confidence level. Results with lower levels should be sent off for human verification or correction. Many business use cases, however, can tolerate lower accuracy. This judgment is very domain-specific, and should involve both business and technical stakeholders.

Think about the business processes at your own organization: are there areas that could be automated by this type of analysis? Do you need to collect and input information from documents supplied by your customers? Perhaps you could improve that process by adapting this example to your own needs.

7.2.6 Remove the API

Before moving on to the next section, we need to remove the API to avoid any additional charges. To do this, cd into the `chapter7/text-analysis/text-analysis -api` directory and run

```
$ source ../.env && aws s3 rm s3://${CHAPTER7_IMAGE_BUCKET} --recursive
$ serverless remove
```

This will remove all of the uploaded images from the bucket and tear down the stack.

7.3 An AI-enabled data processing pipeline with Kinesis

For our second example, we will build a data processing pipeline. This pipeline will be exposed through an asynchronous API, and will serve as our pattern 2 example. In building this example, we will explore a number of new services and technologies in detail, including Kinesis, Translate, and Comprehend:

- Kinesis is Amazon's real-time streaming service, which is used to create data- and video-processing pipelines.
- Translate is Amazon's machine-driven language translation service.
- Comprehend is Amazon's natural language processing (NLP) service, which can be used to perform tasks like sentiment analysis or keyword detection.

Consider the domain of retail and e-commerce. A large retail outlet might have multiple product departments such as "outdoor," "automotive," "pets," and so on. Customer service is an important part of the retail trade. In particular, responding quickly and effectively to customer complaints is important, as it can transform a disgruntled customer into a brand advocate if done correctly. The problem is that customers have many channels on which to complain, including website product reviews, email, Twitter, Facebook, Instagram, blog posts, and so forth.

Not only are there many channels on which product feedback can be placed, global retailers have to handle feedback in multiple languages as well. Though humans are needed to deal with the customers, detecting the negative feedback across all of these channels and geographic territories is something that is amenable to an AI-driven solution.

Our example system will be an AI-enabled pipeline that can be used to filter feedback from multiple channels in multiple languages. The aim of our pipeline is to alert the appropriate department when a piece of negative feedback is detected about one of their products.

This AI-enabled pipeline augments and extends the retailer's digital capability, while not interfering directly with line-of-business systems.

Our pipeline is depicted in figure 7.10. At the start of the pipe, raw data is sent to a collection API; this can be inbound from multiple feeds, such as a Twitter feed, Facebook comments, inbound emails, and other social channels. The API feeds the raw text into a Kinesis stream.

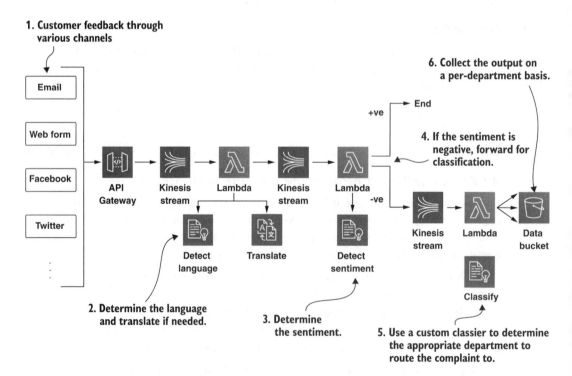

Figure 7.10 Processing pipeline

AWS provides two key streaming technologies: Managed Streaming for Kafka (MSK) and Kinesis. Of these, Kinesis is the simplest to use, so we will focus on it for this system. Data in the stream triggers a downstream Lambda, which uses Comprehend to determine the language of the inbound text. If the language is not English, then the Lambda runs on-the-fly translation with AWS Translate before posting it down the pipe. The next downstream Lambda runs sentiment analysis against the translated text using Comprehend. If a positive sentiment is detected, then no further processing is carried out for the message. However, should the sentiment be strongly negative, the text is sent to a customer classifier built using AWS Comprehend. This analyzes the text and attempts to determine the product department pertaining to the message. Once a department has been identified, the message can be dispatched to the appropriate team to allow them to address the negative comment. In this case, we will output results to an S3 bucket.

By using a combination of AI services in this way, a pipeline such as this can provide enormous cost savings for an enterprise, because the filtering and categorization of feedback is performed automatically without requiring a team of people.

Kinesis vs. Kafka

Until recently, one of the reasons for choosing Kinesis over Kafka was that Kafka required installation, setup, and management on EC2 instances. With the release of AWS Managed Streaming for Kafka (MSK), this situation has changed. Though a full discussion on the merits of Kafka is outside the scope of this book, we would note that the technology is highly scalable and versatile. We suggest that you investigate Kafka in more depth if you are building a system that requires a lot of streaming at scale.

Even taking MSK into account, it is still true that Kinesis is more fully integrated into the AWS stack and is simpler to get up and running quickly, so we will use it for the purposes of our example system. Kinesis can be used in several ways:

- Kinesis Video Streams—For video and audio content
- Kinesis Data Streams—For general data streaming
- Kinesis Data Firehose—Supports streaming of Kinesis data to targets such as S3, Redshift, or Elasticsearch
- Kinesis Analytics—Supports real-time stream processing with SQL

In this chapter, we are using Kinesis Data Streams to build our pipeline.

7.3.1 Get the code

The code for our pipeline is in the book repository in the directory `chapter7/pipeline`. This contains the following sub directories that map to each stage in the process:

- `pipeline-api`—Contains the API Gateway setup for the system
- `translate`—Contains the language detection and translation service
- `sentiment`—Contains the sentiment analysis code
- `training`—Contains utility scripts to help train a custom classifier

- classify—Contains the code that triggers our custom classifier
- driver—Contains code to exercise the pipeline

As with the preceding examples, we will briefly describe the code for each service before deploying. Once all of our units have been deployed, we will test our pipeline end to end. Let's get started with the simple first step, deploying the API.

7.3.2 Deploying the API

The code for the API is in the directory chapter7/pipeline/pipeline-api and consists of a serverless.yml file along with a simple API. The Serverless configuration defines a single ingest method, which pushes data posted to the API into Kinesis. The Kinesis stream is also defined in the Serverless configuration, which is shown in the following listing.

Listing 7.9   `serverless.yml` Kinesis definition

```
resources:
  Resources:                                       ┐ Define Kinesis
    KinesisStream:                        ◁─────────┘ stream
      Type: AWS::Kinesis::Stream
      Properties:
        Name: ${env:CHAPTER7_PIPELINE_TRANSLATE_STREAM}
        ShardCount: ${env:CHAPTER7_PIPELINE_SHARD_COUNT}
```

The code for the API is very simple in that it just forwards inbound data to the Kinesis stream. The API accepts inbound JSON POST requests and expects the format shown in the next listing.

Listing 7.10   JSON data format for pipeline API

```
{                                    ┐ The original
  originalText: ...        ◁─────────┘ text         ┐ The source of
  source: 'twitter' | 'facebook'...        ◁────────┘ the feedback   ┐ The ID of the
  originator: '@pelger'                              ◁───────────────┘ feedback originator
}
```

Before deploying the API, we need to set up our environment. We have provided a template .env file in the chapter7/pipeline directory called default-environment.env. Make a copy of this file in the chapter7/pipeline directory with the filename .env. The file should have the contents outlined in the next listing.

Listing 7.11   Environment file for Pipeline

```
TARGET_REGION=eu-west-1                              ┐ Kinesis shard
CHAPTER7_PIPELINE_SHARD_COUNT=1            ◁─────────┘ count           ┐ Name of Kinesis
CHAPTER7_PIPELINE_TRANSLATE_STREAM=c7ptransstream        ◁────────────┘ translation stream
CHAPTER7_PIPELINE_SENTIMENT_STREAM=c7psentstream        ◁──┐ Name of Kinesis
                                                           │ sentiment stream
```

```
CHAPTER7_PIPELINE_CLASSIFY_STREAM=c7pclassifystream
CHAPTER7_PIPELINE_TRANSLATE_STREAM_ARN=...
CHAPTER7_PIPELINE_SENTIMENT_STREAM_ARN=...
CHAPTER7_PIPELINE_CLASSIFY_STREAM_ARN=...
CHAPTER7_CLASSIFIER_NAME=chap7classifier
CHAPTER7_CLASSIFIER_ARN=...
...
```

**Name of Kinesis
classify stream**

Next we can go ahead and deploy the API by opening a command shell in the
`chapter7/pipeline/pipeline-api` directory and executing

```
$ npm install
$ serverless deploy
```

This will create our first Kinesis stream, and also our ingestion API. Figure 7.11 illustrates the state of our pipeline after deployment of the API. The highlighted section
represents what has been deployed so far.

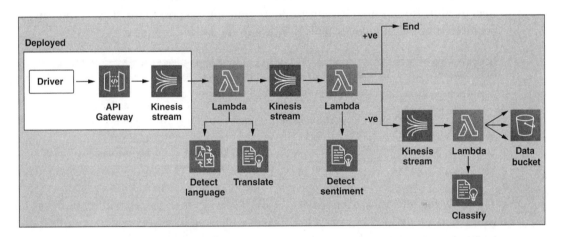

Figure 7.11   Pipeline after API deployment

On deployment, the framework will output the URL for our API. Before proceeding
to the next stage, add this into the `.env` file as shown in the following listing, substituting your specific value.

Listing 7.12   Additional entries in `.env` file following API deployment

```
CHAPTER7_PIPELINE_API=<your API url>
```

7.4 *On-the-fly translation with Translate*

The first stage in our pipeline after ingestion is to detect the language and translate to
English if needed. These tasks are handled by our translation service, the code for which
is in the directory `chapter8/pipeline/translate`. The Serverless configuration

is fairly standard, except that the main handler function is triggered by the Kinesis stream that we defined in our API deployment. This is shown in the following listing.

Listing 7.13 Handler triggered by Kinesis

```
functions:
  translate:
    handler: handler.translate
    events:                           ┐ Connect to
      - stream:              ⊲────┘  the stream.
          type: kinesis
          arn: ${env:CHAPTER7_PIPELINE_TRANSLATE_STREAM_ARN}
          batchSize: 100
          startingPosition: LATEST
          enabled: true
          async: true
```

The configuration defines a second Kinesis stream that our Sentiment service will connect to, and also sets up the appropriate permissions to post to the stream and call the required translation services. This is shown in the following listing.

Listing 7.14 Handler IAM permissions

```
- Effect: Allow
      Action:
                                                    ┐ Comprehend
        - comprehend:DetectDominantLanguage  ⊲─┘  permissions
        - translate:TranslateText            ⊲──┐ Translate
        - kinesis:PutRecord        ⊲──┐ Kinesis │ permissions
        - kinesis:PutRecords          │ permissions
      Resource: "*"
```

The code for our translation service in `handler.js` is triggered with data from the Kinesis stream defined by our API. This is as a block of Base64-encoded records in the event parameter to our handler function. The next listing shows how our service consumes these records.

Listing 7.15 Translation service

```
module.exports.translate = function (event, context, cb) {
  let out = []
  asnc.eachSeries(event.Records, (record, asnCb) => {  ⊲──┐ Loop over
    const payload = new Buffer(record.kinesis.data,       │ each record.
      'base64').toString('utf8')              ⊲──┐ Decode
    let message                                    │ the record.
    try {
      message = JSON.parse(payload)   ⊲──┐ Convert
    } catch (exp) {                       │ to object
    ...
  })
```

Our service uses Comprehend and Translate in combination. Comprehend is used to detect the language in our message, and Translate is used to convert to English if the detected language requires it. The next listing shows the relevant calls from the source code.

Listing 7.16   Detect language and translate

```
...
let params = {
  Text: message.originalText
}                                                            Detect
comp.detectDominantLanguage(params, (err, data) => {   <──  language
...
  params = {
    SourceLanguageCode: data.Languages[0].LanguageCode,
    TargetLanguageCode: 'en',
    Text: message.originalText
  }                                                          Translate
  trans.translateText(params, (err, data) => {         <──  to English
  ...
```

Once the service has translated the text, if required, it posts an updated message into the second Kinesis stream. This will later be picked up by our sentiment detection service, which we will deploy shortly.

To deploy the translation service, open a command shell in the `chapter7/pipeline/translate` directory and run

```
$ npm install
$ serverless deploy
```

This will create the second stage in our pipeline. Figure 7.12 illustrates the state of our pipeline after the latest deployment.

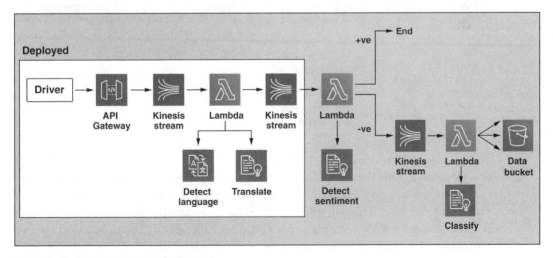

Figure 7.12   Pipeline after API deployment

We're halfway through the deployment of our pipeline. In the next section, we will check that everything is working so far.

7.5   *Testing the pipeline*

Now that we have part of our pipeline deployed, let's put some data through it to check that it's working correctly. To do this, we are going to take advantage of a free open source public data set. Let's grab some of this data now and use it to test our pipeline.

First `cd` into `chapter7/pipeline/testdata` directory. This contains a script that will download and unpack some test data, which you can run using

```
$ bash ./download.sh
```

We are using a subset of the Amazon product review data held at http://snap.stanford .edu/data/amazon/productGraph/. Specifically we are using data in the automotive, beauty, office, and pet categories. Once the script has completed, you will have four JSON files in the directory `testdata/data`. Each file contains a number of reviews, with review text and an overall score. You can open up the files in a text editor and take a look through them to get a feel for the data.

There is another script in the `testdata` directory called `preproc.sh`. This takes the downloaded review data and processes it into a format for training and testing our custom classifier. We will look at the classifier in the next section, but for now let's process our data by running this script:

```
$ cd pipeline/testdata
$ bash preproc.sh
```

This will create a number of additional files in the `data` directory. For each downloaded file, it creates a new JSON file with the structure shown in the next listing.

Listing 7.17   Amazon reviews data format

```
{
  train: [...],          ◁────┐ Training
  test: {                     │ data
    all: [...],                        ┌ Negative
    neg: [...],          ◁────┘ │ test data
    pos: [...]           ◁────┐ Positive
  }                           │ test data
}
```

What the script has done is to split the input data into two sets, one for training and one for testing, with the bulk of the records in the training set. Within the test set, we have used the `overall` field in the original data to determine if this review data is positive or negative. This will allow us to test our sentiment filter later on. The script has also created a CSV (comma separated value) file, `data/final/training.csv`. We will use this file in the next section to train our classifier.

Now that we have our data downloaded and prepared, we can check that our pipeline is functioning correctly so far. There is a test utility for this in the directory `pipeline/driver`. This has two small Node.js programs: `driver.js`, which calls our API with test data, and `streamReader.js`, which reads data from a nominated Kinesis stream so that we can see what data exists in that stream. We won't go into the code here.

Let's first post some data to our API. Open a command shell in `pipeline/driver`, install dependencies, and then run the driver:

```
$ npm install
$ node driver.js office pos
$ node driver.js office neg
$ node driver.js beauty neg
```

This will call the API with three random reviews: two from the office products data set, and one from the beauty data set. The driver also allows us to specify whether the data should be positive or negative. Next let's check that the data is indeed in our Kinesis streams. First run

```
$ node streamReader.js translate
```

This will read data back from our translate stream and display it on the console. The stream reader code polls Kinesis every second to display the latest data. To stop the reader, press Ctrl-C. Next, repeat this exercise for the sentiment stream:

```
$ node streamReader.js sentiment
```

You should see the same data displayed to the console, with some additional fields that were added by the translation service.

7.6 *Sentiment analysis with Comprehend*

Now that we have tested our pipeline, it's time to implement the next stage, which is detecting the sentiment of the inbound text. The code for this is in the directory `pipeline/sentiment` and uses AWS Comprehend to determine the sentiment. The Serverless configuration is very similar to the previous services, so we won't cover it here, except to note that the configuration creates an S3 bucket to collect the negative review data for further processing.

> ### Sentiment analysis
>
> Sentiment analysis is a complex process involving the use of natural language processing (NLP), text analysis, and computational linguistics. It is a difficult task for computers to perform, because at the root it involves the detection, to some extent, of emotions expressed in text form. Consider the following sentence that might be written by a reviewer about a hotel that they just stayed in:
>
> *We hated leaving the hotel and felt sad to get home.*
>
> While this is in fact expressing a positive sentiment about the hotel, all of the words in this sentence are negative if taken in isolation. With the application of deep learning

(continued)

techniques, sentiment analysis is becoming more and more accurate. However sometimes a human is still required to make a judgement call.

By using AWS Comprehend, we don't have to be concerned about all of this complexity; we merely need to process the results and call a human in when the API can't make an accurate determination.

The code for the service is in `handler.js`, and is illustrated in the next listing.

Listing 7.18   Sentiment analysis handler

```
{
module.exports.detect = function (event, context, cb) {
  asnc.eachSeries(event.Records, (record, asnCb) => {
    const payload = new Buffer(record.kinesis.data,
      'base64').toString('utf8')                         ◁──┐  Unpack the message
    let message = JSON.parse(payload)                        │  from Kinesis.
    ...
    let params = {
      LanguageCode: 'en',
      Text: message.text
    }
    comp.detectSentiment(params, (err, data) => {       ◁──┐  Detect
      ...                                                    │  sentiment

      if (data.Sentiment === 'NEGATIVE' ||
          data.Sentiment === 'NEUTRAL' ||                     Write negative, neutral,
          data.Sentiment === 'MIXED') {                ◁──┘  or mixed message to S3
        writeNegativeSentiment(outMsg, (err, data) => {
          asnCb(err)
        })
      } else {
        if (data.SentimentScore.Positive < 0.85) {     ◁──┐  Even if positive,
          writeNegativeSentiment(outMsg, (err, data) => {    │  write depending on
            ...                                              │  confidence level
        }
      }
    })
  ...
}
```

After unpacking the message, the code calls Comprehend to detect the message sentiment. Any negative messages are written to an S3 bucket for onward processing. Positive messages are dropped. However, you could do further computation at this point; for example, monitoring the ratio of positive to negative sentiment and alerting on anomalous conditions.

As with all AI services, it is important to interpret the returned confidence level appropriately for the business problem. In this case, we have decided to err on the side of caution. This means

- Any overall negative, neutral, or mixed messages are treated as negative sentiments and sent on for classification.
- Any overall positive messages with a confidence level of more than 85% are discarded.
- Any overall positive message with a confidence level of less than 85% are treated as negative and sent on for classification.

Remember that in this scenario, once classified, messages that aren't discarded will be sent to a human for processing. We could easily change these rules to suit our business process—for example, by discarding the neutral and positive messages regardless of confidence level if we were less concerned about picking up all complaints, and only wanted to focus on strongly negative results. The point is to understand that our results come with an associated confidence level and to interpret this accordingly.

Let's now deploy the sentiment analysis service. `cd` into the `pipeline/sentiment` directory and run the following commands:

```
$ npm install
$ serverless deploy
```

Once the service is deployed, we can retest our pipeline by running the driver again to post some positive and negative messages, as shown in the next listing.

Listing 7.19   Amazon reviews data format

```
$ cd pipeline/driver
$ node driver.js office pos        ◁──┐  Send positive
 $ node driver.js beauty pos           │  message
$ node driver.js beauty neg    ◁──┐  Send negative
 $ node driver.js auto neg          │  message
```

To check that our pipeline is working correctly, run the `streamReader` utility in the `driver` directory, this time telling it to read from the classify stream:

```
$ node streamReader.js classify
```

This will read data back from our classifier stream and display it on the console. The stream-reader code polls Kinesis every second to display the latest data. To stop the reader, hit Ctrl-C. You should see the message output, along with some additional data from the sentiment analysis. Note that strongly positive messages will be discarded, so not all of the messages sent by the driver will make it to the classifier stream.

Following this deployment, the current state of our pipeline is shown in figure 7.13.

> **TIP** Though we are using translation and sentiment analysis services as part of a data pipeline, these can, of course, be used in isolation. Perhaps you can think of instances in your current work or organization where you could apply these services.

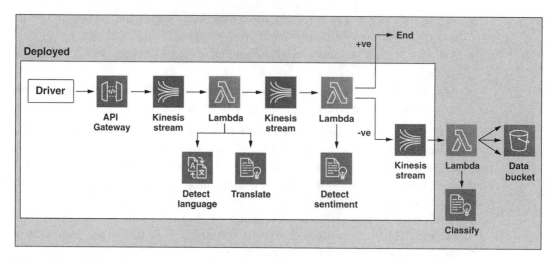

Figure 7.13   Pipeline after sentiment service deployment

7.7   *Training a custom document classifier*

For the final stage in our pipeline, we are going to use a custom classifier. From the inbound message text, our classifier will be able to determine which department the message is pertaining to: Automotive, Beauty, Office, or Pets. Training a classifier from scratch is a complex task that normally requires some level of in-depth knowledge of machine learning. Thankfully AWS Comprehend makes the job much easier. Figure 7.14 illustrates the training process.

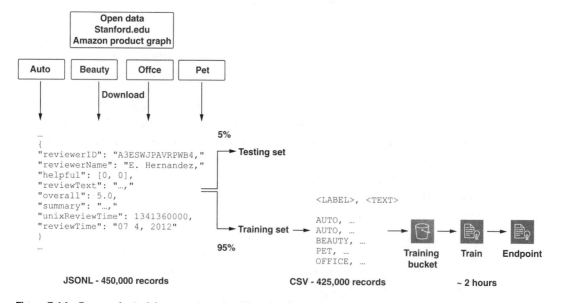

Figure 7.14   Process for training a custom classifier with Comprehend

All of the code to train our custom classifier is in the directory `pipeline/training`. To train our classifier, we need to do the following:

- Create a data bucket.
- Upload training data to the bucket.
- Create an IAM role for the classifier.
- Run the training data to create a classifier.
- Create an endpoint to make the classifier available.

Document classification models

Document classification is the problem of assigning one or more classes or types to a document. In this context, a document can range from a large manuscript to a single sentence. This is typically performed using one of two approaches:

- *Unsupervised classification*—Clusters documents into types based on textual analysis
- *Supervised classification*—Provides labeled data to a training process to build a model that is customized for our needs

In this chapter we are using supervised classification to train a model. By using Comprehend, we don't need to get into the details of the training process; we just need to supply a labeled data set for Comprehend to train on.

7.7.1   Create a training bucket

Before we create our training bucket, we need to update our `.env` file. Open this in a text editor as before, and add the line indicated in the next listing, substituting your own unique bucket name.

Listing 7.20   Environment file for pipeline

```
CHAPTER7_PIPELINE_TRAINING_BUCKET=<your training bucket name>
```

To create the bucket, `cd` into the directory `pipeline/training` and run the following:

```
$ cd pipeline/training
$ npm install
$ cd resources
$ serverless deploy
```

7.7.2   Upload training data

As you'll recall from the previous section where we tested our pipeline, our data processing script created a CSV file for training. We now need to upload this to our training bucket. `cd` into the directory `pipeline/testdata` and run

```
$ source ../.env &&  aws s3 sync ./data/final s3://
    ${CHAPTER7_PIPELINE_TRAINING_BUCKET}
```

This will push the training data set to S3. Note that the training file is around 200MB, so this may take a while to upload depending on your outbound connection speed.

The training data file is just a `csv` file containing a set of labels and associated text, as shown in the next listing.

Listing 7.21   Training data file structure

```
<LABEL>, <TEXT>
```

In our case the label is one of AUTO, BEAUTY, OFFICE, or PET. Comprehend will use this file to build a custom classifier using the text data to train the model and match it to the appropriate label.

7.7.3   Create an IAM role

Next we have to create an Identity and Access Management (IAM) role for the classifier. This will restrict the AWS cloud services that the classifier can access. To create the role, `cd` into the directory `pipeline/training` and run

```
$ bash ./configure-iam.sh
```

This will create the role and write the newly created role ARN to the console. Add the role ARN to the `.env` file, as shown in the following listing.

Listing 7.22   Update pipeline environment with role ARN

```
CHAPTER7_DATA_ACCESS_ARN=<your ARN>
```

> **NOTE**   AWS Identity and Access Management (IAM) capabilities are pervasive throughout AWS. AWS IAM defines roles and access permissions across the platform. A full description is outside the scope of this book, but you can find the full AWS IAM documentation here: http://mng.bz/NnAd.

7.7.4   Run training

We're now ready to start training the classifier. The code to do this is in `pipeline/training/train-classifier.js`. This code simply calls Comprehend's `createDocumentClassifier` API, passing in the data access role, classifier name, and a link to the training bucket. This is shown in the next listing.

Listing 7.23   Training the classifier

```
const params = {
  DataAccessRoleArn: process.env.CHAPTER7_DATA_ACCESS_ARN,      ◁─┐  Set training
  DocumentClassifierName: process.env.CHAPTER7_CLASSIFIER_NAME,      parameters.
  InputDataConfig: {
    S3Uri: `s3://${process.env.CHAPTER7_PIPELINE_TRAINING_BUCKET}`
  },
```

```
    LanguageCode: 'en'
}
comp.createDocumentClassifier(params, (err, data) => {          ◁──┐ Start
    ...                                                              training.
```

To start training, `cd` into the directory `pipeline/training` and run

```
$ bash ./train.sh
```

It should be noted at this point that the training process may take a while to complete, usually over an hour, so now might be a good time to take a break! You can check on the status of the training process by running the script `status.sh` in the same directory. This will output a status of TRAINED once the classifier is ready to use.

7.8   *Using the custom classifier*

Now that we have trained our classifier, we can complete the last stage in the pipeline: deploying a classification service to call our newly trained custom classifier. Recall that we have already determined the language of the message, translated to English if required, and filtered to include only negative messages in the processing bucket. Now we need to determine which department these messages are related to by running our newly trained classifier.

To make the classifier available, we need to create an endpoint. Do this by running the script `endpoint.sh` in the `pipeline/training` directory:

```
$ cd pipeline/training
$ bash ./endpoint.sh
```

> **WARNING** Once the endpoint for the classifier is created, you will be charged per hour that it is available, so please ensure that you delete all resources for this chapter once you're done!

Before we deploy our classification service, we need to update the `.env` file to provide the name of our output bucket. Open this in a text editor and edit the line indicated in the next listing, substituting your own unique bucket name.

Listing 7.24   Pipeline processing bucket

```
CHAPTER7_PIPELINE_PROCESSING_BUCKET=<your processing bucket name>
```

The code for out classification service is in the `pipeline/classify` directory. This holds the `serverless.yml` and `handler.js` files for the service. The following listing shows how the classifier is executed from the main handler function in the service.

Listing 7.25   Invoking the custom classifier endpoint

```
    ...
    let params = {                                           ◁──┐ Add the endpoint ARN
        EndpointArn: process.env.CHAPTER7_ENDPOINT_ARN,          to the parameters.
```

```
      Text: message.text
    }
    comp.classifyDocument(params, (err, data) => {          Invoke the classifier
      if (err) { return asnCb(err) }                        through the endpoint.
      let clas = determineClass(data)                 Process
      writeToBucket(clas, message, (err) => {         the results.
        if (err) { return asnCb(err) }                  Write the message
        asnCb()                                          to the output bucket.
      })
    })
    ...
```

While we have trained our own custom classifier, the consumption pattern is similar to the other services that we have encountered previously, so the code should seem familiar. The function `determineClass` that is called in listing 7.25 is shown in the following listing.

Listing 7.26   Interpreting the custom classification results

```
function determineClass (result) {
  let clas = classes.UNCLASSIFIED
  let max = 0
  let ptr

  result.Classes.forEach(cl => {            Find the classification
    if (cl.Score > max) {                    with the highest score.
      max = cl.Score
      ptr = cl
    }
  })
  if (ptr.Score > 0.95) {          Only accept scores
    clas = classes[ptr.Name]        greater that 95%.
  }
  return clas
}
```

The function returns the classification class with the highest score, given that the score is greater than 95%. Otherwise it will return a result of UNCLASSIFIED. It is important to note that like the other services we have encountered, interpretation of the confidence level is domain-specific. In this case, we have opted for a high degree of accuracy (greater than 95%). Unclassified results will need to be processed by a human rather than sent directly to a department.

To deploy the classification service, `cd` into the `pipeline/classify` directory and run

```
$ npm install
$ serverless deploy
```

We have now fully deployed our pipeline! For the final step in this chapter, let's test it end to end.

7.9 *Testing the pipeline end to end*

To test our full pipeline, let's first push some data into it. We can do this by using the test driver as before. `cd` into the directory `pipeline/driver`, and push in some data by running

```
$ node driver.js [DEPT] [POS | NEG]
```

Do this several times, substituting random department names: `auto`, `beauty`, `office`, or `pet`. Also, randomly use both positive and negative values. The messages should flow through the pipeline, and negative messages will end up in the processing bucket under one of five possible paths: auto, beauty, office, pet, or unclassified. We have provided a script to help check the results. `cd` into the `pipeline/driver` directory and run

```
$ node results.js view
```

This will fetch the output results from the bucket and print them to the console. You should see output similar to the following:

```
beauty
I'm not sure where all these glowing reviews are coming from...
NEGATIVE
{
  Positive: 0.0028411017265170813,
  Negative: 0.9969773292541504,
  Neutral: 0.00017945743456948549,
  Mixed: 0.0000021325695342966355
}

office
I bought this all in one HP Officejet for my son and his wife...
NEGATIVE
{
  Positive: 0.4422852396965027,
  Negative: 0.5425800085067749,
  Neutral: 0.015050739049911499,
  Mixed: 0.00008391317533096299
}

unclassified
didnt like it i prob will keep it and later throw it out...
NEGATIVE
{
  Positive: 0.00009981004404835403,
  Negative: 0.9993864297866821,
  Neutral: 0.0005127472686581314,
  Mixed: 9.545062766846968e-7
}
```

Remember that only the negative messages will be in the results bucket; positive values should have been discarded by the sentiment filter. Take some time to review the results. Some messages will be unclassified, meaning that the confidence level of the classification step was below 95%.

A next logical step in the process would be to send alert emails, based on the pipeline output, to the appropriate department. This could easily be done using Amazon's SES (Simple Email Service) service, and we leave this as an exercise for the reader to complete!

As a further exercise, you could write a script to push a larger volume of data into the pipeline and see how the system behaves. You could also try making up your own comments or "tweets" and send them into the pipeline to determine how accurate the system is when presented with different data items.

7.10 *Removing the pipeline*

Once you have finished with the pipeline, it's important to remove it in order to avoid incurring additional costs from AWS. To do this, we have provided some scripts that will remove all of the elements of the pipeline in the directory `chapter7/pipeline`. `cd` into this directory and run

```
$ bash ./remove-endpoint.sh
$ bash ./check-endpoint.sh
```

This will remove the endpoint, which may take a few minutes to complete. You can re-run the `check-endpoint.sh` script; this will show a status of `DELETING` against our endpoint. Once the script no longer lists our endpoint, you can proceed to remove the rest of the system by running

```
$ bash ./remove.sh
```

This will remove the custom classifier and all of the other resources deployed in this section. Be sure to check that all of the resources were indeed removed by the script!

7.11 *Benefits of automation*

Let's take a moment to think through how this type of processing could benefit an organization. As of April 2019, Amazon.com has a product catalog with hundreds of millions of listings. Let's consider a smaller retailer that lists, say, 500,000 items across a number of different departments. Let's assume that customers provide feedback on the following five channels:

- Twitter
- Facebook
- Site reviews
- Email
- Other

Let's also assume that on an average day, 2% of the products will receive some attention on each of these channels. That means that on a daily basis, the company has around 50,000 items of feedback to review and process. On an annual basis, that equates to 18,250,000 individual pieces of feedback.

Given that it would take a human an average of, say, two minutes to process each piece of feedback, an individual could process only 240 of these in a standard eight-hour work day. This means that a team of over 200 people would be needed to manually process all of the feedback items.

Our AI-enabled pipeline can handle this load easily, 24 hours a day, 365 days a year, dramatically reducing costs and drudgery.

Hopefully this chapter has inspired you to investigate further how you can apply AI as a Service to tackle problems like these in your own day-to-day work.

Summary

- There are various architectural patterns for applying AI as a Service to existing systems:
  - Synchronous API
  - Asynchronous API
  - Stream In
  - Fully Connected Streaming
- Key text fields can be extracted from a document using AWS Textract. We demonstrated an example in the specific case of extracting information from a passport scan.
- Using the example of an existing e-commerce/retail platform, we can build an AI-enabled data processing pipeline using Kinesis and Lambda.
- AWS Translate can be used to translate languages on the fly.
- Using product review data from Amazon, it is possible to build a sentiment analysis service.
- A document classifier is built using Comprehend by splitting Amazon review data into a training and test set.
- Combining all of these techniques into a data processing pipeline results in a system that translates, filters, and classifies data. This is an example of how to combine several AI services to achieve a business goal.

WARNING Please ensure that you fully remove all cloud resources deployed in this chapter in order to avoid additional charges!

Part 3

Bringing it all together

In chapter 8 we build a serverless web crawler and examine some of the challenges associated with data collection. In chapter 9 we use AI as a Service to analyze data scraped with our serverless crawler, and examine how to efficiently orchestrate and control our analysis jobs. If you have mastered all of the content so far, then this content will be challenging but hopefully rewarding and enlightening.

Once you have mastered this final part, you will be up to speed with the current state of the art and ready to apply the tools, services, and techniques in your own work. Good luck!

Gathering data at scale for real-world AI

This chapter covers

- Selecting sources of data for AI applications
- Building a serverless web crawler to find sources for large-scale data
- Extracting data from websites using AWS Lambda
- Understanding compliance, legal aspects, and politeness considerations for large-scale data gathering
- Using CloudWatch Events as a bus for event-driven serverless systems
- Performing service orchestration using AWS Step Functions

In chapter 7, we dealt with the application of natural language processing (NLP) techniques to product reviews. We showed how sentiment analysis and classification of text can be achieved with AWS Comprehend using streaming data in a serverless architecture. In this chapter, we are concerned with data gathering.

207

According to some estimates, data scientists spend 50-80% of their time collecting and preparing data.[1][2] Many data scientists and machine learning practitioners will say that finding good quality data and preparing it correctly are the biggest challenges faced when performing analytics and machine learning tasks. It is clear that the value of applying machine learning is only as good as the quality of the data that is fed into the algorithm. Before we jump straight into developing any AI solution, there are a few key questions to be answered concerning the data that will be used:

- What data is required and in what format?
- What sources of data are available?
- How will the data be cleansed?

A good understanding of data gathering concepts is key to a functional machine learning application. Once you have learned to source and adapt data to your application's needs, your chances of producing the desired results are greatly increased!

8.1   Scenario: Finding events and speakers

Let's consider a problem that a lot of software developers have—finding relevant conferences to attend. Imagine that we wanted to build a system to solve this problem. Users will be able to search for conferences on topics of interest, and see who's speaking at the conference, what the location is, and when it takes place. We can also imagine extending this to recommend conferences to users who have searched for or "liked" other events.[3]

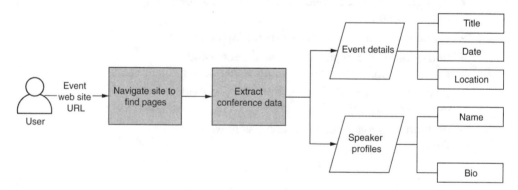

Figure 8.1   Our data gathering application will crawl conference websites and extract event and speaker information.

[1]   Gil Press, "Cleaning Big Data: Most Time-Consuming, Least Enjoyable Data Science Task, Survey Says," Forbes, March 23, 2016, https://www.forbes.com/sites/gilpress/2016/03/23/data-preparation-most-time-consuming-least-enjoyable-data-science-task-survey-says.

[2]   Steve Lohr, "For Big-Data Scientists, 'Janitor Work' Is Key Hurdle to Insights," New York Times, August 17, 2014, https://www.nytimes.com/2014/08/18/technology/for-big-data-scientists-hurdle-to-insights-is-janitor-work.html.

[3]   This is an interesting challenge for the reader. The AWS Personalize service (available in Developer Preview at the time of writing) is a managed machine learning recommendation service that should be suitable for this application.

The first challenge in building such a system is in collecting and cataloging the data on conference events. There is no existing, complete, structured source of such data. We can find websites for relevant events using an internet search engine, but then comes the problem of finding and extracting the event location, dates, and speaker and topic information. This is a perfect opportunity to apply web crawling and scraping! Let's summarize our requirements with figure 8.1.

8.1.1 Identifying data required

The first step in identifying your data is to start with the problem you are solving. If you have a clear picture of what you are going to achieve, work back from there, and determine what data is required and what attributes it should have. The kind of data required is significantly impacted by two factors:

- Are *training and validation* necessary?
- If so, will your data have to be labelled?

Throughout this book, we have been using managed AI services. A major advantage of this approach is that it often eliminates the need for training. Services that do not require you to train with your own data come with pre-trained models that are ready for use with your test data set. In other cases, you might need a training step.

TRAINING, VALIDATION, AND TEST DATA In the development of machine learning models, a data set is typically divided into three sets, as shown in figure 8.3.

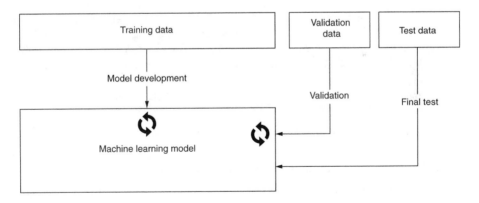

Figure 8.2 Training, validation, and test data during model development and test

A larger proportion of the data, the training set, is used to train the algorithm. The validation set (or development set) is used to select the algorithm and measure its performance. Finally, the test set is an independent set used to check how well the algorithm generalizes with data not used in training.

You might remember the topic of supervised and unsupervised learning from chapter 1. It is important to understand which approach you are using because supervised learning will require data to be annotated with labels.

In chapter 1, we presented a table of managed AWS AI services. This table is extended in appendix A, showing the data requirements and training support for each service. You can use this as a reference in planning your AI-enabled application.

If you are not using managed AI services, but instead selecting an algorithm and training a custom model, the effort required for gathering and preparing data is large. There are many considerations to getting data that will produce accurate results that work well within the domain of test data.

Selecting representative data

When selecting data to train a machine learning model, it is critical to ensure that the data is representative of data in the wild. Problems occur when your data makes assumptions that result in a prejudiced outcome. Selection of good training data is important to reduce *overfitting*. Overfitting occurs when a model is too specific to a training data set and is not able to generalize.

A team of researches at the University of Washington illustrated the issue of *selection bias* by training a machine learning model to detect whether a picture contained a wolf or a husky dog. By deliberately choosing wolf pictures with snow in the background and husky dog pictures with grass in the background, they trained an algorithm that was actually only effective at detecting grass vs. snow. When they presented the result to a set of test subjects, people still reported that they trusted the algorithm's ability to detect huskies and wolves![a]

We also know that training with data from systems that are the output of human biases can result in the algorithms inheriting existing harmful societal biases. This was infamously shown when Microsoft's "Tay" Twitter bot was shut down after it started generating racist, hateful tweets.[b]

[a] Ribeiro, Singh and Guestrin, "'Why Should I Trust You?' Explaining the Predictions of Any Classifier," University of Washington, August 9, 2016, https://arxiv.org/pdf/1602.04938.pdf.
[b] Ashley Rodriguez, "Microsoft's AI millennial chatbot became a racist jerk after less than a day on Twitter," Quarts, March 24, 2016, http://mng.bz/BED2.

A few rules can be applied to choosing good data:

- Data should have representations of all scenarios that may be encountered "in the wild" (like huskies on backgrounds other than snow!).
- For classification, you should have sufficient, and preferably roughly equal, representations of all classes.
- For labelling, consider whether the labels can be assigned without ambiguity, or how to deal with it if not. You might have cases where the label to assign is not clear ("Is that a husky or a dog?").

- Regularly inspect a reasonably-sized random selection of your data manually to verify that there is nothing unexpected occurring. It is worth taking some time for this, because bad data will never produce good results!

In this book, we are largely concerned with using pre-trained, managed services. For a more in-depth understanding of machine learning training optimization, data wrangling, and feature engineering, we recommend *Real-World Machine Learning* by Brink, Richards, and Fetherolf from Manning Publications, 2017.

8.1.2 Sources of data

One of the key points discussed in chapter 1 was how recent successes in the field of AI have been made possible by the availability of vast volumes of data. The internet itself is a public source of data, and by using the internet in our daily lives, we are constantly contributing to the growing volumes of incredibly detailed data. Big technology companies (Google, Facebook, Amazon) have had great success in AI. A large factor in this is their access to data and expertise in data gathering.[4] For everyone else, there are many ways of sourcing data for AI applications. Appendix C contains a list of public data sets and other data sources that may be a great fit for your application.

8.1.3 Preparing data for training

Once you have gathered data for training, there is still plenty of work to be done:

- Deal with missing data. You might need to remove records, interpolate or extrapolate data, or use some other means of avoiding problems with missing fields. In other cases, it is better to leave missing fields empty, as this can be an important input into the algorithm. For more on this topic, take a look at chapter 1, "Exploring Data," of *Exploring Data Science* by John Mount and Nina Zumel.[5]
- Get the data in the right format. This could mean applying a consistent format for date or currency values. In image recognition, it might mean cropping, resizing, and changing color formats. Many pre-trained networks are trained on 224x224 RGB data, so if you want to analyse very high-resolution data (where too much information will be lost if images are resized), then these networks may not be suitable without modification.

We have briefly covered some of the data sources available to machine learning engineers. It should be clear that the internet has been a major source of large-scale data volumes. Much internet data is not available via an API or in structured files, but is published on websites intended to be consumed with a web browser. Gathering data from this valuable trove requires crawling, scraping, and extraction. This is the topic we will cover next.

---

[4] Tom Simonite, "AI and 'Enormous Data' Could Make Tech Giants Harder to Topple," Wired, 13 July 2017, http://mng.bz/dwPw.

[5] *Exploring Data Science,* John Mount and Nina Zumel, Manning Publications, 2016, https://www.manning.com/books/exploring-data-science.

8.2   Gathering data from the web

The remainder of this chapter will look in more detail at gathering data from web-sites. Though some data may be available in pre-packaged, structured formats, accessi-ble as either flat files or through an API, this is not the case with web pages.

Web pages are an unstructured source of information such as product data, news articles, and financial data. Finding the right web pages, retrieving them, and extract-ing relevant information are non-trivial. The processes required to do this are known as *web crawling* and *web scraping*:

- *Web crawling* is the process of fetching web content and navigating to linked pages according to a specific strategy.
- *Web scraping* follows the crawling process to extract specific data from content that has been fetched.

Figure 8.4 shows how the two processes combine to produce meaningful, structured data.

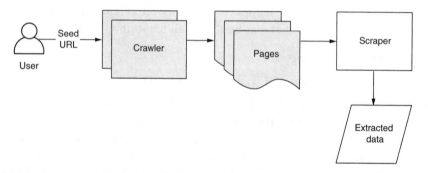

Figure 8.3   Web page crawling and scraping process overview. In this chapter, we are concerned with the *crawler* part of this picture and the pages it produces as output.

Recall our conference speaker information-gathering scenario from the start of the chapter. Our first step in creating a solution for this scenario will be to build a server-less web crawling system.

8.3   Introduction to web crawling

The crawler for our scenario will be a *generic* crawler. Generic crawlers can crawl any site with an unknown structure. Site-specific crawlers are usually created for large sites, with specific selectors for findings links and content. An example of a site-specific crawler could be one written to crawl particular products from amazon.com, or auctions from ebay.com.

Examples of well-known crawlers include

- Search engines such as Google, Bing, Yandex, or Baidu
- GDELT Project (https://www.gdeltproject.org), an open database of human society and global events

- OpenCorporates (https://opencorporates.com), the largest open database of companies in the world
- Internet Archive (https://archive.org), a digital library of internet sites and other cultural artifacts in digital form
- CommonCrawl (https://commoncrawl.org/), an open repository of web crawl data

One challenge for web crawling is the sheer number of web pages to visit and analyze. When we are performing the crawling task, we may need arbitrarily large compute resources. Once the crawling process is complete, our compute resource requirement drops. This scalable, bursty compute requirement is an ideal fit for on-demand, cloud computing, and Serverless!

8.3.1 Typical web crawler process

To understand how a web crawler might work, consider how a web browser allows a user to navigate a web page manually:

1 The user enters a web page URL into a web browser.
2 The browser fetches the page's first HTML file.
3 The HTML file is parsed by the browser to find other required content such as CSS, JavaScript, and images.
4 Links are rendered. When the user clicks on a link, the process is repeated for a new URL.

The following listing shows the HTML source for a very simple example web page.

Listing 8.1 Example web page HTML source

```
<!DOCTYPE html>
<html>
  <body>
    <a href="https://google.com">Google</a>          External link
    <a href="https://example.com/about">About</a>    Absolute internal link
    <a href="/about">About</a>                       Relative internal link

    <img src="/logo.png" alt="company logo"/>        Image resource

    <p>I am a text paragraph</p>                     Paragraph text

    <script src="/script.js"></script>               JavaScript source
  </body>
</html>
```

We have shown the structure of a very basic page. In reality, a single HTML page can contain hundreds of hyperlinks, both internal and external. The set of pages required to be crawled for a given application is known as the *crawl space*. Let's talk about the architecture of a typical web crawler and how it is structured to deal with various sizes of crawl space.

8.3.2   *Web crawler architecture*

A typical web crawler architecture is illustrated in figure 8.4. Let's get an understanding of each component of the architecture and how it relates to our conference website scenario before describing how this might be realized with a serverless approach.

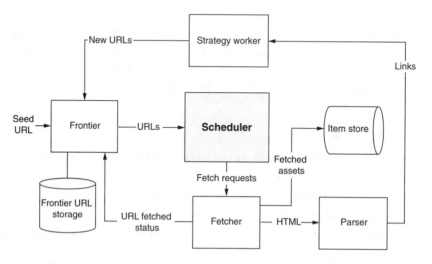

Figure 8.4   Components of a web crawler. There are distinct responsibilities for each component that can guide us in our software architecture.

- The *frontier* maintains a database of URLs to be crawled. This is initially populated with the conference websites. From there, URLs of individual pages on the site are added here.
- The *fetcher* takes a URL and retrieves the corresponding document.
- The *parser* takes the fetched document, parses it, and extracts required information from it. We will not be looking for specific speaker details or anything conference-specific at this point.
- The *strategy worker or generator* is one of the most crucial components of a web crawler, since it determines the *crawl space*. URLs generated by the strategy worker are fed back into the frontier. The strategy worker decides
  - Which links should be followed
  - The priority of links to be crawled
  - The crawl depth
  - When to revisit/recrawl pages if required
- The *item store* is where the extracted documents or data are stored.
- The *scheduler* takes a set of URLs, initially the seed URLs, and schedules the *fetcher* to download resources. The scheduler is responsible for ensuring that the crawler behaves politely toward web servers, that no duplicate URLs are fetched, and that URLs are normalized.

Is crawling really amenable to serverless architecture?

If at this point you're wondering whether serverless architecture really is a valid choice for the implementation of a web crawler, you have a good point! Web crawlers, operating at scale, require fast, efficient storage; caching; and plenty of compute power for multiple, resource-intensive page rendering processes. Serverless applications, on the other hand, are typically characterized by short-term, event-driven computation and the absence of fast, local disk storage.

So, is the system in this chapter worthy of production use, or are we embarking on a wild experiment to see how far we can push our cloud-native ideology?! There are definite advantages to using a more traditional "farm" of servers such as Amazon Elastic Compute Cloud (EC2) instances. If your crawling needs require a constantly-running workload at large volumes, you might be better off choosing a traditional approach.

We must remember the hidden cost of maintaining and running this infrastructure, the operating system, and any underlying frameworks. Also, our crawling scenario is for on-demand extraction of data regarding specific conference websites. This "bursty" behavior is suitable to an elastic, utility computing paradigm. A serverless implementation may not be optimal from a caching perspective, but for our scenario, that does not have a major impact. We are more than happy with this approach, given that we are paying $0 while the system is not running and we don't have to worry about operating system patches, maintenance, or container orchestration and service discovery.

For our web crawler, we are dealing with conferences. Since these constitute a minority of all web pages, there is no need to crawl the entire web for such sites. Instead, we will provide the crawler with a "seed" URL.

On the conference sites themselves, we will crawl local hyperlinks. We will not follow hyperlinks to external domains. Our goal is to find the pages that contain the required data, such as speaker information and dates. We are not interested in crawling the entire conference site, and for this reason we will also use a *depth limit* to stop crawling after reaching a given depth in the link graph. The crawl depth is the number of links that have been followed from the seed URL. A depth limit stops the process from going beyond a specified depth.

BASIC CRAWLERS VERSUS RENDERING CRAWLERS

Basic crawlers will fetch only HTML pages and will not evaluate JavaScript. This leads to a much simpler and faster crawl process. However, this may result in us excluding valuable data.

It is now very common to have web pages that are rendered dynamically in the browser by JavaScript. Single-page applications (SPAs) using frameworks like React or Vue.js are examples of this. Some sites use server-side rendering with these frameworks, and others perform pre-rendering to return fully-rendered HTML to search engine crawlers as a search engine optimization (SEO) technique. We cannot rely on these being universally employed. For these reasons, we are opting to employ full rendering of web pages, including JavaScript evaluation.

There are a number of options for rendering web pages when there is no user or screen available:

- Splash (https://scrapinghub.com/splash), a browser designed for web scraping applications.
- Headless Chrome (http://mng.bz/r2By) with the Puppeteer API. This simply runs the popular Chrome browser and allows us to control it programatically.
- Headless Firefox (http://mng.bz/V8qG) with Selenium (https://www.seleniumhq.org). This option is a Firefox-based alternative to Puppeteer.

For our solution, we are going to use headless Chrome. We have chosen this option because there are readily available Serverless Framework plugins for use with AWS Lambda.

Legal and compliance considerations for web crawling

The legality of web crawling can be a contentious area. On one hand, the site owner is making content publicly available. On the other hand, heavy-handed crawling can have an adverse impact on the site's availability and server load. Needless to say, the following does not represent legal advice. Here are just a few best practices that are regarded as polite behavior:

- Identify your crawler using the `User-Agent` string. Provide a way for site owners to contact you, e.g. `AIaaSBookCrawler/1.0; +https://aiasaservicebook.com)`.
- Respect a site's `robots.txt`. This file allows site owners to say what pages you may and may not crawl.[a]
- Use a site's API, if available, instead of web scraping.
- Limit the number of requests per second per domain.
- Cease crawling a site immediately if requested by the site owner.
- Only crawl publicly accessible content. Never use login credentials.
- Use caching to reduce load on the target server. Don't refetch the same page repeatedly in a short amount of time.
- Material gathered from websites generally falls under copyright and intellectual property legislation. Make sure that you respect this.

In particular, we need to make sure that we limit the concurrency per domain/IP address, or that we choose a reasonable delay between requests. These requirements will be a consideration in our serverless crawler architecture.

At the time of writing, the AWS Acceptable Use Policy prevents "Monitoring or crawling of a System that impairs or disrupts the System being monitored or crawled" (https://aws.amazon.com/aup/).

Note also that some websites implement mechanisms to prevent web scraping. This can be done by detecting IP address or user agent. Solutions like CloudFlare (https://www.cloudflare.com/products/bot-management/) or Google reCaptcha (https://developers.google.com/recaptcha/docs/invisible) use more elaborate approaches.

---

[a] For more about robots.txt, see http://www.robotstxt.org.

8.3.3 Serverless web crawler architecture

Let's take a first look at how we will map our system to the canonical architecture developed in chapter 1. Figure 8.5 provides us with a breakdown of the system's layers and how services collaborate to deliver the solution.

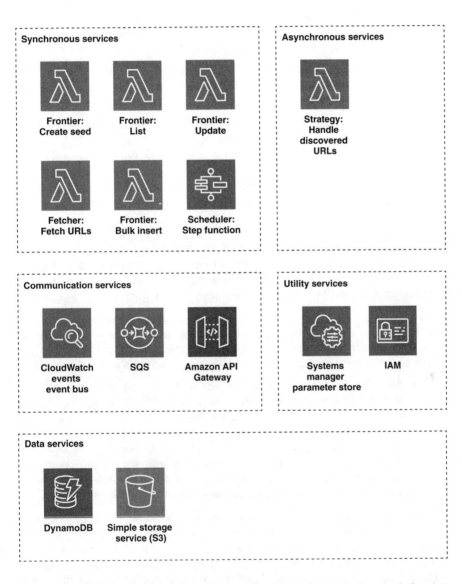

Figure 8.5 Serverless web crawler system architecture. The system is composed of custom services implemented using AWS Lambda and AWS Step Functions. SQS and the CloudWatch Events service are used for asynchronous communication. Internal API Gateways are used for synchronous communication. S3 and DynamoDB are used for data storage.

The system architecture shows the layers of the system across all services. Note that, in this system, we have no front-end web application:

- Synchronous tasks in the frontier and fetch services are implemented using AWS Lambda. For the first time, we introduce AWS Step Functions to implement the scheduler. It will be responsible for orchestrating the fetcher based on data in the frontier.
- The strategy service is asynchronous and reacts to events on the event bus indicating that new URLs have been discovered.
- Synchronous communication between internal services in our system is handled with API Gateway. We have chosen CloudWatch Events and SQS for asynchronous communication.
- Shared parameters are published to Systems Manager Parameter Store. IAM is used to manage privileges between services.
- DynamoDB is used for frontier URL storage. An S3 bucket is used as our item store.

TIP   If you want to learn more about web scraping, look at chapter 6, "Intelligent Web Crawling," of *Collective Intelligence in Action* by Satnam Alag.[6]

Build or buy? Evaluating third-party managed services

There's a certain irony in writing a book that espouses the virtues of managed services, emphasizes the importance of focusing on your core business logic, and also dedicates a chapter to building a web crawler from scratch.

Our crawler is quite simple and also domain-specific. This is some justification for writing our own implementation. However, we know from experience that simple systems grow in complexity over time. Therefore, implementing your own *anything* should be your last resort. Here are two rules of thumb for modern application development:

- Minimize the amount of code you write! The majority of code you write should concern unique business logic. Where possible, avoid writing code for any part of your system that is mundane and implemented in many other software systems, frequently called *undifferentiated heavy lifting*.[a]
- Use cloud managed services. While you can follow *rule 1* by using libraries, frameworks, and components, these can have their own maintenance burden, and you still have to maintain the infrastructure they run on. Integrating with cloud managed services relieves you of this significant burden.

Such services can be found outside the realm of your chosen cloud provider. Even if Amazon Web Services has no off-the-shelf web crawling and scraping services, look beyond AWS and evaluate the third-party offerings. This is a worthwhile exercise for any service you are thinking of building. For example, if you want to implement a search feature in your application, you might evaluate a fully-managed Elasticsearch

---

[6]   *Collective Intelligence in Action*, Satnam Alag, Manning Publications, 2019, http://mng.bz/xrJX.

service such as Elastic (https://www.elastic.co) or a managed search and discovery API like Algolia (https://www.algolia.com/).

If you are interested in evaluating third-party web scraping services, take a look at the following:

- Grepsr (https://www.grepsr.com)
- Import.io (https://www.import.io)
- ScrapingHub ScrapyCloud (https://scrapinghub.com/scrapy-cloud)

---

a The origin of the term *undifferentiated heavy lifting* is unclear. However, Jeff Bezos, CEO of Amazon, mentioned it in a speech at Web 2.0 Summit in 2006. He said, "There is a huge amount of undifferentiated heavy lifting, which we call 'muck,' in between an item and a successful product. We believe creating new products today is 70% muck and 30% new idea execution. We want to reverse that ratio." (Source: Dave Kellogg, Web 2.0 Summit: Jeff Bezos, November 8, 2006, http://mng.bz/Az2x.

8.4 Implementing an item store

We will start our walkthrough of the crawler implementation with the simplest service of all, the item store. As part of our conference-site crawling process, the item store will store a copy of each page crawled on each conference website. First, grab the code so you can explore in more detail.

8.4.1 Getting the code

The code for the item store is in the directory `chapter8-9/item-store`. Similar to our previous examples, this directory contains a `serverless.yml` file declaring our APIs, functions, and other resources. We will explain the contents as we go, before deploying and testing the item store.

8.4.2 The item store bucket

Taking a look at `serverless.yml` in the item store, we see an S3 Bucket and not much else! We are implementing the simplest possible store.

Other services may write directly to our bucket or list objects and fetch objects using the AWS SDK S3 API. All that is required is that they have the correct permissions in their IAM roles and policies.

8.4.3 Deploying the item store

Deploying the item store is straightforward. Given that we are deploying an S3 bucket, we will define its globally-unique name in a `.env` file within the `chapter8-9` directory:

```
ITEM_STORE_BUCKET=<your bucket name>
```

No further configuration is required. The default region is `eu-west-1`. If you want to specify a different region, provide it using the `--region` argument to the `serverless deploy` command:

```
npm install
serverless deploy
```

That's it! The item store is deployed and ready. Let's move on to the next service in our crawler application.

8.5   *Creating a frontier to store and manage URLs*

Our frontier will store all seed URLs for conference sites and newly-discovered URLs found during the crawl process. We are using DynamoDB for storage. Our goal here is to leverage DynamoDB's API for inserting and querying, with a minimal layer of abstraction on top.

8.5.1   *Getting the code*

The code for the frontier service is in the directory `chapter8-9/frontier-service`. This directory contains a `serverless.yml` file declaring our APIs, functions, and other resources. We will explain the contents as we go, before deploying and testing the frontier service.

8.5.2   *The frontier URL database*

The frontier URL database stores all URLs that are intended to be fetched, have been fetched, or failed to have been fetched. The service is required to have an interface supporting the following actions:

- Insert a *seed URL*.
- Update the status of a URL to `PENDING`, `FETCHED`, or `FAILED`.
- Insert a batch of newly-discovered URLs (links) that have been deemed eligible for fetching.
- Get a set of URLs for a given seed URL, filtered by a status parameter and a maximum record limit.

The data model for our frontier database is illustrated by the example in table 8.1.

Table 8.1   Frontier URL database example

Seed	URL	Status	Depth
`http://microxchg.io`	`http://microxchg.io`	FETCHED	0
`http://microxchg.io`	`http://microxchg.io/2019/index.html`	FETCHED	1
`http://microxchg.io`	`http://microxchg.io/2019/all-speakers.html`	PENDING	2
`https://www.predictconference.com`	`https://www.predictconference.com`	PENDING	0

Our "primary key" in this instance is a combination of the seed and the URL. The *seed* attribute is the *partition key* or *hash*, whereas the *url* attribute is the *sort key* or *range*. This ensures we don't insert duplicates into the database.

In addition to our table key, we will define a *secondary index*. This allows us to quickly search based on seed URL and status.

We can see from the sample data in table 8.1 that the full URL is included in the url field, not just the relative path. This allows us to support external URLs linked from the seed in the future, and saves us the inconvenience of having to reconstruct URLs when we go to fetch the content.

The DynamoDB table resource definition for the *frontier* table can be found in the service's serverless.yml file, and is shown in the following listing.

Listing 8.2 Frontier DynamoDB table definition

```
frontierTable:
    Type: AWS::DynamoDB::Table                          The table name is
    Properties:                                         defined as frontier.
      TableName: ${self:provider.environment.FRONTIER_TABLE}     ◄─┘
      AttributeDefinitions:
       - AttributeName: seed
         AttributeType: S
       - AttributeName: url
         AttributeType: S
       - AttributeName: status
         AttributeType: S           The table's key is comprised
      KeySchema:                ◄─┘ of the seed and url attributes.
        - AttributeName: seed
          KeyType: HASH
        - AttributeName: url            A secondary index, frontierStatus, is
          KeyType: RANGE               defined to allow queries to be run
      LocalSecondaryIndexes:           using the seed and status attributes.
        - IndexName: ${self:provider.environment.FRONTIER_TABLE}Status  ◄─
          KeySchema:
            - AttributeName: seed
              KeyType: HASH
            - AttributeName: status    In this case, we choose provisioned
              KeyType: RANGE           throughput with five read and write
          Projection:                  capacity units. Alternatively, we could
            ProjectionType: ALL        specify BillingMode: PAY_PER_REQUEST
      ProvisionedThroughput:        ◄─ to deal with unpredictable loads.
        ReadCapacityUnits: 5
        WriteCapacityUnits: 5
```

Serverless databases

We have already presented a few examples of working with DynamoDB. DynamoDB is a NoSQL database, suitable for unstructured document storage. It is possible, and sometimes very desirable, to model relational data in DynamoDB.[ab] In general, DynamoDB is more suitable when you have a clear picture of how the data will be accessed, and can design keys and indices to accommodate the access patterns. Relational databases are more suitable when you are storing structured data, but

(continued)

want to support arbitrary access patterns in the future. This is what Structured Query Language (SQL), the interface supported by an RDBMS, is very good at.

Relational databases are optimized for a lower number of long-running connections from servers. As a result, a large number of short-lived connections from Lambda functions can result in poor performance. As an alternative to the *serverful* RDBMS, Amazon Aurora Serverless is a serverless relational database solution that avoids the need to provision instances. It supports auto-scaling and on-demand access, allowing you to pay per second of usage. It is also possible to run queries against Aurora Serverless with the Data API using the AWS SDK in a Lambda function (http://mng.bz/ZrZA). This solution avoids the problem of creating short-lived database connections.

[a] Amazon has an example of relational model in DynamoDB on their blog: http://mng.bz/RMGv.
[b] Many advanced DynamoDB topics, including relational modeling, are covered in Rick Houlihan's AWS re:Invent 2018 talk, "Amazon DynamoDB Deep Dive: Advanced Design Patterns for DynamoDB (DAT401)," https://www.youtube.com/watch?v=HaEPXoXVf2k.

8.5.3   Creating the frontier API

We have described the DynamoDB table that is central to the frontier service. We need a way to get URLs for conference sites into the system. Let's now take a look at the API Gateway and Lambda functions that allow external services to interact with the frontier in order to achieve this.

The APIs supported by the frontier service are shown in table 8.2.

Table 8.2   Frontier service APIs

Path	Method	Lambda Function	Description
`frontier-url/{seed}/{url}`	POST	`create`	Adds a URL for a seed
`frontier-url/{seed}`	POST	`create`	Adds a new seed
`frontier-url/{seed}/{url}`	PATCH	`update`	Updates the status of a URL
`frontier-url`	PUT	`bulkInsert`	Creates a batch of URLs
`frontier-url/{seed}`	GET	`list`	Lists URLs for a seed by status, up to a specified maximum number of records

The definition for each API can be found in the `serverless.yml` configuration for `frontier-service`. This configuration also defines a Systems Manager Parameter Store variable for the service's API. We are not using DNS for the API, so it cannot be discovered by other services using a known name. Instead, the API Gateway's generated URL is registered in Parameter Store to be found by services with the correct IAM permissions.

For simplicity, all of our Lambda code is implemented in `handler.js`. It includes the logic to create and execute the DynamoDB SDK calls. If you take a look at this code, you'll recognize much of it as being similar to our handlers from chapters 4 and 5. One significant difference is that we have introduced a library called *Middy* to alleviate much of the boilerplate. Middy is a middleware library that allows you to intercept calls to a Lambda before and after they are invoked, in order to perform common actions (https://middy.js.org). A middleware is simply a set of functions that hook into the lifecycle of your event handler. You can use any of Middy's built-in middlewares or any third-party middleware, or write your own.

For our frontier handlers, we set up the Middy middleware as shown in the next listing.

Listing 8.3 Frontier handler middleware initialization

```
const middy = require('middy')
...

const { cors, jsonBodyParser, validator, httpEventNormalizer,
    httpErrorHandler } = require('middy/middlewares')

const loggerMiddleware = require('lambda-logger-middleware')
const { autoProxyResponse } = require('middy-autoproxyresponse')
...

function middyExport(exports) {
    Object.keys(exports).forEach(key => {
        module.exports[key] = middy(exports[key])
            .use(loggerMiddleware({ logger: log }))
            .use(httpEventNormalizer())
            .use(jsonBodyParser())
            .use(validator({ inputSchema: exports[key].schema }))
            .use(cors())
            .use(autoProxyResponse())
            .use(httpErrorHandler())
    })
}

middyExport({
    bulkInsert,
    create,
    list,
    update
})
```

Middy wraps the plain Lambda handler.

lambda-logger-middleware logs requests and responses in a development environment.[7] We use it with the Pino logger, introduced in chapter 6.

cors automatically adds CORS headers to the response.

jsonBodyParser automatically parses the body and provides an object.

validator validates the input body and parameters against a JSON schema we define.

middy-autoproxy response converts simple JSON object responses to Lambda Proxy HTTP responses.[8]

httpEventNormalizer adds default empty objects for queryStringParameters and pathParameters.

httpErrorHandler handles errors that contain the properties statusCode and message, creating a matching HTTP response.

---

[7] https://github.com/eoinsha/lambda-logger-middleware.
[8] https://www.npmjs.com/package/middy-autoproxyresponse.

This middleware configuration can easily be replicated across all our services to avoid common, repetitive Lambda boilerplate.

8.5.4 *Deploying and testing the frontier*

The frontier service is configured with the `serverless-offline` and `serverless-dynamodb-local` plugins, as outlined in chapter 6. As a result, we can run the API and Lambda functions with a DynamoDB environment locally. To get this up and running, we must install the DynamoDB database:

```
npm install
serverless dynamodb install
npm start
```

The `npm start` command kicks off the script to run our offline frontier service. By default, the API runs on `localhost` port 4000. You can test the API from the command line using cURL:

```
# Create a new seed URL
curl -X POST http://localhost:4000/frontier-url/dummy-seed

# List all pending URLs for a given seed
curl http://localhost:4000/frontier-url/dummy-seed?status=PENDING
```

Once you are satisfied that everything is working as expected locally, deploy the frontier to your AWS account:

```
sls deploy
```

You can use the AWS command line or the Management Console to inspect the DynamoDB table and index that have been created. Then move on to the service where all the real work happens—the fetcher!

8.6 Building the fetcher to retrieve and parse web pages

Now that we have a frontier service that can respond to requests for batches of URLs to be fetched, we are ready to implement our fetcher. The code for this service is in the `chapter8-9/fetch-service` directory. Figure 8.6 shows the physical architecture of the fetcher implementation and the order of steps it performs as it retrieves conference website pages.

This service accepts *fetch* requests for a batch of URLs. The page retrieval, rendering, and parsing steps are executed for each URL in series.

> **NOTE** We haven't defined any Lambda triggers for the fetch handler. Rather than using an API Gateway or an asynchronous event, we are going to allow this handler to be invoked directly using the AWS Lambda SDK. This is a special case because our fetcher implementation results in a long-running Lambda, fetching multiple pages. An API Gateway would time out in 30 seconds maximum. An event-based trigger is unsuitable, as we want to have synchronous invocation from the scheduler.

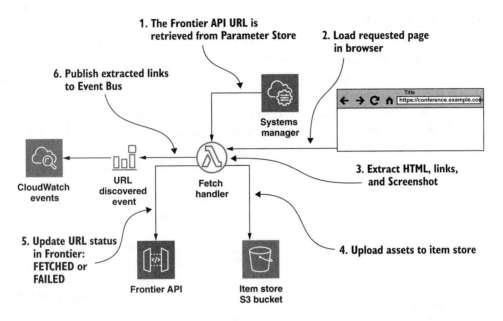

Figure 8.6 The fetcher implementation integrates with the parameter store, the frontier API, an embedded headless web browser, the item store, and the event bus.

8.6.1 Configuring and controlling a headless browser

The configuration of the service (`serverless.yml`) includes a new plugin, `serverless-plugin-chrome` (https://github.com/adieuadieu/serverless-chrome), as shown in the following listing.

Listing 8.4 The fetch service `serverless.yml` loads and configures the Chrome plugin

```
service: fetch-service

plugins:
...
  - serverless-plugin-chrome                          The plugin is specified in the serverless.yml
...                                                    plugins section. It results in the browser
custom:                                                being opened before the handler is invoked.
  chrome:
    flags:                                            Browser command-line arguments are
      - --window-size=1280,1696                       provided. To create a useful screenshot, we
      - --hide-scrollbars                             provide a resolution and hide any scrollbars.
...
```

This plugin automatically installs the Google Chrome web browser in *headless* mode (i.e., with no user interface) when the Lambda function is loaded. We can then control the browser programatically using the `chrome-remote-interface` module (https://github.com/cyrus-and/chrome-remote-interface).

8.6.2 Capturing page output

Our primary goal is to gather the HTML and links. The links will be processed by the strategy worker to determine whether or not they should be fetched. We capture a screenshot of the page so that we have the option to develop a front-end application with a better visualization of the fetched content.

In figure 8.5 we showed a *parser* component in the crawler architecture. In our implementation, the parser is implemented as part of the fetcher. This is both a simplification and an optimization. In our fetcher, we already incurred the overhead of loading a web browser and having it parse and render the page. It is a very simple step to use the browser's DOM API to query the page and extract links.

All of the browser interaction and extraction code is encapsulated in a Node.js module, browser.js. An extract is shown in the following listing.

Listing 8.5 Browser module load function

```
return initBrowser().then(page =>                                    ← Load the correct URL and wait
    page.goto(url, { waitUntil: 'domcontentloaded' }).then(() =>        for the document to be loaded.
        Promise.all([
            page.evaluate(`
JSON.stringify(Object.values([...document.querySelectorAll("a")]       ← Query the page's Document
    .filter(a => a.href.startsWith('http')))                              Object Model (DOM) to
    .map(a => ({ text: a.text.trim(), href: a.href }))                    extract links using JavaScript.
    .reduce(function(acc, link) {
        const href = link.href.replace(/#.*$/, '')
        if (!acc[href]) {
            acc[href] = link
        }
        return acc
    }, {})))
`),
        page.evaluate('document.documentElement.outerHTML'),   ← Capture the page's
        page.evaluate(`                                           generated HTML.
function documentText(document) {                        ← Grab the text from the page and
    if (!document || !document.body) {                      any '<iframe>'s within.
        return ''
    }
    return document.body.innerText + '\\n' +
        [...document.querySelectorAll('iframe')].map(iframe => documentText(ifram
        e.contentDocument)).join('\\n')
}
documentText(document)
`),
        page.screenshot()                                   ← Create a screenshot
    ]).then(([linksJson, html, text, screenshotData]) => ({    image of the page.
        links: JSON.parse(linksJson).reduce(
            (acc, val) =>
                acc.find(entry => entry.href === val.href) ? acc : [...acc, val],
            []
```

```
      ),
      html,
      text,
      screenshotData
    }))
  )
 )
}
```

When the `browser` module's `load` function is invoked with a URL, it performs the following actions.

8.6.3   *Fetching multiple pages*

The fetch service's Lambda handler accepts multiple URLs. The idea is to allow our Lambda function to load and process as many pages as feasible. We optimize these invocations so that all URLs sent to a `fetch` invocation are from the same seed URL. This increases the likelihood that they have similar content and can benefit from caching performed in the browser. URLs are fetched in sequence by our Lambda function. This behavior could easily be altered, adding support for parallel fetchers to optimize the process even further.

All links found on a page are published to our system's event bus. This allows any other service subscribing to these events to react asynchronously. For our event bus, we are using CloudWatch Events. The fetch service publishes discovered links in batches of up to 10 (the CloudWatch limit), shown in the next listing.

Listing 8.6   Generating CloudWatch events for discovered URLs

```
const cwEvents = new AWS.CloudWatchEvents({...})
...
function dispatchUrlDiscoveredEvents(item, links) {       We can only send 10 events at a
  if (links.length > 0) {                                 time using the CloudWatch
    if (links.length > 10) {                              Events API, so we extract 10 and
      return dispatchUrlDiscoveredEvents(item, links.splice(0, 10))   then process the rest recursively.
        then(() => dispatchUrlDiscoveredEvents(item, links))
    }

    const eventEntries = links.map(link => ({             The Detail property is the
      Detail: JSON.stringify({ item, link }),             JSON payload of the event.
      Source: 'fetch-service',
      DetailType: 'url.discovered'        The event type is used to match events on
    }))                                   the receiving event in a CloudWatch rule.

    return cwEvents.putEvents({ Entries: eventEntries })
      promise().then(() => {})                                    We identify
  }                                                               the origin of
  return Promise.resolve()             The event batch is sent     the event.
}                                      using the CloudWatch
                                       Events API in the AWS SDK.
```

CloudWatch Events as an event bus

In chapter 2, we described messaging technology and the distinction between queue systems and pub/sub systems. For our "URL Discovered" messages, we would like a pub/sub model. This allows multiple subscribers to respond to such events, and does not make any assumptions about what they do. The approach aids us in our mission to reduce coupling between services.

In AWS, we have a few pub/sub options:

- Simple Notification Service (SNS)
- Kinesis Streams, used in chapter 7
- Managed Streaming for Kafka (MSK) for users already using Kafka
- DynamoDB Streams, a system that publishes changes to DynamoDB data, built on top of Kinesis Streams
- CloudWatch Events, a simple service requiring almost no setup

CloudWatch Events has the advantage of requiring little setup. We don't need to declare any topic or configure shards. We can just send events using the AWS SDK. Any service wishing to react to these events needs to create a CloudWatch rule to match incoming events and trigger the target. Examples of possible targets include SQS, Kinesis, and of course, Lambda.

For each successful page fetch, the Frontier URL Update API is invoked to mark the URL as FETCHED. Any failed page loads result in the URL being marked as FAILED.

8.6.4   *Deploying and testing the fetcher*

To deploy the fetcher to AWS, test locally. First, we install module dependencies:

```
npm install
```

Next, we use a serverless local invocation. Our local invocation will attempt to copy content to our item store S3 bucket. It will also publish events to CloudWatch events relating to links discovered in the page that is fetched. As a result, ensure your AWS credentials are configured either using the AWS_ environment variables or using an AWS profile. Run the invoke local command, passing the test event provided with the Fetch service code:

```
source ../.env
serverless invoke local -f fetch --path test-events/load-request.json
```

You should see Google Chrome run and load a web page (https://fourtheorem.com). On some platforms, the invocation may not exit even after it has completed, and may have to be killed manually. When the invocation is complete, you can navigate to the S3 bucket for the item store in the AWS Management Console. There you will find a single folder containing an HTML file and a screenshot. Download them and see the results of your excellent work so far! We are now ready to deploy to AWS:

```
serverless deploy
```

8.7 Determining the crawl space in a strategy service

The process of determining a crawl space in any web crawler is specific to the domain and application. In our scenario, we are making a number of assumptions that will simplify our crawl strategy:

- The crawler follows local links only.
- The crawl strategy for each *seed* is independent. We don't require any handling of duplicate content across links found by crawling different seeds.
- Our crawl strategy obeys a crawl depth limit.

Let's explore the crawler service implementation. You can find the code in `chapter8-9/strategy-service`. The diagram in figure 8.7 presents the physical structure of this service.

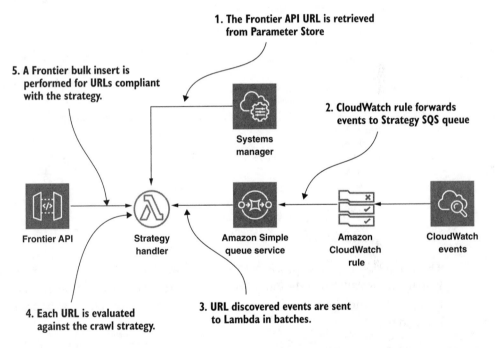

Figure 8.7 The strategy service implementation is tied to CloudWatch Events via SQS. It also integrates with the parameter store and the frontier API.

You can see that this service is quite simple. It handles a batch of events as shown in listing 8.7. An extract from the `handler.js` can be found in `chapter8-9/strategy-service`.

Listing 8.7   Page crawl strategy

```
const items = event.Records.map(({ body }) => {
    const { item, link } = JSON.parse(body)        ◁─┐   Each record in the event is parsed
    return {                                       ◁─┤   to extract the link and the page
        seed: item.seed,                                 where it was discovered.
        referrer: item.url,
        url: link.href,                                  A Frontier record for the new page is created.
        label: link.text,                                It contains the referring page's URL, the link
        depth: item.depth + 1                            text label, and the incremented crawl depth.
    }
}).filter(newItem => {                                                  Items that exceed the maximum
    if (newItem.depth > MAX_DEPTH) {               ◁─────               crawl depth are excluded.
        log.debug(`Rejecting ${newItem.url} with depth (${newItem.depth})
        beyond limit`)
    } else if (!shouldFollow(newItem.seed, newItem.url)) {  ◁─┐   Items from a different
        log.debug(`Rejecting ${newItem.url}                    ├   domain are excluded.
        from a different domain to seed ${newItem.seed}`)
    } else {
        return true
    }
    return false                                          The Frontier's Bulk Insert API is
})                                                        called with eligible items using
log.debug({ items }, 'Sending new URLs to Frontier')      the Axios HTTP library.[9]
return items.length > 0
    ? signedAxios({method: 'PUT', url: frontierUrl, data: items})   ◁─────┘
        .then(() => ({}))
        .catch(err => {
            const { data, status, headers } = err.response || {}
            if (status) {
                log.error({ data, status, headers }, 'Error found')
            }
            throw err
        })
    : Promise.resolve({})
```

The events we have just processed were sent by the fetch service using the Cloud-Watch Events API. To understand how they are received by the strategy service, refer to figure 8.7 and the `serverless.yml` extract from `strategy-service`, shown in listing 8.8.

Listing 8.8   CloudWatch events received by strategy service via SQS

```
Resources:
    strategyQueue:                            We define a SQS queue. This is the trigger for
        Type: AWS::SQS::Queue          ◁──┘   the handleDiscoveredUrls Lambda handler.
        Properties:
            QueueName: ${self:custom.strategyQueueName}
```

---

[9] https://github.com/axios/axios.

```yaml
strategyQueuePolicy:
  Type: AWS::SQS::QueuePolicy
  Properties:
    Queues:
      - !Ref strategyQueue
    PolicyDocument:
      Version: '2012-10-17'
      Statement:
        - Effect: Allow
          Action:
            - sqs:SendMessage
          Principal:
            Service: events.amazonaws.com
          Resource: !GetAtt strategyQueue.Arn
```

The SQS queue is given a resource policy granting the CloudWatch Events service permission to send messages to the queue.

```yaml
discoveredUrlRule:
  Type: AWS::Events::Rule
  Properties:
    EventPattern:
      detail-type:
        - url.discovered
    Name: ${self:provider.stage}-url-discovered-rule
    Targets:
      - Arn: !GetAtt strategyQueue.Arn
        Id: ${self:provider.stage}-url-discovered-strategy-queue-target
        InputPath: '$.detail'
```

A CloudWatch rule is defined to match events of a given pattern.

The rule matches events with DetailType: url-discovered.

The SQS queue is specified as the target for the rule.

The body of the messages sent to the target is the message payload.

Let's deploy the strategy service straight to AWS:

```
npm install
serverless deploy
```

We are now ready to build the final part of the crawler.

8.8 Orchestrating the crawler with a scheduler

The last component of the web crawler, the scheduler, is where the process of crawling a site starts and is tracked until the end. Designing this kind of process with a serverless mindset is challenging for anyone used to larger, monolithic architectures. In particular, for any given site, we need to enforce the following requirements:

- A maximum number of concurrent fetches per site must be enforced.
- The process must wait a specified amount of time before proceeding to perform the next batch of fetches.

These requirements are related to *flow control*. It would be possible to achieve flow control using a purely event-driven approach. However, in order to make an effort to cluster requests to the same site within the same Lambda function, the architecture would already be reasonably complex and difficult to reason about.

Before we address the challenge of flow control, make sure you have the code for this service ready to explore.

8.8.1   Grabbing the code

The scheduler service code can be found in `chapter8-9/scheduler-service`. In the `serverless.yml`, you will find a new plugin, `serverless-step-functions`. This introduces a new AWS service that will help us to orchestrate the crawling process.

8.8.2   Using Step Functions

Our scheduler will implement flow control and orchestration of the process using an AWS Step Function. Step Functions have the following capabilities:

- They can run for up to one year.
- Step Functions integrate to many AWS services, including Lambda.
- Support is provided for wait steps, conditional logic, parallel task execution, failures, and retries.

Step Functions are defined in JSON using a specific syntax called *Amazon States Language (ASL)*. The `serverless-step-function` plugin allows us to define ASL for our function in the serverless configuration file under the `stepFunctions` section. We are using YAML in our Serverless Framework configuration. This format is converted to JSON before the resources are created as part of the underlying Cloud-Formation stack. Figure 8.8 illustrates the flow of the scheduler Step Function.

We have already learned how the other component services are built. We covered the APIs and event handling they use to interact with the rest of the system. The end-to-end crawl process, as managed by the scheduler, has also been shown. In particular, the `Wait` and `Check Batch Count` steps in the process show how control flow is easily managed with a Step Function. The ASL code listing for the Step Function state machine is shown in listing 8.9.

Listing 8.9   The ASL for the scheduler service state machine

```
StartAt: Seed URL
States:
  Seed URL:
    Type: Task
    Resource: !GetAtt PutSeedLambdaFunction.Arn   <─┐
    Next: Get URL Batch
    InputPath: '$'
    ResultPath: '$.seedResult'
    OutputPath: '$'
  Get URL Batch:
    Type: Task
    Resource: !GetAtt GetBatchLambdaFunction.Arn  <─┐
    Next: Check Batch Count
    InputPath: '$'
    ResultPath: '$.getBatchResult'
    OutputPath: '$'
  Check Batch Count:
    Type: Choice                                  <─┘
```

The state machine invokes the putSeed Lambda to start the crawl process.

A batch of URLs is retrieved using the getBatch Lambda function.

The number of URLs in the batch is checked in a Choice state. This is an example of how simple flow control is implemented in a Step Function. If the count is zero, the state machine terminates with the Done state. Otherwise, it advances to the Fetch state.

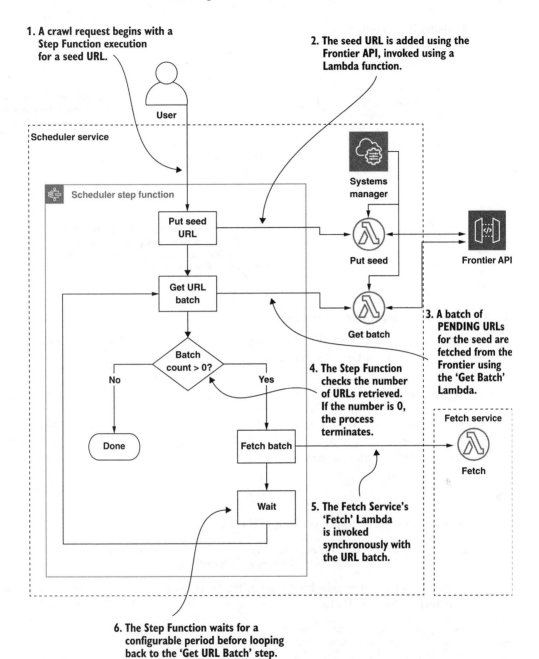

1. A crawl request begins with a Step Function execution for a seed URL.

2. The seed URL is added using the Frontier API, invoked using a Lambda function.

3. A batch of PENDING URLs for the seed are fetched from the Frontier using the 'Get Batch' Lambda.

4. The Step Function checks the number of URLs retrieved. If the number is 0, the process terminates.

5. The Fetch Service's 'Fetch' Lambda is invoked synchronously with the URL batch.

6. The Step Function waits for a configurable period before looping back to the 'Get URL Batch' step.

Figure 8.8 The scheduler is implemented as an AWS Step Function. It makes synchronous invocations to Lambdas defined within the scheduler service, as well as the fetch Lambda in the fetch service.

Listing 8.9   (continued)

```
        Choices:
          - Not:
              Variable: $.getBatchResult.count
              NumericEquals: 0
            Next: Fetch
          Default: Done
      Fetch:
        Type: Task
        Resource: ${ssm:/${self:provider.stage}/fetch/lambda-arn}
        InputPath: $.getBatchResult.items
        ResultPath: $.fetchResult
        Next: Wait
      Wait:
        Type: Wait
        Seconds: 30
        Next: Get URL Batch
      Done:
        Type: Pass
        End: true
```

> The fetch service's Lambda, discovered using the parameter store, is invoked with the batch of URLs from the frontier.

> Once the fetch is complete, the state machine waits 30 seconds to ensure polite crawling behavior. The state machine then loops back to the Get URL Batch state to process more pages.

8.8.3   Deploying and testing the scheduler

Once we have deployed the scheduler, you should be able to initiate a crawl process for any given seed URL. Let's begin!

```
npm install
serverless deploy
```

We now have all services in place to run a crawl. A crawl process is initiated by starting a Step Function execution. This can be done using the AWS command line. First, we use the `list-state-machines` command to find the ARN of the `CrawlScheduler` Step Function:

```
aws stepfunctions list-state-machines --output text
```

An example of the output returned follows:

```
STATEMACHINES 1561365296.434 CrawlScheduler arn:aws:states:eu-west-
    1:123456789123:stateMachine:CrawlScheduler
```

Next, we start a State Machine execution by providing the ARN and passing JSON containing the seed URL:

```
aws stepfunctions start-execution \
  --state-machine-arn arn:aws:states:eu-west-
    1:1234567890123:stateMachine:CrawlScheduler \
  --input '{"url": "https://fourtheorem.com"}'
```

As an alternative to using the CLI, we can start a Step Function execution in the AWS Management Console. Navigate to the Step Functions service in your browser and select the `CrawlScheduler` service. You should see something similar to the screen in figure 8.9.

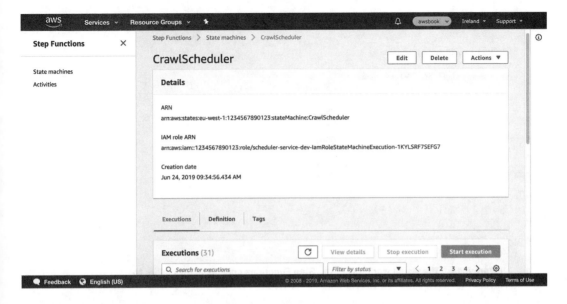

Figure 8.9 The Step Function view in the AWS Management Console allows you to start a new execution and view the progress of existing executions. You can also inspect or edit the ASL JSON from here.

Select *Start Execution*. From here, you can enter the JSON object to be passed to the start state. In our case, the JSON object requires one property—the URL of the site to be crawled. This is shown in figure 8.10.

Once the execution has started, the console will take you to the execution view. From here, you can see a very useful visualization of the progress of the Step Function

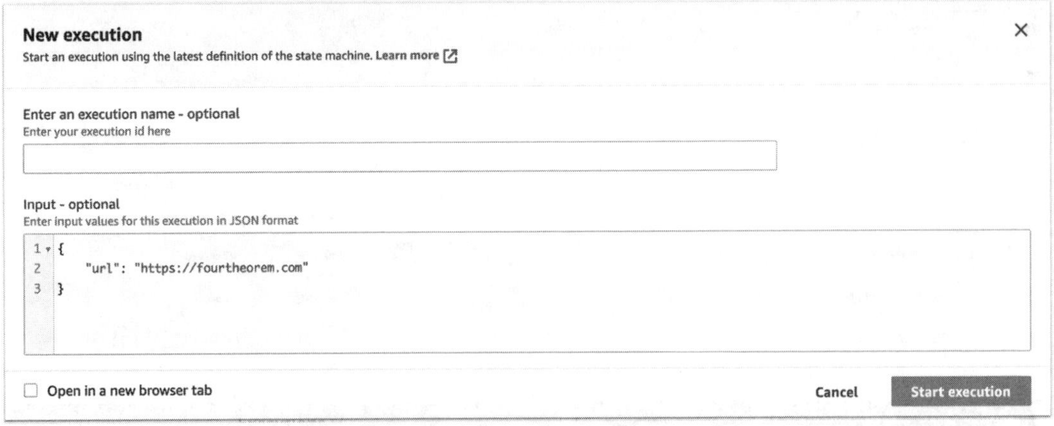

Figure 8.10 A crawl process can be started by providing the site URL in the Start Execution option on the Step Functions console.

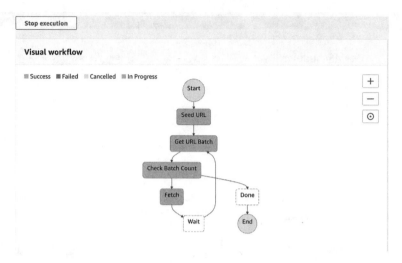

Figure 8.11   The visual workflow in the Step Functions console allows users to monitor the progress of an execution.

execution, shown in figure 8.11. By clicking on any state, you can see the input data, output data, and any error.

When the Step Function execution is complete, take a look at the contents of the item store S3 bucket. You should find a nice collection of files relating the most important pages linked from the seed URL. An example of one page's contents is shown in figure 8.12.

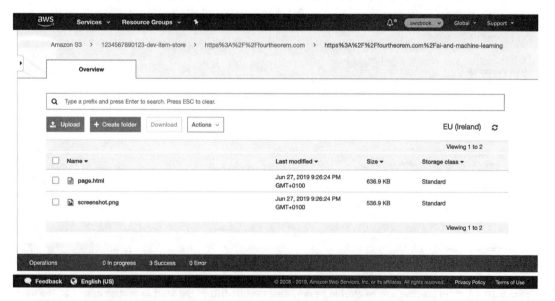

Figure 8.12   The item store can be browsed from the S3 Console. This allows us to inspect the generated HTML and visually check the page's screenshot.

This type of data, gathered from many conference websites, will form the basis for intelligent data extraction in chapter 9. However, before you move on, take some time to navigate the components of the crawler in the AWS Console. Start with the Step Function, following each phase in order. Look at the CloudWatch logs for the fetch service, the strategy service, and the frontier. The flow of data and events should match the diagrams in figure 8.9, and this exercise should help to cement everything we have described in the chapter.

In the next chapter, we will dive into extracting specific information from textual data using named entity recognition.

Summary

- The type of AI algorithm or managed service dictates what data is required for AI applications.
- If you don't have the right data already, look at finding publicly available data sources or generating your own datasets.
- Web crawlers and scrapers find and extract data from websites.
- DynamoDB secondary indexes can be used to perform additional queries.
- It is possible to architect and build a serverless application for web crawling, particularly for specific small sets of sites.
- Event-driven serverless systems can use CloudWatch events (or EventBridge) as an event bus.
- Processes requiring control flow can be orchestrated using AWS Step Functions.

WARNING Chapter 9 continues to build on this system and we provide instructions on how to remove the deployed resources at the end of Chapter 9. If you are not planning on working on Chapter 9 for some time, please ensure that you fully remove all cloud resources deployed in this chapter in order to avoid additional charges!

Extracting value from large data sets with AI

Chapter 8 dealt with the challenge of gathering unstructured data from websites for use in machine learning analysis. This chapter builds on the serverless web crawler from chapter 8. This time, we are concerned with using machine learning to extract meaningful insights from the data we gathered. If you didn't work through chapter 8, you should go back and do so now before proceeding with this chapter, as we will be building directly on top of the web crawler. If you are already comfortable with that content, we can dive right in and add the information extraction parts.

9.1 Using AI to extract significant information from web pages

Let's remind ourselves of the grand vision for our chapter 8 scenario—finding relevant developer conferences to attend. We want to facilitate a system that allows people to search for conferences and speakers of interest to them. In chapter 8's web crawler, we built a system that solved the first part of this scenario—gathering data on conferences.

However, we don't want users to have to manually search through all of the unstructured website text we have gathered. Instead, we want to present them with conferences, the event locations and dates and a list of people who may be speaking at these conferences.

Extracting this meaningful data from unstructured text is a non-trivial problem—at least, it was before the recent advancement of managed AI services.

Let's revisit the requirements overview diagram for our scenario from chapter 8. This time, we are highlighting the relevant parts for this chapter.

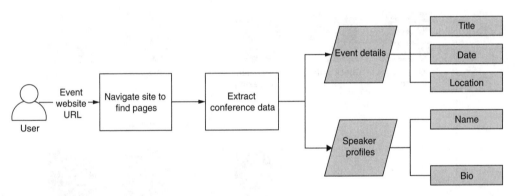

Figure 9.1 This chapter deals with extraction of event and speaker information from the data we already gathered.

9.1.1 Understanding the problem

The challenge of extracting important information from unstructured text is known as *named entity recognition (NER)*. A *named entity* can be a person, location, or organization. It can also refer to dates and numerical quantities. NER is a challenging problem and the subject of much research. It is certainly not a completely solved problem. Since its results cannot be guaranteed to be 100% accurate, we must take this into consideration. Human result-checking may be required, depending on the application. For example, suppose you have a system that is required to detect locations in a body of text. Now suppose one of the sentences in the text mentions the Apollo 11 command module, "Columbia." NER might identity this as a location instead part of a spacecraft! Every named entity recognition system will give a likelihood score for each recognition result, and this value never reaches 100%.

For our conference event information extraction scenario, we are aiming to extract the names of people, locations, and dates from website data. This will then be stored and made accessible to users.

9.1.2 Extending the architecture

We are about to design and deploy a serverless system to extract the required information from conference web pages. Let's take a look at the architecture components for this chapter, using the categories outlined in the canonical serverless architecture from chapter 1. This is shown in figure 9.2.

There is less variety of services and communication channels than with previous chapters. From an AWS service point of view, this chapter will be relatively simple. The

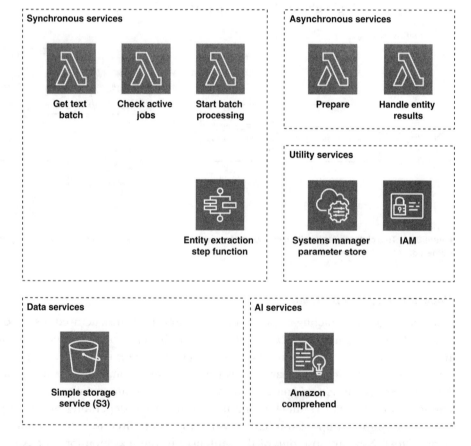

Figure 9.2   Serverless entity extraction system architecture. The system is composed of synchronous Lambda functions orchestrated using a step function. Data is stored in the item store S3 bucket introduced in chapter 8. Bucket notifications from S3 trigger our asynchronous services.

new aspects being introduced include Amazon Comprehend features and S3 event notifications as a trigger for data processing.

9.2 Understanding Comprehend's entity recognition APIs

Amazon Comprehend has more than one supported interface for entity recognition. Before we go into further detail on how data flows through the system, let's take some time to understand how Comprehend works and what impacts that may have on our architecture.

The three entity recognition interfaces in Amazon Comprehend are outlined in table 9.1

Table 9.1   Amazon Comprehend modes of operation

API	Description	Limits
On-demand entity recognition	A single piece of text is analyzed. Results are returned synchronously.	Up to 5,000 characters only.
Batch entity recognition	Multiple pieces of text are analyzed. Results are returned synchronously.	Up to 25 documents, each up to 5,000 characters only.
Asynchronous entity recognition	Multiple large pieces of text are analyzed. Text is read from S3 and results are written to S3 asynchronously.	Only one request per second, 100 KB per document, 5 GB max for all documents.

For full details on Comprehend limits, see the Amazon Comprehend *Guidelines and Limits* documentation.[1]

For our purposes, we wish to analyze documents larger than 5,000 characters, so we must choose the asynchronous mode of operation. This mode requires us to use two APIs: *StartEntititesDetectionJob* to initiate analysis, and *DescribeEntitiesDetectionJob* if we wish to poll the status of the job.

Comprehend returns entity recognition results as an array. Each array element contains the following properties:

- `Type`—The entity type that has been recognized: PERSON, LOCATION, ORGANI-ZATION, COMMERCIAL_ITEM, EVENT, DATE, QUANTITY, TITLE, or OTHER.
- `Score`—The confidence score in the analysis result. This is a value between 0 and 1.
- `Text`—The text of the entity that has been recognized.
- `BeginOffset`—The begin offset of the entity within the text.
- `EndOffset`—The end offset of the entity within the text.

---

[1]   Amazon Comprehend Guidelines and Limits, http://mng.bz/2WAa.

To get a feel for how Comprehend works, let's run a once-off test using the AWS Command Line Interface. Using the shell is a useful way to familiarize yourself with any new AWS service.

> **TIP** Chapter 2 and appendix A introduced the AWS CLI. In addition to the normal AWS CLI, Amazon has released an interactive version called *AWS Shell* (https://github.com/awslabs/aws-shell). It supports interactive help and command auto-completion. If you use the AWS CLI to learn and explore new services, it's worth looking at AWS Shell.

We are going to analyze some sample text available in the code repository under `chapter8-9/sample-text/apollo.txt`. The paragraph of text is taken from the *Apollo 11* page on Wikipedia.[2] The sample text is shown in the next listing.

Listing 9.1 Sample text for entity recognition: `apollo.txt`

```
Apollo 11 was the spaceflight that first landed humans on the Moon.
Commander Neil Armstrong and lunar module pilot Buzz Aldrin formed the
American crew that landed the Apollo Lunar Module Eagle on July 20, 1969,
at 20:17 UTC. Armstrong became the first person to step onto the lunar
surface six hours and 39 minutes later on July 21 at 02:56 UTC; Aldrin
joined him 19 minutes later. They spent about two and a quarter hours
together outside the spacecraft, and they collected 47.5 pounds (21.5 kg)
of lunar material to bring back to Earth. Command module pilot Michael
Collins flew the command module Columbia alone in lunar orbit while they
were on the Moon's surface. Armstrong and Aldrin spent 21 hours 31 minutes
on the lunar surface at a site they named Tranquility Base before lifting
off to rejoin Columbia in lunar orbit.
```

We can run on-demand entity recognition using the CLI using the following commands:

```
export INPUT_TEXT=`cat apollo.txt`

aws comprehend detect-entities --language-code=en --
    text $INPUT_TEXT > results.json
```

The output of this command, saved to `results.json`, gives an indication of how Comprehend provides analysis results for entity recognition tasks. Table 9.2 shows some of the results obtained for this command in tabular format.

Table 9.2 Comprehend entity recognition sample results

Type	Text	Score	BeginOffset	EndOffset
ORGANIZATION	Apollo 11	0.49757930636405900	0	9
LOCATION	Moon	0.9277622103691100	62	66

---

[2] Apollo 11, Wikipedia, reproduced under the Creative Commons Attribution-ShareAlike License, https://en.wikipedia.org/wiki/Apollo_11.

Table 9.2 Comprehend entity recognition sample results

Type	Text	Score	BeginOffset	EndOffset
PERSON	Neil Armstrong	0.9994082450866700	78	92
PERSON	Buzz Aldrin	0.9906044602394100	116	127
OTHER	American	0.6279735565185550	139	147
ORGANIZATION	Apollo	0.23635128140449500	169	175
COMMERCIAL_ITEM	Lunar Module Eagle	0.7624998688697820	176	194
DATE	"July 20, 1969"	0.9936476945877080	198	211
QUANTITY	first person	0.8917713761329650	248	260
QUANTITY	about two and a quarter hours	0.9333438873291020	395	424
QUANTITY	21.5 kg	0.995818555355072	490	497
LOCATION	Earth	0.9848601222038270	534	539
PERSON	Michael Collins	0.9996771812438970	562	577
LOCATION	Columbia	0.9617793560028080	602	610

It's clear that very accurate results can be obtained from Comprehend entity recognition with very little effort.

In order to get these kinds of results for every web page crawled from conference sites, we will use the asynchronous entity recognition API. This means we will have to handle the following characteristics of this API:

- Entity recognition jobs on Comprehend take longer to run in asynchronous mode. Each job may take from 5 to 10 minutes. This is much longer than synchronous jobs, but the trade-off is that asynchronous jobs can process much larger documents.
- To avoid hitting API throttling limits, we will avoid more than one request per second, and submit multiple web pages to each job.
- The asynchronous API in Amazon Comprehend writes results to a configured S3 bucket. We will process results by using notification triggers on the S3 bucket.

The web crawler from chapter 8 wrote a text file (page.txt) for each web page to an S3 bucket. In order to start entity recognition, we will make a copy of this in a separate staging folder in S3. This way, we can check the contents of the staging folder for new text files to be processed. When processing has started, we will delete the file from the staging area. The original file (page.txt) will remain in place in the sites folder permanently, so it is available for further processing if required later.

Let's go ahead and implement the simple service that will create a copy of the text file in the staging area.

9.3 Preparing data for information extraction

The staging area that contains files ready to be processed will be a directory in the item store S3 bucket called `incoming-texts`. We will use S3 notification triggers to react to new `page.txt` files arriving in the bucket from the web crawler. Each file will then be copied to `incoming-texts/`.

9.3.1 Getting the code

The code for the preparation service is in the directory `chapter8-9/preparation-service`. This directory contains a `serverless.yml`. We will explain the contents as we go before deploying and testing the preparation service.

9.3.2 Creating an S3 event notification

The preparation service is largely composed of one simple function with an event notification. Let's explore `serverless.yml` in detail to see how this works. The next listing shows an extract of this file, where we encounter our first S3 bucket event notification.

> ### Listing 9.2 Preparation service `serverless.yml` file extract

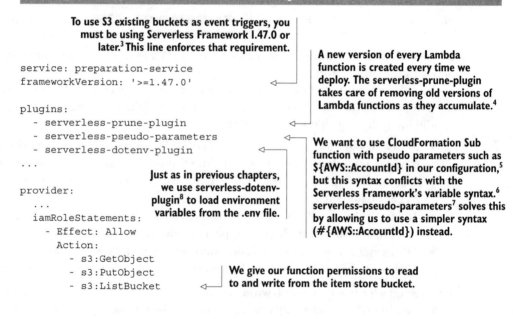

To use S3 existing buckets as event triggers, you must be using Serverless Framework 1.47.0 or later.[3] This line enforces that requirement.

```
service: preparation-service
frameworkVersion: '>=1.47.0'

plugins:
  - serverless-prune-plugin
  - serverless-pseudo-parameters
  - serverless-dotenv-plugin
...

provider:
  ...
  iamRoleStatements:
    - Effect: Allow
      Action:
        - s3:GetObject
        - s3:PutObject
        - s3:ListBucket
```

A new version of every Lambda function is created every time we deploy. The serverless-prune-plugin takes care of removing old versions of Lambda functions as they accumulate.[4]

We want to use CloudFormation Sub function with pseudo parameters such as ${AWS::AccountId} in our configuration,[5] but this syntax conflicts with the Serverless Framework's variable syntax.[6] serverless-pseudo-parameters[7] solves this by allowing us to use a simpler syntax (#{AWS::AccountId}) instead.

Just as in previous chapters, we use serverless-dotenv-plugin[8] to load environment variables from the .env file.

We give our function permissions to read to and write from the item store bucket.

---

[3] Serverless Framework, Using Existing Buckets, http://mng.bz/1g7q.

[4] Serverless Prune Plugin, https://github.com/claygregory/serverless-prune-plugin.

[5] The Sub Function and CloudFormation variables, http://mng.bz/P18R.

[6] Serverless Framework Variables, http://mng.bz/Jx8Z.

[7] Serverless Pseudo Parameters Plugin, http://mng.bz/wpE5.

[8] Serverless Dotenv Plugin, http://mng.bz/qNBx.

```
     Resource:
       - arn:aws:s3:::${env:ITEM_STORE_BUCKET}/*
...
functions:
  prepare:
    handler: handler.prepare
    events:
      - s3:
          bucket: ${env:ITEM_STORE_BUCKET}
          event: s3:ObjectCreated:*
          rules:
            - suffix: page.txt
          existing: true
```

The S3 event handling function is defined in handler.js. The function name is exported as prepare.

The Lambda trigger is defined as an S3 notification. The notifications will match any object (file) created in the bucket with the suffix page.txt.

This ensures that the Serverless Framework will not attempt to create the bucket. Instead it will create a notification trigger on the existing item store bucket.

We have just declared the function, its resources, and triggers for the preparation handler. We can now move on to the implementation of this function.

CloudFormation and S3 notification triggers

CloudFormation is a fantastic way to define Infrastructure as Code in a way that supports logically grouped resources and rollback in the event of any failure. One disadvantage, however, is that CloudFormation is not as flexible as the AWS SDK for creating all resource types.

One example of this is with bucket notifications. Using CloudFormation, notifications can only be added when the bucket resource is created.[a] We would prefer to be able to add notifications to existing buckets for any service in our system.

The Serverless Framework provides a great workaround for this problem. By using an s3 event type with the property `existing: true`, the framework uses the AWS SDK under the hood to add a new notification to an existing bucket. This is achieved using *CloudFormation custom resources*, a useful workaround when official CloudFormation support falls short of your needs. For more information on custom resources, see the AWS documentation.[b]

[a] CloudFormation AWS::S3::NotificationConfiguration, http://mng.bz/7GeQ.
[b] AWS CloudFormation Templates Custom Resources, http://mng.bz/mNm8.

9.3.3 Implementing the preparation handler

The goal of the preparation service's `handler` module is to perform any processing required in order for the text to be ready for entity recognition. In our case, this is simply a case of putting the text in the right folder with the right filename for processing. The preparation service's `handler` module is shown in the following listing.

Listing 9.3 Preparation service `handler.js` extract

```
...
const s3 = new AWS.S3({ endpoint: process.env.S3_ENDPOINT_URL })

function prepare(event) {                          Every S3 notification event is
  const record = event.Records[0]          ◄──┘   an array of length I.
  const bucketName = record.s3.bucket.name
  const key = decodeURIComponent(record.s3.object.key)    ◄─┐  Object keys are
  const object = { Bucket: bucketName, Key: key }            │  URL-encoded
  ...                                                         │  when they arrive
  return s3                                                   │  in S3 events.
    .getObject(object)
    .promise()
    .then(({ Body: body }) => body)                 The key for the staging area copy is
    .then(body => body.toString())                  created by replacing the prefix and the
    .then(text => {                                 filename from the incoming key string.
      const textObjectKey = `incoming-texts/
    ${key.substring(KEY_PREFIX.length).replace(/page.txt$/
    , 'pending.txt')}`
      ...                                                                          ◄─
      return s3                                                                    ◄─
        .putObject({ Body: text, Bucket: bucketName, Key: textObjectKey })
        .promise()
    })                                              The S3 object's contents
}                                                   are written to the target key.
```

9.3.4 Adding resilience with a dead letter queue (DLQ)

Before we deploy the preparation services, let's deal with the issue of resilience and retries. If our event handler fails to process the event, we risk the event being lost. Lambda will retry our function twice.[9] If our function does not successfully handle the event during any of these invocation attempts, there will be no further automatic retries.

Luckily, we can configure a dead-letter queue (DLQ) for any Lambda function. This is where unprocessed events go after automatic retries have failed. Once they are in the DLQ, it is up to us to decide how to reprocess them.

A DLQ may be an SQS queue or SNS topic. SNS (Simple Notification Service) is used for pub/sub messaging, a topic covered in chapter 2. SQS (Simple Queue Service) is used for point-to-point messaging. We are going to use an SQS queue for our DLQ, since we only need one consumer. The DLQ interaction is illustrated in figure 9.3.

This is how we will handle unprocessed messages:

- We set an SQS queue as the DLQ for the `prepare` Lambda function.
- Unprocessed messages are sent to our queue after all retry attempts have failed.
- We can inspect the SQS queue in the AWS Console intermittently. In a production scenario, we would ideally set up a CloudWatch alarm to alert us when the

---

[9] Lambda Asynchronous Invocation, http://mng.bz/5pN7.

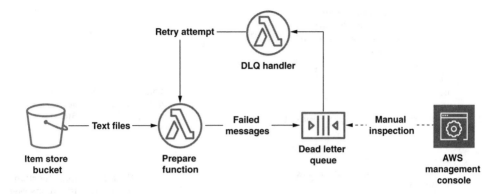

Figure 9.3   A DLQ facilitates inspection and reprocessing of events that have caused a Lambda execution failure.

number of messages in this queue exceeds zero. To keep it simple, we are not going to create a CloudWatch alarm in this chapter.[10]

- We will create a second Lambda function whose sole purpose is to retrieve messages from the DLQ and pass them back to the original `prepare` Lambda function. This can be invoked manually when we notice unprocessed messages and have taken steps to remedy the underlying problem.

9.3.5   Creating the DLQ and retry handler

In chapters 2 and 3, we used an SQS queue to trigger a Lambda function. In the case of the DLQ, we don't want our retry Lambda to be automatically triggered. Since we will manually invoke the retry Lambda, the retry handler must manually read messages from the SQS queue. Let's take a look at the additions to `serverless.yml`. The following listing shows the relevant extracts. You can find the complete configuration file in `chapter8-9/preparation-service`.

> **Listing 9.4   Preparation service `serverless.yml` DLQ extract**

```
custom:
    ...
    dlqQueueName: ${self:provider.stage}PreparationDlq
    ...
provider:
    ...
    iamRoleStatements:
    ...
      - Effect: Allow
        Action:
          - sqs:GetQueueUrl
```

The DLQ queue name is different for each deployed stage to avoid naming conflicts.

The Lambda requires four permissions to read and process the messages in the DLQ

---

[10] For details on creating a CloudWatch Alarm based on the SQS queue message count, see http://mng.bz/ 6AjR.

```
          - sqs:DeleteMessage
          - sqs:SendMessage
          - sqs:ReceiveMessage
        Resource:
          - !GetAtt preparationDlq.Arn
functions:
  prepare:
    ...
    onError: !GetAtt preparationDlq.Arn        ◁──┐

    ...
  retryDlq:
    handler: dlq-handler.retry                 ◁──┐
    environment:
      DLQ_QUEUE_NAME: ${self:custom.dlqQueueName}
    ...
resources:
  Resources:
    preparationDlq:
      Type: AWS::SQS::Queue
      Properties:
        QueueName: ${self:custom.dlqQueueName}
        MessageRetentionPeriod:                ◁──┐
```

> **onError is used to set the DLQ of the prepare Lambda function to the SQS queue ARN.**

> **The retry Lambda function is configured without any event triggers. The DLQ queue is configured using an environment variable.**

> **We set the message retention period for the DLQ to one day. This should be reasonably long so undelivered messages can be manually recovered. The maximum message retention value is 14 days.**

The Lambda handler is implemented in the `retry` function in `dlq-handler.js`. When invoked, its goal is to perform the following sequence of actions:

1 Retrieve a batch of messages from the DLQ.
2 For each message, extract the original event from the message.
3 Invoke the `prepare` function by loading the `handler` module and calling `prepare` directly with the event, and wait for a success or failure response.
4 If the event has succeeded, delete the message from the DLQ.
5 Proceed to process the next message until all messages in the batch have been processed.

DLQ handling is a common pattern that we wish to apply to multiple Lambda functions, so we have extracted it into a separate, open source NPM module, `lambda-dlq-retry`.[11] The use of this module makes the retry implementation simpler. Let's take a look at `dlq-handler.js`, shown in the following listing.

Listing 9.5   Preparation service DLQ handler

```
const lambdaDlqRetry = require('lambda-dlq-retry')  ◁──┐
const handler = require('./handler')           ◁──┐
const log = require('./log')
```

> **The lambda-dlq-retry module is imported.**

> **The module containing the prepare function for the preparation service is required.**

---

[11] lambda-dlq-retry is available at https://github.com/eoinsha/lambda-dlq-retry.

```
module.exports = {
  retry: lambdaDlqRetry({ handler: handler.prepare, log })
}
```

We export a DLQ retry handler, created for us by the lambda-dlq-retry module using the specified handler. You may pass a logger instance. If debug logging is turned on, this will produce log entries relating to DLQ retries.

It's worth mentioning that `lambda-dlq-retry` processes messages in batches of up to 10. This can be configured by setting an alternative value in the environment variable, `DLQ_RETRY_MAX_MESSAGES`.

9.3.6 *Deploying and testing the preparation service*

We have created four Lambda functions so far in this chapter. It's worthwhile reviewing these before we deploy and run them so we can start gaining a clear understanding of how they work together. Figure 9.4 revisits our service architecture from the beginning of the chapter. The sections we have covered already are highlighted.

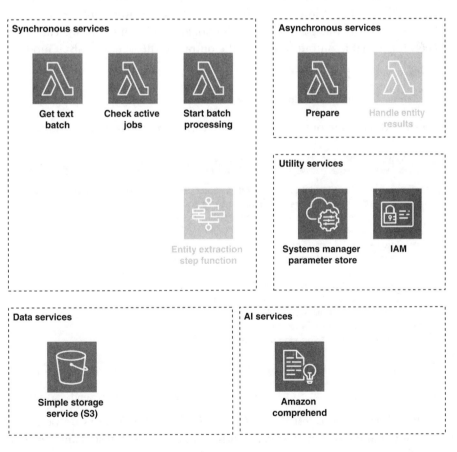

Figure 9.4 So far, we have implemented Lambda functions for text preparation, getting a batch of text files, starting entity recognition, and checking recognition progress.

Before we deploy the preparation service, make sure you have set up .env in the chapter8-9 directory as outlined in chapter 8. This contains the item store bucket name environment variable. Once that's done, we can proceed with the usual steps to build and deploy!

```
npm install
sls deploy
```

To test our function, we can manually upload a file to the item store bucket with the suffix page.txt. We can then check to see if it is copied to the incoming-texts staging area. We can use the sample text we already have from our simple Comprehend test:

```
source ../.env
aws s3 cp ../sample-text/apollo.txt \
  s3://${ITEM_STORE_BUCKET}/sites/test/page.txt
```

To check the logs for the prepare function, we can use the Serverless logs command. This will take CloudWatch logs for the function and print them on the console. Because we used the pino module for logging in chapter 8, we can format them nicely for readable output by piping the output to the pino-pretty module:

```
npm install -g pino-pretty

sls logs -f prepare | pino-pretty
```

You should see some output similar to that shown in the following listing.

Listing 9.6   Preparation service log output

```
START RequestId: 259082aa-27ec-421f-9caf-9f89042aceef Version: $LATEST
[1566803687880] INFO (preparation-service/
    1 on 169.254.238.253): Getting S3 Object
    object: {
      "Bucket": "item-store-bucket",
      "Key": "sites/test/page.txt"
    }
[1566803687922] INFO (preparation-service/
    1 on 169.254.238.253): Uploading extracted text
    bucketName: "item-store-bucket"
    key: "sites/test/page.txt"
    textObjectKey: "incoming-texts/test/pending.txt"
```

You can then check the S3 bucket for the contents of the file in the staging area:

```
aws s3 ls s3://${ITEM_STORE_BUCKET}/incoming-texts/test/pending.txt
```

Lastly, we are going to test the DLQ retry functionality. There's no point in having a process to handle recovery from a failure if it has not been tested and verified to work! To simulate an error, we are going to withdraw read permissions to the S3 bucket.

Comment out the `GetObject` permission from the Lambda IAM role policy in `serverless.yml` as follows:

```
...
    - Effect: Allow
      Action:
#         - s3:GetObject
        - s3:PutObject
...
```

Deploy the updated preparation service with the modified IAM role:

```
sls deploy
```

We can run the same test again using a different S3 key (path):

```
aws s3 cp ../sample-text/apollo.txt s3://${ITEM_STORE_BUCKET}/sites/test2/
    page.txt
```

This time, we should observe an error in the `prepare` function logs:

```
START RequestId: dfb09e2a-5db5-4510-8992-7908d1ac5f13 Version: $LATEST
...
[1566805278499] INFO (preparation-service/
    1 on 169.254.13.17): Getting S3 Object
  object: {
    "Bucket": "item-store-bucket",
    "Key": "sites/test2/page.txt"
  }
[1566805278552] ERROR (preparation-service/1 on 169.254.13.17): Error in handler
  err: {
    "type": "Error",
    "message": "Access Denied",
```

You'll see this error two more times: once after one minute, and again after two additional minutes. This is because AWS Lambda is automatically retrying. After the three attempts have failed, you should see the message arriving in the DLQ.

We will use the AWS Console to inspect errors before attempting redelivery:

1 Browse to the SQS console and select the preparation service DLQ from the queue list. You will notice that the message count is set to 1.

2 Right-click on the queue in the list and select the View/Delete Messages option. Select Start Polling for Messages, and then select Stop Now once our undelivered S3 event message has come into view.

3 To see the full message, select More Details. We now see the full text of the S3 event that resulted in an error in the `prepare` Lambda function.

4 This is valuable information for troubleshooting the original message. By selecting the second tab, Message Attributes, we can also see the error message along with the request ID. This ID matches the Lambda function invocation, and can be used to correlate the error back to the logs in CloudWatch. You may notice that the "error code" is shown here to be 200. This value can be ignored, as it is always set to 200 for DLQ messages.

Next, test redelivery by restoring the correct permissions in `serverless.yml`. Uncomment the `s3:GetObject` line and redeploy with `sls deploy`. We can choose to trigger the retry Lambda through the AWS Console, the AWS CLI, or using the Serverless Framework `invoke` commands. The following command uses the AWS CLI:

```
aws lambda invoke --function-name preparation-service-dev-retryDlq /tmp/dlq-
    retry-output
```

If you run this and inspect the output in `/tmp/dlq-retry-output`, you should see a simple JSON object (`{"count": 1}`). This means that one message has been processed and delivered! We can inspect the output of the retry Lambda as we did before, using the `sls logs` command:

```
sls logs -f retryDlq | pino-pretty
```

This will show that the S3 event has been successfully processed this time.

9.4   Managing throughput with text batches

Now we have a separate staging area, along with a preparation service to populate it with text from conference web pages as files are created by the web crawler. We have also decided to use the asynchronous Comprehend API and process text in batches. Our next step is to create a simple Lambda to retrieve a batch of text files to be processed.

9.4.1   Getting the code

The `getTextBatch` function can be found in the `extraction-servicehandler` module. The extraction service includes the rest of the functionality for this chapter, as it deals with extraction and reporting of extraction results:

```
cd ../extraction-service
```

9.4.2   Retrieving batches of text for extraction

The source code for `getTextBatch` is shown in the next listing. This function uses the S3 `listObjectsV2` API to read files in the staging area up to a specified limit.

Listing 9.7   The `getTextBatch` function

```
const MAX_BATCH_SIZE = 25
const INCOMING_TEXTS_PREFIX = 'incoming-texts/'
...

function getTextBatch() {
  ...
    return s3
      .listObjectsV2({
        Bucket: itemStoreBucketName,           Read up to 25 keys from the
        Prefix: INCOMING_TEXTS_PREFIX,    ◁──┘  staging area (incoming-texts).
```

```
      MaxKeys: MAX_BATCH_SIZE
    })
    .promise()
    .then(({ Contents: items }) =>
      items.map(item => item.Key.substring(INCOMING_TEXTS_PREFIX.length))
    )
    .then(paths => {
      log.info({ paths }, 'Text batch')
      return {
        paths,
        count: paths.length
      }
    })
}
```

> **Modify file names to remove the incoming-texts/ prefix from the batch results.**

> **The batch of transformed file names is returned along with a count indicating the batch size.**

We will wait to deploy the extraction service in full, so let's test this using the `sls invoke local` command. Bear in mind that although we are executing the function locally, it is calling out to S3. As a result, your `AWS_` environment variables should be set here to ensure you are authorized to execute these SDK calls.

We run the function locally as follows:

```
sls invoke local -f getTextBatch
```

You should see some output similar to the following listing.

Listing 9.8 Sample output from `getTextBatch`

```
{
    "paths": [
        "test/pending.txt",
        "test2/pending.txt"
    ],
    "count": 2
}
```

9.5   *Asynchronous named entity abstraction*

We already have a means to get a batch of text from conference web pages. Let's now build a function to take a set of text files and initiate entity recognition. Remember that we are using asynchronous entity recognition in Comprehend. With this method, input files are stored in S3. We can poll Comprehend to check the status of the recognition job, and results are written to a specified path in an S3 bucket.

9.5.1   *Get the code*

The code for the extraction service is in the directory `chapter8-9/extraction-service`. Our `startBatchProcessing` and `checkActiveJobs` functions can be found in `handler.js`.

9.5.2   *Starting an entity recognition job*

The AWS SDK for Comprehend provides us with the `startEntitiesDetectionJob` function.[12] It requires us to specify an input path for *all* text files in S3 to be processed. We want to ensure that no text files are omitted from processing. To achieve this, we will copy files to be processed to a batch directory, and only delete the source files once the `startEntitiesDetectionJob` call has succeeded.

This can be seen in the `startBatchProcessing` Lambda function in the extraction service's `handler.js`, shown in the next listing.

Listing 9.9   Extraction service handler `startBatchProcessing` function

```
                                              The event is passed an array of paths. The
                                              paths are relative to the incoming_texts
                                              prefix. This set of paths makes up the batch.
function startBatchProcessing(event) {
  const { paths } = event            ◄─┘
  const batchId = new Date().toISOString().replace(/[^0-9]/g, '')          ◄─┐

  return (                                                     We generate a batch ID
    Promise.all(     ◄─┐                                     based on the current time.
      paths              All files in the batch are copied to the    This is used to create the
        .map(path => ({  batch directory before processing.          batch directory in S3.
          Bucket: itemStoreBucketName,
          CopySource: encodeURIComponent(
The S3 copyObject ┌──▷  `${itemStoreBucketName}/${INCOMING_TEXTS_PREFIX}${path}`
API requires the  │    ),
CopySource property│    Key: `${BATCHES_PREFIX}${batchId}/${path}`
to be URL-encoded.│  }))
                     .map(copyParams => s3.copyObject(copyParams).promise())
    )
      // Start Processing
      .then(() => startEntityRecognition(batchId))                   ◄─┐
      // Delete the original files so they won't be reprocessed
      .then(() =>
        Promise.all(                    ◄─┐  When the batch recognition has started,
          paths.map(path =>                  we proceed to deleting all input paths in
            s3                               the incoming_texts directory.
              .deleteObject({
                Bucket: itemStoreBucketName,
                Key: `${INCOMING_TEXTS_PREFIX}${path}`
              })
              .promise()                         We pass the batch ID to our
          )                               startEntityRecognition function so all files
        )                                   in the batch can be analyzed together.
      )
      .then(() => log.info({ paths }, 'Batch process started'))
      .then(() => ({ batchId }))
  )
}
```

---

[12] startEntitiesDetectionJob, AWS SDK for Javascript, http://mng.bz/oRND.

We can now see how, by copying files into a batch directory, we ensure that each file in `incoming_texts` will be processed. Any error in starting the batch recognition job will leave the file in `incoming_texts` so it can be reprocessed using a subsequent batch.

We just saw a reference to the `startEntityRecognition` function. This is the function responsible for creating the parameters for Comprehend's `startEntities-DetectionJob` API. Listing 9.10 shows the code for this function.

Listing 9.10 Extraction service `startBatchProcessing` Lambda function

> For ease of manual troubleshooting, we use the generated batch ID as the job name.

> The job requires an IAM role with permissions to read and write to the S3 bucket. The role definition can be found in extraction-service/serverless.yml.

> We need to tell Comprehend that each file in the S3 folder represents a single document. The other option is ONE_DOC_PER_LINE.

> The path to the files in the batch is the path where our files have just been copied.

> Comprehend results are written to an output folder designated by the batch ID.

```
function startEntityRecognition(batchId) {
  return comprehend
    .startEntitiesDetectionJob({
      JobName: batchId,                                  ◁
      DataAccessRoleArn: dataAccessRoleArn,              ◁
      InputDataConfig: {
        InputFormat: 'ONE_DOC_PER_FILE',                 ◁
        S3Uri: `s3://${itemStoreBucketName}/${BATCHES_PREFIX}${batchId}/`  ◁
      },
      LanguageCode: 'en',
      OutputDataConfig: {
        S3Uri: `s3://${itemStoreBucketName}/
${ENTITY_RESULTS_PREFIX}${batchId}`              ◁
      }
    })
    .promise()
    .then(comprehendResponse =>
      log.info({ batchId, comprehendResponse }, 'Entity detection started')
    )
}
```

The `startBatchProcessing` function is the core of the functionality in this chapter. It passes the extracted text through to AWS Comprehend, the managed AI service that performs the extraction of significant data.

9.6 *Checking entity recognition progress*

Before we try out our entity recognition job processing, we will take a look at `check-ActiveJobs`. This is a simple Lambda function that will use the Comprehend API to report on the status of jobs that are *in progress*. For manual progress checking, you can also take a look at the Comprehend section of the AWS Management Console. When we know how many jobs are in progress, we can know when to start more jobs and control the number of concurrent Comprehend job executions. The code for `check-ActiveJobs` is shown in the next listing.

Listing 9.11   Extraction service `checkActiveJobs` Lambda function

```
function checkActiveJobs() {
  return comprehend
    .listEntitiesDetectionJobs({
      Filter: { JobStatus: 'IN_PROGRESS' },
      MaxResults: MAX_COMPREHEND_JOB_COUNT
    })
    .promise()
    .then(({ EntitiesDetectionJobPropertiesList: jobList }) => {
      log.debug({ jobList }, 'Entity detection job list retrieved ')
      return {
        count: jobList.length,
        jobs: jobList.map(
          ({ JobId: jobId, JobName: jobName, SubmitTime: submitTime }) => ({
            jobId,
            jobName,
            submitTime
          })
        )
      }
    })
}
```

The listEntitiesDetectionJobs API is invoked, filtering on in-progress jobs. To limit the number potentially returned, we cap the number of results to a maximum. We have chosen 10 for this value.

The results are transformed to give us an output containing the total number of in-progress jobs (not exceeding our maximum job count value of 10) and a summary of each job.

We now have three Lambda functions that can be used together to perform entity recognition for batches of files:

1 `getTextBatch` to select a limited number of files for processing.
2 `startBatchProcessing` to start execution of entity recognition for a batch of files.
3 `checkActiveJobs` to report on the number of recognition jobs in progress. This will come in handy later when we tie all of our entity extraction logic together.

We have tested `getTextBatch` already using `sls invoke local`. Next, we will deploy the extraction service and start processing on a batch of sample text files, to see how these functions fit together in practice.

9.7   *Deploying and testing batch entity recognition*

To test our function, we are going to first deploy the extraction service. This is done in the same way as all our other Serverless Framework deployments:

```
cd extraction-service
npm install
sls deploy
```

We can now use the Serverless Framework CLI to invoke our remote function. We will pass the `startBatchProcessing` Lambda function a simple JSON-encoded array of paths. For this example, we will use the two files already present in our incoming-texts S3 directory. These files contain the Apollo 11 sample text. Later, we will be performing entity recognition on real conference web page data!

```
sls invoke -f startBatchProcessing --data \
  "{\"paths\":[\"test/pending.txt\", \"test2/pending.txt\"]}"
```

If the execution is successful, you should see something like the following output—a JSON object containing the batch ID:

```
{
    "batchId": "20190829113049287"
}
```

Next, we will run checkActiveJobs to report on the number of active Comprehend jobs.

Listing 9.12 checkActiveJobs **output**

```
{
    "count": 1,                                    The total number
    "jobs": [                                      of jobs in progress
        {
            "jobId": "acf2faa221ee1ce52c3881e4991f9fce",    The job ID is generated
                                                            by Comprehend.
            "jobName": "20190829113049287",                The job name matches the
            "submitTime": "2019-08-29T11:30:49.517Z"       batch ID we generated.
        }
    ]
}
```

After 5–10 minutes, running checkActiveJobs again will report zero in-progress jobs. At this point, you can inspect the output of the job.

The extraction-service directory contains a shell script that may be used to conveniently find, extract, and output the results of a batch job. To run it, execute the following command:

```
./scripts/get-batch_results.sh <BATCH_ID>
```

The <BATCH_ID> placeholder can be replaced with the batch ID value you saw when startBatchProcessing was executed. Running this script will print JSON representing Comprehend entity recognition results for each sample text. In our example so far, both files in the batch have the same sample text about Apollo 11.

9.8 *Persisting recognition results*

We have seen how to manually run entity extraction functions from the command line and verify the NER output. For our end-to-end application for conference site crawling and analysis, we want to persist our entity extraction results. This way, we can use an API to serve extracted names for people, locations, and dates for our conference-seeking audience!

Entity result processing will be driven by the arrival of Comprehend results in the output folder that we configured when we started the entity recognition job. Just as with the preparation service, we'll use an S3 bucket notification. You will find the configuration of the `processEntityResults` function in the `serverless.yml` for the extraction service. The relevant section is reproduced in the next listing.

Listing 9.13   `serverless.yml` extract for `processEntityResults`

```
processEntityResults:
    handler: handler.processEntityResults
    events:
      - s3:
          bucket: ${env:ITEM_STORE_BUCKET}          ⟵  The notification configuration is in the
          event: s3:ObjectCreated:*                      same bucket as the preparation
          rules:                                         service S3 bucket notification. This
            - prefix: entity-results/                    time, the key suffix/prefix is different.
            - suffix: /output.tar.gz       ⟵
          existing: true                         All Comprehend results are persisted
                                                 to entity-results, as we specified in
                                                 the call to startEntitiesDetectionJob.

                    Comprehend writes other, temporary
                    files. We are only interested in the final
                         results, stored in output.tar.gz.
```

When results arrive, we'll use our notified Lambda function to extract results and persist them in the frontier service. Because the frontier service maintains state for all URLs, it's convenient to store the results along with the crawling/extraction state. Let's break down all the required steps:

1 The S3 notification triggers the `processEntityResults` function.
2 The object is fetched from S3 as a stream.
3 The stream is unzipped and extracted.
4 Each JSON line in the output is parsed.
5 The structure of each Comprehend result entry is transformed to a more accessible data structure. The results are grouped by entity type (PERSON, LOCATION, and so on).
6 The seed and URL for the web page are derived from the path (key) of the S3 object.
7 The transformed recognition results are sent to the frontier service.

The Lambda function and associated internal functions (`handleEntityResult-Lines`, `storeEntityResults`) can be found in the extraction service's `handler.js` module.

9.9 *Tying it all together*

The last task in our conference site crawling and recognition application is to tie all of the functionality together so all sites are automatically analyzed as the crawler makes new page data available.

Just as we did in chapter 8, we are going to employ AWS Step Functions for this job.

9.9.1 Orchestrating entity extraction

Figure 9.5 shows the control logic implemented in the step function and how it relates to the Lambda functions we have built.

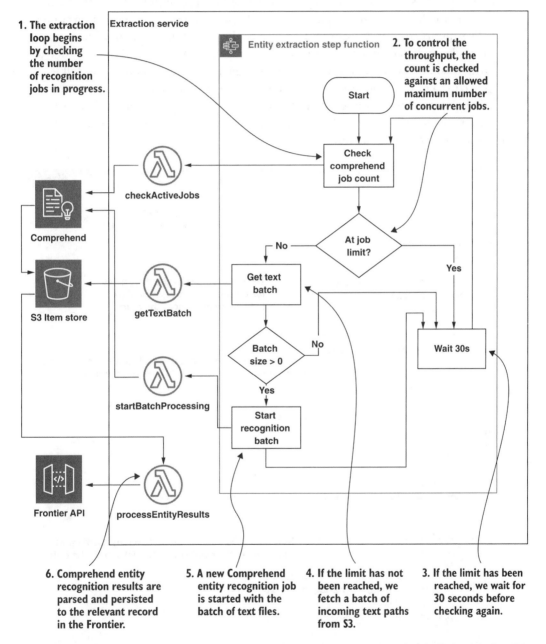

1. The extraction loop begins by checking the number of recognition jobs in progress.

2. To control the throughput, the count is checked against an allowed maximum number of concurrent jobs.

6. Comprehend entity recognition results are parsed and persisted to the relevant record in the Frontier.

5. A new Comprehend entity recognition job is started with the batch of text files.

4. If the limit has not been reached, we fetch a batch of incoming text paths from S3.

3. If the limit has been reached, we wait for 30 seconds before checking again.

Figure 9.5 The logical steps in the extraction service are orchestrated using an AWS step function. This ensures we have control over how many machine learning jobs are executed concurrently. It is also extensible to support advanced error recovery scenarios.

Our conference data extraction process is a continuous loop that checks for newly crawled page text, and starts asynchronous entity recognition according to a configured limit of concurrent jobs. As we have seen, the result processing is a separate, asynchronous process, driven by the arrival of Comprehend results in the S3 bucket.

Figure 9.5 is a slight simplification of the step function. Step functions don't actually support continuously executing events; the maximum execution time is one year. It is also mandatory to have a reachable End state in the function. In order to deal with this, we have added some additional logic to the step function. We will terminate execution of the function after 100 iterations. This is a safety measure to avoid forgetting about a long-running job, potentially resulting in surprising AWS costs! The following listing shows a condensed view of the step function YAML. The full version is contained in the extraction service's `serverless.yml`.

Listing 9.14 Condensed entity extraction step-function configuration

```yaml
StartAt: Initialize
States:                              The start state initializes
  Initialize:                        the iteration count to 100.
    Type: Pass
    Result:
      iterations: 100
    ResultPath: $.iterator           The Iteration task is the start point
    Next: Iterator                   for the loop. It invokes a Lambda
  Iterator:                          function to decrement the count.
    Type: Task
    Resource: !GetAtt IteratorLambdaFunction.Arn
    ResultPath: $.iterator
    Next: ShouldFinish               Check the number of iterations. When the loop has been
  ShouldFinish:                      performed 100 times, the state machine terminates.
    Type: Choice
    Choices:
      - Variable: $.iterator.iterations
        NumericEquals: 0
        Next: Done
    Default: Check Comprehend
  Check Comprehend:
    Type: Task
    Resource: !GetAtt CheckActiveJobsLambdaFunction.Arn
    ...

  Check Job Limit:                   Now that we've run the checkActiveJobs function, we
    Type: Choice                     can compare the number of active jobs to the limit (10).
    Choices:
      - Variable: $.activeJobsResult.count
        NumericGreaterThanEquals: 10
        Next: Wait
    Default: Get Text Batch
  Get Text Batch:
    Type: Task
    Resource: !GetAtt GetTextBatchLambdaFunction.Arn
    ...
```

```
Check Batch Size:
   Type: Choice
   Choices:
      - Variable: $.textBatchResult.count
        NumericEquals: 0
        Next: Wait
   Default: Start Batch Processing
Start Batch Processing:
   Type: Task
   Resource: !GetAtt StartBatchProcessingLambdaFunction.Arn
   ...

Wait:
   Type: Wait
   Seconds: 30
   Next: Iterator
Done:
   Type: Pass
   End: true
```

> **Retrieve the batch of incoming texts. If there are no texts available, we wait. If there is at least one item, we start an entity recognition job.**

> **The wait period of 30 seconds is one variable that controls the throughput of data. We could also increase the maximum batch size and the number of concurrent Comprehend jobs.**

The simple iterator function is provided in the `handler.js` module contained in `extraction-service`.

9.9.2 *End-to-end data extraction testing*

We have completed building our final serverless AI application! You have covered a great deal of serverless architecture, learned many incredibly powerful AI services, and built some pretty amazing AI-enabled systems. Congratulations on reaching this milestone! It's time to reward yourself by running our end-to-end conference data crawling and extraction application in full. Let's kick off the web crawler with the URL of a conference website. Then, sit back and observe our automated extraction logic kick into action, as the details of conferences and speakers detected using AI start to appear.

Just as we did at the end of chapter 8, we will start the web crawler with a seed URL. This time, we'll pick a real conference website!

```
aws stepfunctions start-execution \
  --state-machine-arn arn:aws:states:eu-west-
     1:1234567890123:stateMachine:CrawlScheduler \
  --input '{"url": "https://dt-x.io"}'
```

We will also start the entity extraction step function in the same way. This command requires no JSON input:

```
aws stepfunctions start-execution \
   --state-machine-arn arn:aws:states:eu-west-
     1:1234567890123:stateMachine:EntityExtraction
```

In both cases, you will have to replace the step function ARN with the correct values for your deployment. Recall from chapter 8 that the AWS CLI command required to retrieve these is

```
aws stepfunctions list-state-machines --output text
```

Once the state machines are running, you can view them in the AWS Console Step Functions section, and monitor their progress by clicking on the states as transitions occur. Figure 9.6 shows the progress for the entity extraction state machine.

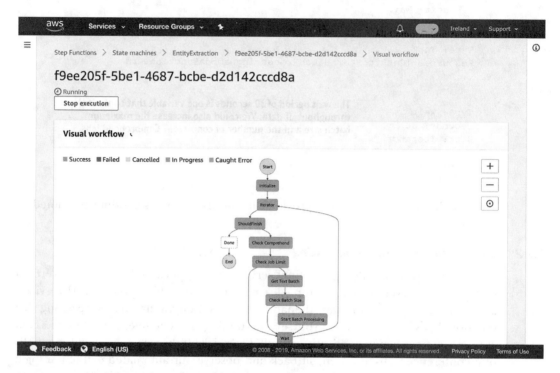

Figure 9.6   Monitoring the progress of the entity extraction state machine

9.9.3   *Viewing conference data extraction results*

Building a front-end UI for the application is beyond the scope of this chapter, so a handy script for inspecting results is available in `scripts/get_extracted _entities.js`. By running this script, a DynamoDB query will be executed to find extracted entities for a given seed URL in the frontier table. These results are then aggregated to generate a CSV file summarizing the number of appearances, and an average score for each entity found using the machine learning process. The script is executed as follows:

```
scripts/get_extracted_entities.js https://dt-x.io
```

The script uses the AWS SDK, so AWS credentials must be configured in the shell. The script will print the name of the CSV file generated. For this example, it will be `https-dt-x-io.csv`. Open the CSV using an application such as Excel to inspect the outcome. Figure 9.7 shows our results for this conference website.

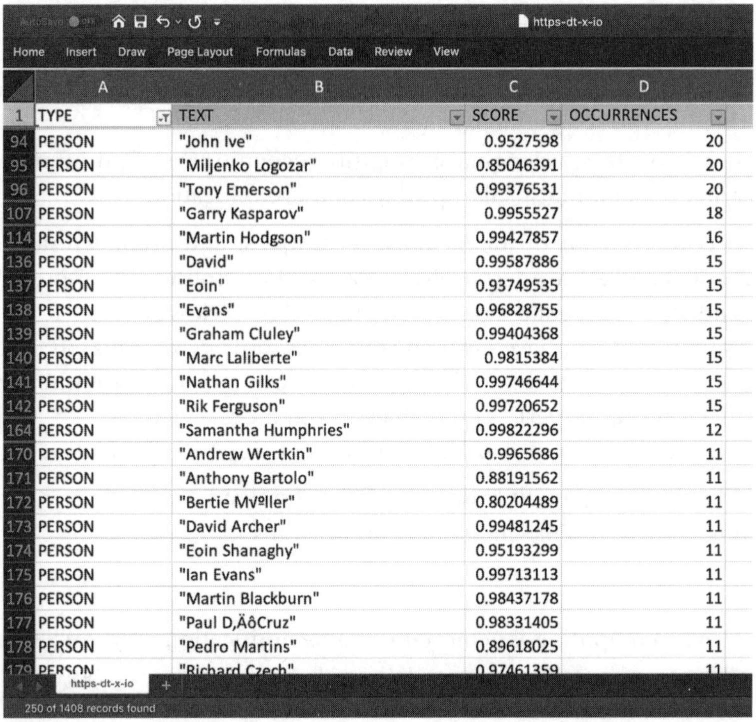

	TYPE	TEXT	SCORE	OCCURRENCES
94	PERSON	"John Ive"	0.9527598	20
95	PERSON	"Miljenko Logozar"	0.85046391	20
96	PERSON	"Tony Emerson"	0.99376531	20
107	PERSON	"Garry Kasparov"	0.9955527	18
114	PERSON	"Martin Hodgson"	0.99427857	16
136	PERSON	"David"	0.99587886	15
137	PERSON	"Eoin"	0.93749535	15
138	PERSON	"Evans"	0.96828755	15
139	PERSON	"Graham Cluley"	0.99404368	15
140	PERSON	"Marc Laliberte"	0.9815384	15
141	PERSON	"Nathan Gilks"	0.99746644	15
142	PERSON	"Rik Ferguson"	0.99720652	15
164	PERSON	"Samantha Humphries"	0.99822296	12
170	PERSON	"Andrew Wertkin"	0.9965686	11
171	PERSON	"Anthony Bartolo"	0.88191562	11
172	PERSON	"Bertie MVºller"	0.80204489	11
173	PERSON	"David Archer"	0.99481245	11
174	PERSON	"Eoin Shanaghy"	0.95193299	11
175	PERSON	"Ian Evans"	0.99713113	11
176	PERSON	"Martin Blackburn"	0.98437178	11
177	PERSON	"Paul D,ÄôCruz"	0.98331405	11
178	PERSON	"Pedro Martins"	0.89618025	11
179	PERSON	"Richard Czech"	0.97461359	11

Figure 9.7 Monitoring the progress of the entity extraction state machine

We have filtered to show only PERSON entities in this case. The results include every person mentioned across all pages of the crawled site! This conference has some great speakers, including both authors of this book!

Feel free to try other conference sites to test the limits of our conference crawler and extractor. As always, bear in mind your usage costs with AWS. Comprehend costs can be expensive as volumes grow,[13] though a free tier is available. If in doubt, stop any running step function state machines, and remove the deployed application as soon as you are done testing. The `chapter8-9` code directory includes a `clean.sh` script to help you with this!

9.10 Wrapping up

You have made it to the end of the last chapter. Congratulations on sticking with it and getting this far! In this book, we have built

- An image recognition system with object detection
- A voice-driven task management app
- A chatbot

[13] Amazon Comprehend Costs, https://aws.amazon.com/comprehend/pricing/.

- An automated identity document scanner
- An AI integration for e-commerce systems, to determine the sentiment behind customer product reviews, categorize them using a custom classifier, and forward them to the correct department
- An event web site crawler that uses entity recognition to find information on conferences, including speaker profiles and event location

We have also covered a lot of ideas, tools, techniques, and architectural practices. Though Serverless and AI are fast-evolving topics, these foundational principles are designed to endure as you build amazing AI-enabled serverless systems.

We are grateful that you have devoted your time to *AI as a Service*. To learn more, check out the fourTheorem blog (https://fourtheorem.com/blog) where you will find more articles on AI, serverless architecture, and more.

For all our updates on these topics, follow us on Twitter and LinkedIn:

- Peter Elger—@pelger—linkedin.com/in/peterelger
- Eóin Shanaghy - @eoins - linkedin.com/in/eoins

Summary

- Event-driven computing is achieved using S3 notifications and AWS Lambda.
- A dead-letter queue captures undelivered messages. It can be implemented with AWS Lambda and SQS to prevent data loss.
- Named entity recognition is the process of automatically identifying entities such as names, places, and dates in text.
- Amazon Comprehend has multiple modes of operation that can be selected depending on the quantity of text being analyzed.
- Comprehend can be used to perform asynchronous batch entity recognition.
- Step functions can be used to control the concurrency and throughput of asynchronous AI analysis jobs.
- The machine learning analysis data produced by Comprehend can be extracted and transformed according to the application's business requirements.

WARNING   Please ensure that you fully remove all cloud resources deployed in this chapter in order to avoid additional charges!

appendix A
AWS account setup and configuration

This appendix is for readers unfamiliar with Amazon Web Services. It explains how to get set up on AWS and how to configure your environment for the examples in the book.

A.1 Set up an AWS account

Before you can start using AWS, you need to create an account. Your account is a basket for all your cloud resources. You can attach multiple users to an account if multiple people need access to it; by default, your account will have one root user. To create an account, you need the following:

- A telephone number to validate your identity
- A credit card to pay your bills

The sign-up process consists of five steps:

1 Provide your login credentials.
2 Provide your contact information.
3 Provide your payment details.
4 Verify your identity.
5 Choose your support plan.

Point your favorite web browser to https://aws.amazon.com, and click the Create a Free Account button.

A.1.1 Providing your login credentials

Creating an AWS account starts with defining a unique AWS account name, as shown in figure A.1. The AWS account name has to be globally unique among all AWS customers. Beside the account name, you have to specify an email address and

265

a password used to authenticate the root user of your AWS account. We advise you to choose a strong password to prevent misuse of your account. Use a password consisting of at least 20 characters. Protecting your AWS account from unwanted access is crucial to avoid data breaches, data loss, or unwanted resource usage on your behalf. It is also worthwhile to spend some time investigating how to use multi-factor authentication (MFA) with your account.

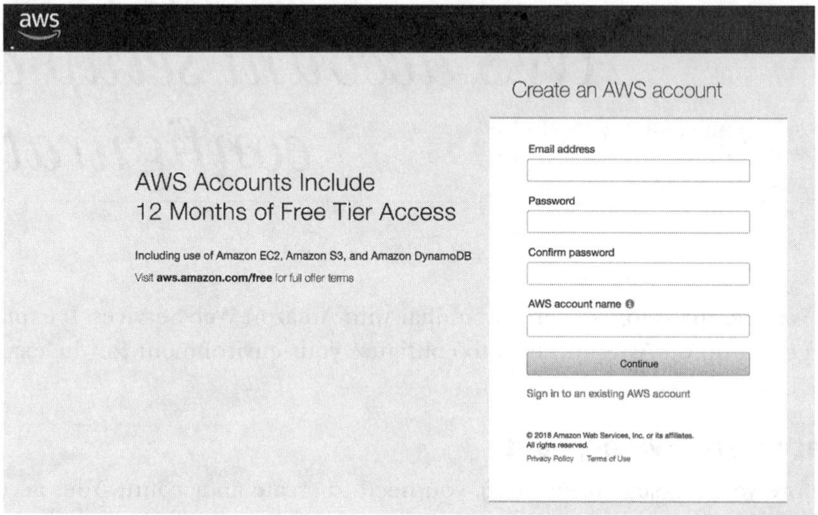

Figure A.1   Creating an AWS account: signup page

The next step, as shown in figure A.2, is adding your contact information. Fill in all the required fields, and continue.

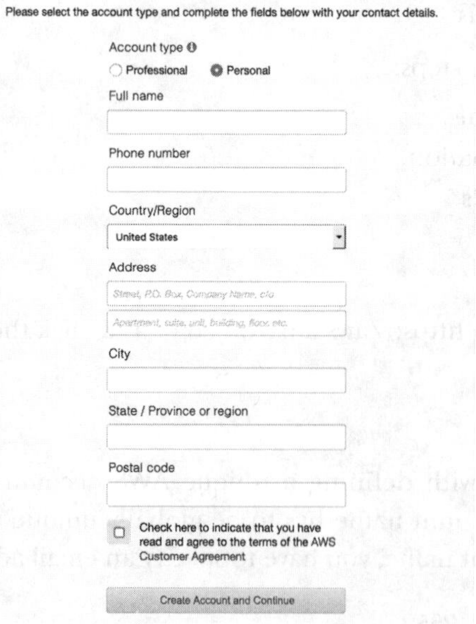

Figure A.2   Creating an AWS account: providing your contact information

A.1.2 Providing your payment details

Next, the screen shown in figure A.3 asks for your payment information. Provide your credit card information. There's an option to change the currency setting from USD to AUD, CAD, CHF, DKK, EUR, GBP, HKD, JPY, NOK, NZD, SEK, or ZAR later if that's more convenient for you. If you choose this option, the amount in USD is converted into your local currency at the end of the month.

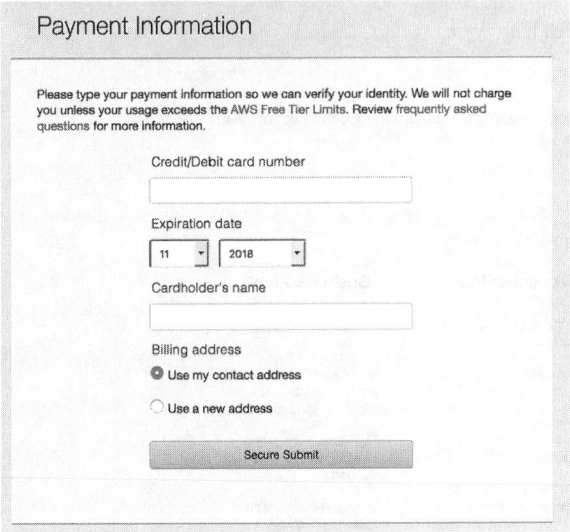

Payment Information

Please type your payment information so we can verify your identity. We will not charge you unless your usage exceeds the AWS Free Tier Limits. Review frequently asked questions for more information.

Credit/Debit card number

Expiration date
11   2018

Cardholder's name

Billing address
● Use my contact address
○ Use a new address

Secure Submit

Figure A.3   Creating an AWS account: providing your payment details

A.1.3 Verifying your identity

The next step is to verify your identity. Figure A.4 shows the first step of the process. After you complete the first part of the form, you'll receive a call from AWS. A robot voice will ask for your PIN. The four-digit PIN is displayed on the website, and you have to enter it using your telephone. After your identity has been verified, you are ready to continue with the last step.

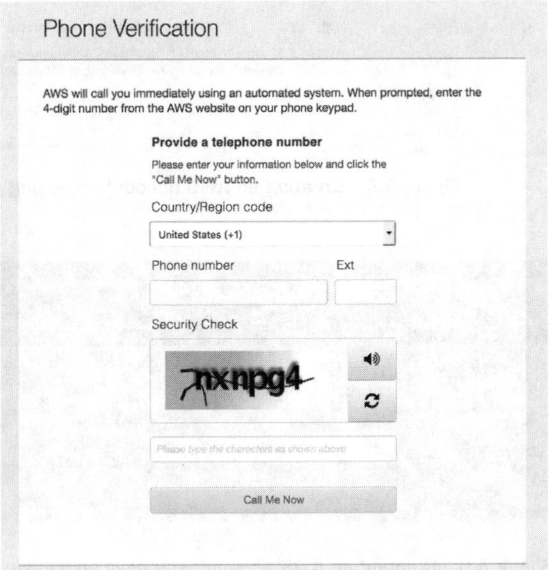

Phone Verification

AWS will call you immediately using an automated system. When prompted, enter the 4-digit number from the AWS website on your phone keypad.

Provide a telephone number

Please enter your information below and click the "Call Me Now" button.

Country/Region code

United States (+1)

Phone number   Ext

Security Check

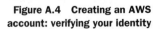

Please type the characters as shown above

Call Me Now

Figure A.4   Creating an AWS account: verifying your identity

A.1.4   *Choosing your support plan*

The last step is to choose a support plan; see figure A.5. In this case, select the Basic plan, which is free. If you later create an AWS account for your business, we recommend the Business support plan. You can even switch support plans later. You may have to wait a few minutes until your account is ready. Click Sign In to the Console, as shown in figure A.6, to sign into your AWS account for the first time!

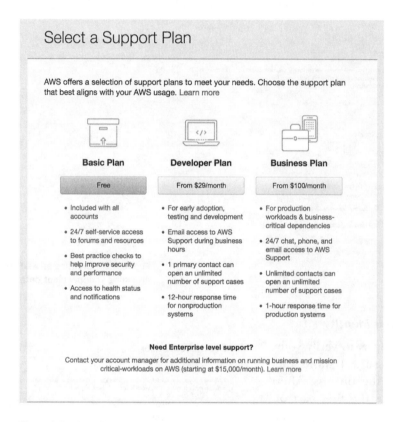

Figure A.5   Creating an AWS account: choosing your support plan

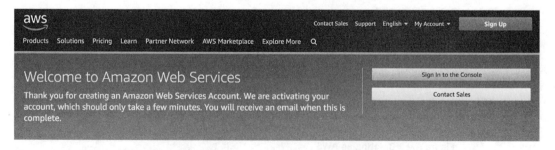

Figure A.6   Creating an AWS account: you have successfully created an AWS account.

A.2   *Signing in*

You now have an AWS account and are ready to sign in to the AWS Management Console. The Management Console is a web-based tool you can use to inspect and control AWS resources; it makes most of the functionality of the AWS API available to you. Figure A.7 shows the sign-in form at https://console.aws.amazon.com. Enter your email address, click Next, and then enter your password to sign in.

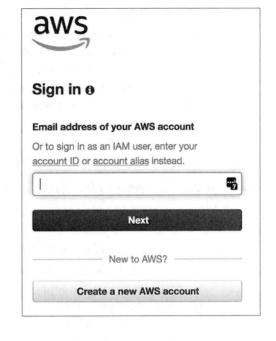

Figure A.7   Creating an AWS account: signing in to the console

After you have signed in successfully, you are forwarded to the start page of the Console, as shown in figure A.8.

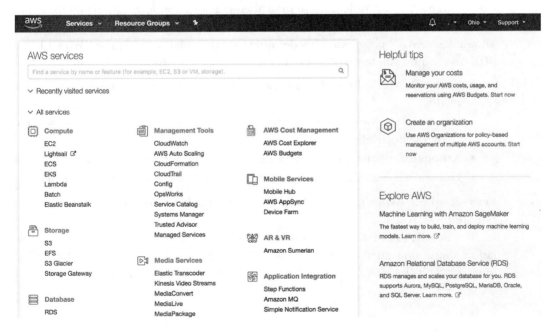

Figure A.8   AWS Console

A.3   *Best practice*

In the previous sections we have covered setting up an AWS root account. If you intend to use this account for experimentation only, this will suffice; however, be aware that for production workloads, using the root account is discouraged. A full treatment of this topic is outside the scope of this book, but we strongly encourage you to use AWS account best practices, such as setting up IAM users, groups, and roles as outlined in this AWS article: http://mng.bz/nzQd. We also recommend the AWS security blog as a great resource for keeping up to date with AWS-related security topics: https://aws.amazon.com/blogs/security/.

A.4   *AWS Command Line Interface*

When you need to create, edit, or inspect AWS cloud resources, you have a number of options:

- Manually, using the AWS Console in a web browser.
- Programatically, using the AWS SDK for your programming language of choice. Many languages are supported, including JavaScript and Python.
- Using third-party tools such as the Serverless Framework. These tools typically use the AWS SDK under the hood.
- Using the AWS Command Line Interface (CLI).

Throughout this book, we will use the Serverless Framework where possible. In some cases, we will execute commands with the AWS CLI. We aim to avoid using the AWS Console. The AWS Console is more than adequate for experimentation and for familiarizing yourself with AWS products. It's also the easiest to use. However, as your knowledge of AWS progresses, it's definitely worth understanding the AWS CLI and SDK. You should aim to use programmatic options for the following reasons:

- Your code (including CLI commands) provides a record of changes you have made.
- You can place your code under version control (for example, Git) and manage changes effectively.
- Actions can be redone quickly, without having to perform many manual steps.
- Human errors that are common with point-and-click interfaces are less likely.

Let's set up the AWS CLI so you have everything ready to run CLI commands when required.

The installation method will depend on your platform. For Windows-based installation, simply download the 64-bit (https://s3.amazonaws.com/aws-cli/AWSCLI64PY3.msi) or 32-bit (https://s3.amazonaws.com/aws-cli/AWSCLI32PY3.msi) installer.

A.4.1 Installing the AWS CLI on Linux

Most Linux package managers offer a quick installation option for the AWS CLI. For Ubuntu or Debian-based systems, use `apt`:

```
sudo apt install awscli
```

For distributions that use yum, like CentOS and Fedora, enter this command:

```
sudo yum install awscli
```

A.4.2 Installing the AWS CLI on MacOS

For MacOS users with Homebrew, the simplest installation method is to use Homebrew:

```
brew install awscli
```

A.4.3 Installing the AWS CLI on other platforms

If your system differs from the options already described, you can try an alternative method, such as using `pip` to install the AWS CLI with Python. For details, refer to the AWS CLI installation documentation (http://mng.bz/X0gE).

A.4.4 Configuring the local AWS environment

To access AWS services from a local development system, we need to create an API access key pair and make it available to our development shell. To do this, first log back into your AWS account, and then select My Security Credentials from the AWS user menu, as illustrated in figure A.9.

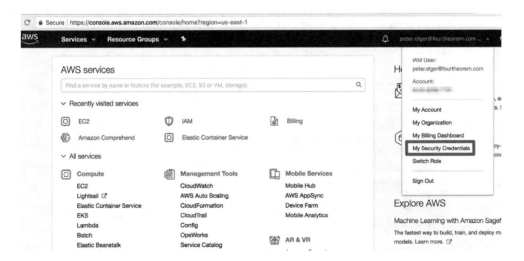

Figure A.9   AWS security credentials menu

Next, select your user name from the AWS user list, and then select Create Access Key from the user summary screen, as illustrated in figure A.10.

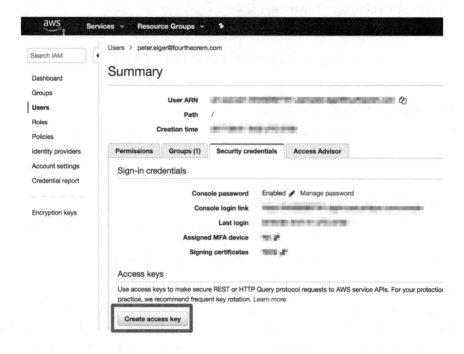

Figure A.10   AWS user summary screen

AWS will create an API access key pair. To use these keys, go ahead and download the CSV file, as shown in figure A.11.

Figure A.11   AWS keys created dialog

Store this CSV file somewhere secure for later reference. The CSV file contains two identifiers: the access key ID and a secret access key. The contents should look similar to the following listing.

Listing A.1 AWS credentials CSV file

```
Access key ID,Secret access key
ABCDEFGHIJKLMNOPQRST,123456789abcdefghijklmnopqrstuvwxyz1234a
```

To use these keys for access, we need to add them to our development shell. For UNIX-like systems, this can be achieved by adding the environment variables to your shell configuration. For example, Bash shell users can add these to their `.bash_profile` file, as shown in the next listing.

Listing A.2 `bash_profile` entries for AWS credentials

```
export AWS_ACCOUNT_ID=<your aws account ID>
export AWS_ACCESS_KEY_ID=<your access key ID>
export AWS_SECRET_ACCESS_KEY=<your secret access key>
export AWS_DEFAULT_REGION=eu-west-1
export AWS_REGION=eu-west-1
```

> **NOTE** We have set both the `AWS_REGION` and `AWS_DEFAULT_REGION` environment variables. This is due to an unfortunate mismatch between the JavaScript SDK and the CLI. The AWS CLI uses `AWS_DEFAULT_REGION`, whereas the SDK uses `AWS_REGION`. We expect this to be corrected in future releases, but for now, the simple fix is to set both variables to the same region.

Windows users will need to set these environment variables using the system configuration dialog in the Control Panel. Note that in order for these environment variables to take effect, you will need to restart your development shell.

Managing your keys

There are various other ways to configure AWS API access through the use of configuration files. For convenience, we have used environment variables for local development.

You should exercise caution in managing access keys to ensure that they are not inadvertently exposed. For example, adding access keys to a public Git repository is a very bad idea!

Note that we are suggesting the use of environment variables for AWS API keys in a *local development environment only*. We do not recommend that you do this in a production environment. There are services available to help with key management, such as AWS Key Management Service (KMS). A full treatment of this topic is outside the scope of this book.

A.4.5   *Checking the setup*

To confirm that the setup is good, run the following commands:

```
$ aws --version
$ aws s3 ls s3://
```

Both should complete with no errors. If this is not the case, then please review all of the preceding steps in this appendix.

appendix B
Data requirements
for AWS managed
AI services

Chapter 1 presented a table of AWS managed AI services. This appendix expands on this table to show the data requirements for each service. This is presented in table B.1. It also indicates whether training is supported in each service. You can use this guide, along with everything you learned about data gathering in chapter 7, to ensure you have the correct data and have performed adequate data preparation.

Table B.1   Data requirements for AI services

Application	Service	Data required	Training support
Machine translation	AWS Translate	Text in the source language	Translate does not support or require custom training. You can, however, define custom terminology that is specific to your domain.
Document analysis	AWS Textract	High quality images of documents	No training is required.
Key phrases	AWS Comprehend	Text	No training is required.
Sentiment analysis	AWS Comprehend	Text	No training is required.
Topic modeling	AWS Comprehend	Text	No training is required.
Document classification	AWS Comprehend	Text with classification labels	Training is required. We covered custom classifiers in chapter 6.

Table B.1   Data requirements for AI services *(continued)*

Application	Service	Data required	Training support
Entity extraction	AWS Comprehend	Text. For custom entity training, labelled entities are required.	Standard entities (names, dates, and locations) can be extracted without training. It is also possible to train AWS Comprehend with custom entities by providing a set of text with entity labels.
Chatbots	AWS Lex	Text utterances	Training is not required. AWS Lex builds models based on sample utterances and configured slots. This was covered in chapter 4.
Speech-to-text	AWS Transcribe	Audio files or streaming audio	No training is required, but it is possible to add custom vocabularies and pronunciations to refine results.
Text-to-speech	AWS Polly	Text, optionally annotated using SSML	No training is required. AWS Polly was covered in chapter 4.
Object, scene, and activity detection	AWS Rekognition	Image or video	No training is required.
Facial recognition	AWS Rekognition	Image or video	No training is required, but custom faces can be added.
Facial analysis	AWS Rekognition	Image or video	No training is required.
Text in images	AWS Rekognition	Image	No training is required.
Time series forecasting	AWS Forecast	Time series data and item metadata	Training is required. AWS Forecast trains models based on historical data and metadata you provide.
Real-time personalization and recommendation	AWS Personalize	Item catalog and user data	Training is required. AWS Personalize can train a model and choose an optimal algorithm based on the data provided.

As you can see, the majority of services do not require a training phase. For these cases, the data gathering and learning process is greatly simplified. Whether training or using pre-trained models, AWS has clear specifications on the kind of data required and the format it should be in.

appendix C
Data sources
for AI applications

Chapter 7 gives an overview of the importance of good data gathering and preparation in building AI-enabled applications. This appendix lists some of the data sources that you may utilize to ensure you have the right data for AI success.

C.1 Public data sets

1 The Registry of Open Data on AWS (https://registry.opendata.aws) includes, among others data sets, petabytes of Common Crawl data (http://common-crawl.org/the-data).

2 Public APIs, such as the Twitter API, provide large volumes of data. We saw in chapter 6 how social media posts can be used to perform classification and sentiment analysis.

3 Google has a search engine for public data sets (https://tool-box.google.com/datasetsearch) and a list of public data sets (https://ai.google/tools/datasets/).

4 Kaggle has a directory of thousands of data sets (https://www.kaggle.com/datasets).

5 Many government data sources are now available. An example of this is the United States open government data on https://data.gov.

6 If you are a dog person who felt there was too much cat content in chapter 2, you will be comforted by the 20,000 dog images available in the Stanford Dogs Data set (http://vision.stanford.edu/aditya86/ImageNetDogs/)!

TIP Many public data sets are subject to licenses. Do your homework and understand the legal implications of using data sets in your work.

C.2   Software analytics and logs

Beyond public, prepackaged data, there are many means of collecting data for your machine learning applications. Existing software systems have analytics and log data which can be prepared and optimised for machine learning algorithms:

- Analytics platforms that collect data on end-user interaction from web and mobile applications are a valuable source of raw data on user behavior and interactions. Google Analytics is one example of this.
- Web server and back end application logs or audit logs may also be a comprehensive source of interactions with and within a system.

C.3   Human data gathering

Where data is not readily available and needs to be either collected or transformed at scale, there are a number of ways to crowdsource this job:

- Data gathering companies provide services to collect (via surveys or other means) or transform data.
- There are API-driven crowdsourcing services. Amazon Mechanical Turk (MTurk) is a well-known example (https://www.mturk.com/).
- Many of us have performed countless Captcha checks as a means of verifying that we are not robots! This service actually provides two benefits. Services like reCAPTCHA also serve as a means of gathering labelled training data for image recognition algorithms.[1]

C.4   Device data

Depending on your application, it may be possible to gather telemetry from existing systems, either using software monitoring tools or hardware sensors:

- Sensors are no longer limited to industrial automation devices. IoT (internet of things) devices are becoming prevalent in many environments and generate potentially vast data sets.
- Still-image or video cameras can be used to gather image data for training and analysis. As an example of this, think of the scale of image capture required for Google StreetView and again, how reCAPTCHA is used as a means to label these images at scale.

---

[1]   James O'Malley, "Captcha if you can: how you've been training AI for years without realising it." TechRadar 12 January 2018, https://www.techradar.com/news/captcha-if-you-can-how-youve-been-training-ai-for-years-without-realising-it.

appendix D
Setting up a DNS
domain and certificate

Several of the systems presented in this book require a common AWS setup that needs to be done via the AWS Management console, rather than programmatically. This is because some manual verification is required. Please ensure that you have completed the following setup before running the example systems.

D.1 Setting up a domain

When you create dynamic HTTP endpoints for AWS resources like S3 buckets and API Gateway, AWS will generate a URL for these endpoints. You can use these generated names when you are not building a production application. It quickly becomes frustrating, however. Every time you remove and destroy these resources, the URLs may change. They are also long and difficult to remember. To avoid these problems, we are going to register a domain. The process is made easy by using the Route 53 service in AWS. Alternatively, if you already have a domain and wish to use it, or you wish to use a subdomain of an already registered domain, consult the Route 53 documentation (http://mng.bz/Mox8).

D.1.1 Registering a domain name

We are going to walk through the process of registering a new domain from scratch using Route 53.

If you don't yet have any domain-related resources on this AWS account, clicking the Route 53 link in the Networking section of the main AWS Console (assuming the All Services control is already expanded) takes you to an introductory screen. If you've already created resources, you're instead sent to the Route 53 dashboard.

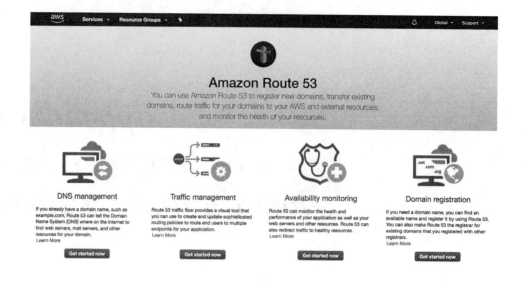

Figure D.1 Amazon Route 53 introduction page showing the service's four distinct elements

Figure D.1 shows the Route 53 introduction page. As you can see, Route 53 is built to deliver four distinct but closely related services: *domain registration* (Amazon is a domain name registrar); *DNS management,* which is the tool you'll use to direct traffic to your domain; *traffic management,* to handle traffic redirection; and *availability monitoring,* to confirm that your target resources are performing the way they're supposed to. We are only going to concern ourselves with domain registration and DNS management.

Click the Get Started Now button beneath Domain Registration, and then click Register Domain. Type the main part of the name—for example, *acme-corporation* if you wish to register *acme-corporation.com.* A drop-down menu displays domains including .com, .org, .net, and so on, with their annual registration cost. Select one, and click Check. Route 54 will search online records to see if that combination is currently available. When you find a domain name that fits your needs, add it to your cart, and go through the checkout process to submit payment for your first year's registration fee. Domain registrations usually cost between $10 and $15 US per year and aren't included in Free Tier usage. In a short time, your new domain will appear in the Route 53 dashboard. It may take a while before your domain registration is complete. At that point, you are ready to proceed to configuring your domain and using it for your newly developed serverless AI application!

NOTE There's nothing forcing you to use Route 53 for your domain registration. In fact, you may find that other providers offer cheaper alternatives. You can use Route 53's other features even for domains registered through other companies.

D.1.2 Configuring your hosted zone

Your domain is now registered, but you haven't told it what to do with incoming requests. Route 53 will automatically create a *Hosted Zone* for your registered domain. Click Hosted Zones in the Route 53 section of the Console and follow the link to the new hosted zone. You will find yourself on a page with two pre-created record sets:

- *Start of authority (SOA)*—Identifies your domain's basic DNS configuration information.
- *NS*—Lists authoritative name servers that can be queried about your domain host. These are the public services that provide answers to domain-name translation requests.

NOTE *Record set*—A set of data records that defines a particular aspect of domain behavior.

Don't mess with either of these record sets. They're not enough on their own to make your new domain name fully available. Later on, we will use the Serverless Framework to automatically add a new record that will tell anyone using your domain name servers (by pointing their browsers to your domain) to request the IP address used by our application.

D.2 Settting up a certificate

Web security is an extensive topic and well beyond the scope of this book. We still want to be sure that we use HTTPS for all web traffic. The days of using plain HTTP are long gone, and it's good to consider security best practices early on. In order to make it easy to manage certificate generation and renewal, we will use AWS Certificate Manager.

D.2.1 Provisioning a new certificate

In the AWS Console, click the link to Certificate Manager in the Networking section. This will bring you to the Certificate Manager dashboard, shown in figure D.2.

Figure D.2   The Certificate Manager introduction page

Select Get Started under the Provision Certificates section, and choose the Request a Public Certificate option. The Request a Certificate page, shown in figure D.3, allows us to specify the domains for our certificate. We are going to request a wildcard certificate to use with all subdomains of our registered domains. For example, if we registered `stuff.org`, the wildcard certificate protects `api.stuff.org` and `www.stuff.org`.

Add `*.stuff.org` (the wildcard domain name) and `stuff.org`. Then, click Next to select the validation method. This will present a page similar to figure D.3.

The AWS Console will request validation for the domains you have added to ensure you are the owner, as shown in figure D.4.

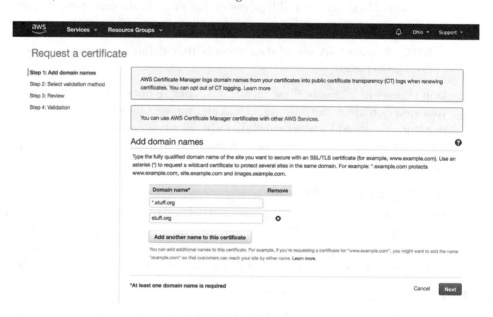

Figure D.3   Selecting domain names to protect with a certificate

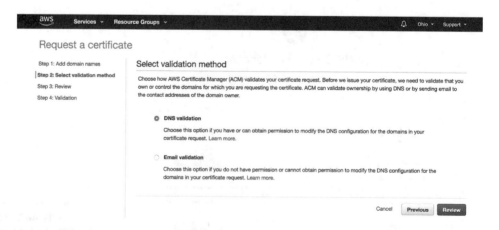

Figure D.4   Choosing a validation method for your certificate

Choose DNS Validation and confirm this selection. Since we registered the domain with Route 53, we have the option to automatically create the special validation DNS entries in the hosted zone. Expand the section for each domain, shown in figure D.5.

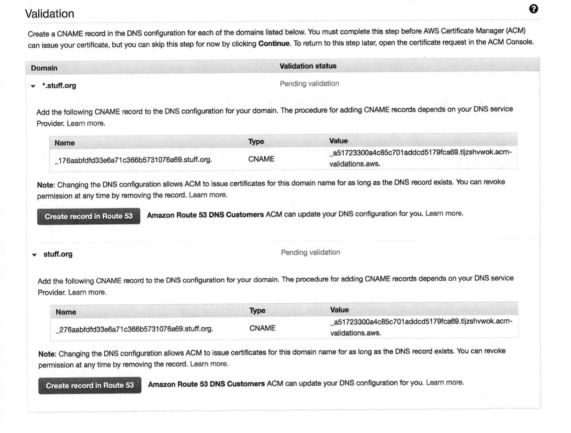

Figure D.5   Creating validation DNS records with Route 53

Click Create Record in Route 53. Confirm this step for each domain before selecting Continue.

You may need to wait up to 30 minutes before your domain has been validated and your certificate provisioning has completed. Once this is done, the Certificate Manager will show your certificate status as *Verified*, as shown in figure D.6.

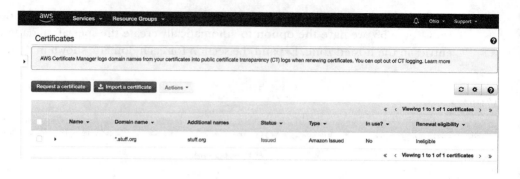

Figure D.6   A verified certificate shown in the Certificate Manager section of the AWS Console

This is excellent work! You have a registered domain and have created an associated SSL/TLS certificate to ensure traffic is encrypted. You will use this domain later to access your newly deployed application.

appendix E
Serverless Framework
under the hood

In this appendix we will look in more detail at serverless technology on AWS, and in particular at the Serverless Framework, which is used for many of the example systems in this book.

As alluded to in chapter 1, the term *serverless* doesn't mean a system without servers; it means that we can construct systems without the need to concern ourselves with the underlying server infrastructure. By using serverless technologies, we are able to move up a level of abstraction and focus more on our application logic and less on the technical "heavy lifting."

A key concept underpinning serverless is Infrastructure as Code (IaC). IaC allows us to treat the entire infrastructure for a system as source code. This means that we can store it in a revision control system such as Git, and apply software development best practices to its creation and maintenance.

All of the major cloud providers support some mechanism for IaC. On AWS, the service that supports IaC is called CloudFormation.

CloudFormation can be configured by creating a template file in either JSON or YAML format. Though it is possible to write templates directly using a text editor, this can quickly become unwieldy for systems of an appreciable size, as the templates are quite verbose. A number of tools are available to help developers work with CloudFormation, such as SAM, the AWS CDK, and the Serverless Framework. There are also other tools such as HashiCorp's Terraform that target multiple clouds, which we won't cover here.

Though the Serverless Framework can be used to deploy any AWS resources, it is oriented toward managing and deploying serverless web applications. Typically this means API Gateway, Lambda functions, and database resources such as

DynamoDB tables. The Serverless configuration file can be thought of as a lightweight domain-specific language (DSL) that describes these types of applications.

Figure E.1 depicts how the Serverless Framework cooperates with CloudFormation.

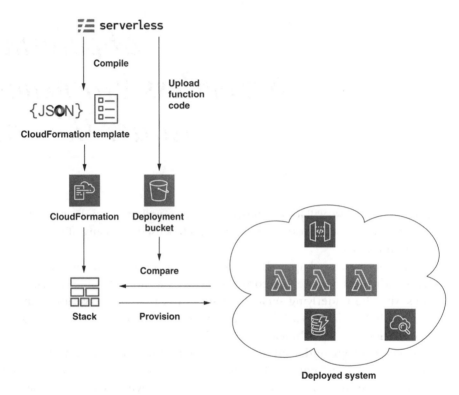

Figure E.1   CloudFormation workflow

On deployment, the Serverless configuration file (serverless.yml) is "compiled" into a CloudFormation template. A deployment bucket is created, and code artifacts for each of the defined Lambda functions are uploaded. Hashes are computed for each of the Lambda functions and included in the template. Serverless then calls the CloudFormation UpdateStack method to delegate the deployment work to Cloud-Formation. CloudFormation then proceeds to query the existing infrastructure. Where differences are found—for example, if a new API Gateway route has been defined—CloudFormation will make the required infrastructure updates to align the deployment with the new compiled template.

E.1   Walkthrough

Let's take a simple Serverless configuration file and walk through the deployment process in detail. First create a new empty directory called hello. cd into this directory and create a file serverless.yml. Add the code shown in the next listing to this file.

Listing E.1 Simple `serverless.yml`

```yaml
service: hello-service

provider:
  name: aws
  runtime: nodejs10.x
  stage: dev
  region: eu-west-1

functions:
  hello:
    handler: handler.hello
    events:
      - http:
          path: say/hello
          method: get
```

Next create a file `handler.js` in the same directory and add the code in the following listing to it.

Listing E.2 Simple handler function

```javascript
'use strict'

module.exports.hello = async event => {
  return {
    statusCode: 200,
    body: JSON.stringify({
      message: 'Hello!',
      input: event
    },
    null, 2)
  }
}
```

Let's now deploy this handler into AWS. You will need to set up an AWS account and also configure your command line before deployment. If you haven't already done this, please refer to appendix A, which walks through the setup process.

To deploy this simple application, run

```
$ serverless deploy
```

Let's take a look at the artifacts that were created during the deployment process. When deploying this application, the framework created a local working directory named `.serverless` in the application directory. If you look in this directory, you should see the files listed in the next listing.

Listing E.3 Serverless working directory

```
cloudformation-template-create-stack.json
cloudformation-template-update-stack.json
hello-service.zip
serverless-state.json
```

These files serve the following purposes:

- `cloudformation-template-create-stack.json` is used to create an S3 deployment bucket for code artifacts, if one doesn't exist already.
- `cloudformation-template-update-stack.json` contains the compiled CloudFormation template to deploy.
- `hello-service.zip` holds the code bundle for our Lambda function.
- `serverless-state.json` holds a local copy of the current deployed state.

Log in to the AWS web console to see exactly what was deployed by the framework. First go to S3 and search for a bucket containing the string `'hello'`; you should find a bucket named something like `hello-service-dev-serverlessdeployment-bucket-zpeochtywl7m`. This is the deployment bucket that the framework used to push code to AWS. If you look inside this bucket, you will see a structure similar to the following listing.

Listing E.4   Serverless deployment bucket

```
serverless
  hello-service
    dev
      <timestamp>
        compiled-cloudformation-template.json
        hello-service.zip
```

`<timestamp>` is replaced with the time when you ran the deployment. As updates are made to the service, the framework will push the updated templates and code to this bucket for deployment.

Next, use the AWS console to navigate to the API Gateway and Lambda web consoles. Click on the Services link in the top right, and search for `lambda` and then `api gateway`, as illustrated in figure E.2.

Figure E.2   Searching for services in the AWS web console.

On the Lambda and Api Gateway consoles, you will see the deployed instances of the service, as shown in figures E.3 and E.4.

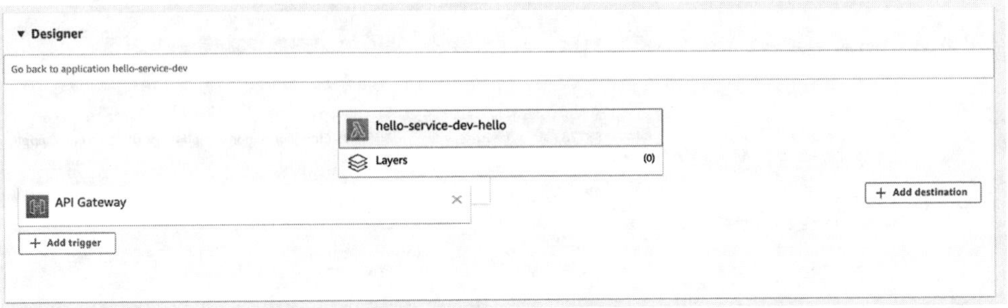

Figure E.3   Deployed Lambda function

Figure E.4   Deployed API Gateway

Finally if you open the CloudFormation web console, you will see the deployed template for the service. This should look similar to figure E.5.

Understanding the deployment process for the framework can help to diagnose issues when things go wrong. The key thing to bear in mind is that `serverless deploy` delegates deployment to CloudFormation `UpdateStack`, and that we can use the AWS Console to look at the stack update history and current state if issues occur.

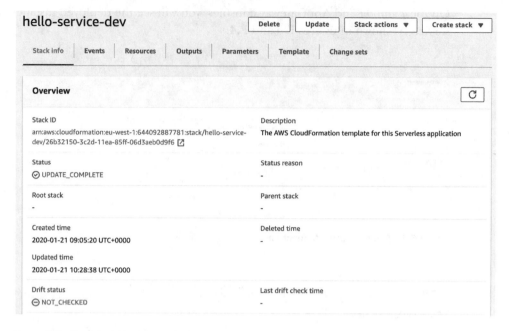

Figure E.5   Deployed CloudFormation stack

E.2   Cleanup

Once you have finished with the example stack, be sure to remove it by running

```
$ serverless remove
```

Make sure that the framework has removed all of the related artifacts described here.

index